THE FACE OF EVIL

ROBERT GILES AND CHRIS CLARK

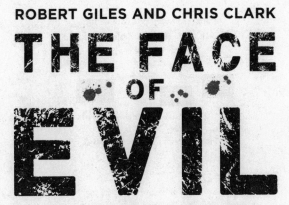

THE FACE OF EVIL

THE TRUE STORY OF SERIAL KILLER ROBERT BLACK

JOHN BLAKE

Published by John Blake Publishing,
3 Bramber Court, 2 Bramber Road,
London W14 9PB, England

www.johnblakebooks.com

www.facebook.com/johnblakebooks ⓕ
twitter.com/jblakebooks ⓔ

First published in paperback in 2017

ISBN: 978-1-78606-287-1

British Library Cataloguing-in-Publication Data:

A catalogue record for this book is available from the British Library.

Design by www.envydesign.co.uk

Printed in Great Britain by CPI Group (UK) Ltd

1 3 5 7 9 10 8 6 4 2

Papers used by John Blake Publishing are natural, recyclable products made from
wood grown in sustainable forests. The manufacturing processes conform to the
environmental regulations of the country of origin.

Every attempt has been made to contact the relevant copyright-holders, but some
were unobtainable. We would be grateful if the appropriate people could contact us.

John Blake Publishing is an imprint of Bonnier Publishing
www.bonnierpublishing.com

CONTENTS

FOREWORD

I have read two books about Robert Black and of those it has been over two decades since the last was published. He was convicted of my sister's murder in 2011, since when a lot more about him has come to light.

Robert Giles met with me last year and let me know he was writing a new book about Robert Black, and had got together with Chris Clark to gather true information and investigate Black's past and his travels.

I have read the chapter about Jennifer's trial and it is very comprehensive and detailed. Some of the details even I had forgotten. I am really grateful that Robert and Chris have produced a book that is up to date.

I remember the trial very well, and remember that Robert Black's face never changed expression and certainly never showed any remorse. I think the only time his expression altered was when the court read out some of the fantasies and sexual things he had done to himself. One thing that all of the people who were present at the trial remember is that when the verdict of 'Guilty' was read out, and he was unanimously found guilty on all counts, nobody in the courtroom cheered or punched their fists in the air. What they did notice was that everybody in the courtroom (including journalists) was in tears. The court clerk (of some thirty years' standing) said it was the first time this was ever seen. Robert Black's face was still expressionless.

Robert Black took our sister from us in 1981. Our family stayed together, and as my dad, Andy, said after the trial, 'Robert Black stole the life of our daughter, Jennifer, but Robert Black didn't steal the lives of me and my family -- we've lived a happy, prosperous life, but we miss Jennifer each and every day.'

We stayed together with the help of God, and he was with us throughout the trial. We have no hatred for Robert Black and we prayed for him through and beyond the trial.

Our family waited over thirty years after Jennifer's death – through all the years without her, the investigation, the trial – to see her killer convicted.

We got the information, the trial and closure, for which we are very grateful. I feel so sad for the families that never received that closure.

It wasn't about bringing someone to justice, or punishment, or revenge. It was about closure. Finding out who did this, and why. We may not have got all the answers, but thank God that we got closure.

MARK CARDY (Jennifer Cardy's older brother)

INTRODUCTION AND BACKGROUND

This book has not been an easy book to write. At times it will not be an easy book to read. The subject matter at its very heart – the murder of children – is an indescribably disturbing one. Any act of murder is horrific by its very nature, both the act of murder and its end result: the taking of a human life. A life ended in an unnatural way and a life ended too soon.

The murder of a child ranks at the very top of the list of murders that produce shock, anger and fear. The general public and the police share feelings of disgust and dread matched with a desire for justice and a determination that the perpetrator or perpetrators should be caught before they have the opportunity to take another child's life. The depths of human depravity can sink no lower. Putting any child through such an ordeal spits in the face of all that is moral and right in our society. It is, simply put, an act of pure evil. It is a life wasted and an innocence lost. Left behind are the broken hearts of the parents, wider family circles, friends, the general public and the police forces that are with them every step of the way. The murder of a child always has been and always will be one of life's unbearable tragedies; a tragedy that is the subject matter of this book.

The United Kingdom has sadly had its fair share of infamous child murderers and killers, too many to list all of them here. In 1948 Peter Griffiths, a twenty-two-year-old former Guardsman, abducted three-year-old June Devaney from a Blackburn Hospital. He raped and battered her to death. Griffiths went to the gallows following his conviction. John Straffen would later go on to become Britain's longest-serving prisoner after he murdered three little girls in the 1950s. Raymond Morris from Walsall was convicted of the 1967 murder of little Christine Darby and sentenced to life; he died in prison in 2014, but remains the prime suspect in two other unsolved child sex murders that took place in and around the Birmingham and West Midlands areas during the mid-1960s. In 2001, Midlands-based farm labourer Brian Field, aged sixty-five by then, was convicted of the brutal 1968 abduction, rape and murder of fourteen-year-old Roy Tuthill, on his way home from school. Field had a history of serious sexual offences against children dating back many years. As with Morris, he remains a suspect in the disappearances and murder of other young boys in the West Midlands.

In the mid-1980s members of a vicious gang of paedophiles led by middle-aged fairground worker Sidney Cooke and operating out of a flat in Hackney, East London, were responsible for the cruel deaths of at least three young boys and, again, are feared to have been responsible for other deaths and disappearances.

Thankfully, most child killers are caught after their first murder of a child; examples of this include the aforementioned Peter Griffiths, Roy Whiting, who murdered eight-year-old schoolgirl Sarah Payne in Sussex in July 2000, and school caretaker Ian Huntley who murdered schoolgirls Holly Wells and Jessica Chapman at his home in the village of Soham, Cambridgeshire, in August 2002. Even though these men were caught after their first murderous attack, it is still one attack too many for the victims' families.

There are cases, however, of child killers who have only been convicted of one child murder and yet are suspected, in some cases very strongly, of involvement in other unsolved child killings. Raymond Morris and Brian Field are examples of this and both have been investigated and questioned in relation to other serious criminal matters. If these suspicions and subsequent investigations and charges turn into convictions then we are dealing with an even more alarming and disturbing prospect: that of a serial child killer. Sadly, in most of these cases, when dealing with suspected repeat offenders, we are left with more questions than answers.

I have already mentioned the gang of child killers led by Sidney Cooke, infamous. in the levels of depravity they exercised upon their young victims. But probably the best-known and infamous example of serial child murder in modern-day British criminal history is the case of the Moors Murders. Young couple Myra Hindley and Ian Brady collaborated on the paedophilia-driven murders of five youngsters of both sexes, aged between ten and seventeen, from July 1963 to October 1965 in the Greater Manchester area. They buried four of their five victims on Saddleworth Moor outside Manchester. The body of twelve-year-old Keith Bennett, abducted and murdered in June 1964, at the time of writing still remains unfound on the moors.

The Moors Murders case has been widely reported and written on since its discovery over forty-seven years ago. Numerous books have been published about the case, countless newspaper articles printed, and documentaries and television dramas made; and even though many of the main players in this dreadful story are now dead, including both perpetrators, it is a story that is unlikely ever to be forgotten.

At that time, in the 1960s, if children were told not to talk to strangers, they usually assumed them to be men. Paedophiles were largely imagined to be dirty, scary-looking old men hanging around outside schools, not young women like Myra Hindley. Her deep involvement as a young woman in this horrific case changed the perception of what could be a threat to our young.

This book, however, is not about Myra Hindley and Ian Brady. It is not about Raymond Morris, Sidney Cooke or any of the other evil child killers and their deeds mentioned above.

No, this is a story about a serial child killer whose life of crime I have been following, studying and researching for over fourteen years. A man whose criminal path may not be as well-known or followed by the British public and media as that of the Moors Murderers or Sidney Cooke's gang but whose crimes are every bit as horrifying and nightmarish. A man who overtakes those other serial child killers in terms of the geographical mobility he was able to take advantage of while committing his crimes, crimes that spread throughout the four corners of the United Kingdom and were committed over a near ten-year period.

A man who in my opinion will overtake those other infamous serial killers of children, both in terms of number of victims and in terms of the many years he got away with abducting and killing little girls. The name of this man, this vicious serial killer of children, is Robert Black.

Robert Black was serving eleven life sentences for four of the most horrific cases of child murder to have ever been committed on the British Isles when he died from a heart attack on 12 January 2016. If the full truth of the past crimes and life this man led ever becomes known then I suspect he could be accounted the worst serial child killer and one of the worst serial killers the UK and Europe has ever had stalking its lands. It was this suspicion that set me on the road to writing this book.

In May 1994 Robert Black was convicted at Newcastle's Moot Hall of the abduction and murder of eleven-year-old Susan Maxwell from Cornhill on Tweed in July 1982, five-year-old Caroline Hogg from Portobello in Edinburgh in July 1983 and ten-year-old Sarah Harper from Morley in Leeds in March 1986. He was also convicted of the attempted abduction of fifteen-year-old Teresa Thornhill in March 1988. He received ten life sentences. Black was an obsessive paedophile and all the attacks had a sexual motive.

For fourteen years from 1976 to the summer of 1990 when he was arrested and subsequently sentenced to life for the abduction and sexual assault of a six-year-old girl whom he abducted from the village of Stow in the Scottish borders, Robert Black was employed by the now defunct courier company, Poster, Despatch and Storage (PDS) as a long-distance delivery-van driver, delivering posters that were used for advertising purposes, mostly on giant billboard campaigns. It was while on these work trips up and down and all over the country in his van that he abducted and murdered his young victims, dumping their bodies in such undignified ways.

He travelled extensively throughout the British Isles and Europe with his job and following his May 1994 conviction, detectives from throughout Europe began to look at cold-case files they had in regard to missing and murdered children to see if any links could be made between these cases and the travels undertaken by Robert Black. The gaps in between the offences in which he had been convicted of were large and empty and, now knowing Black's capabilities, and his history of travelling far and wide, police and criminologists alike were convinced there was a strong possibility of more victims.

One of the police forces that began to look at Black's background and movements was the Northern Ireland police force, the Royal Ulster Constabulary (RUC), who had an unsolved murder case from 1981 that they felt might be connected to Black, particularly when they became aware that Black travelled to Ulster frequently, making deliveries in the late 1970s and early 1980s.

It was this unsolved murder and the possibility of Robert

Black being responsible that got me interested in the case – the thought that a child could have been murdered in Northern Ireland, that in spite of the Troubles was one of the safest places to live in Europe in terms of non-politically motivated crime, both disturbed me and made me wonder if Black was responsible.

The murdered child was a little girl called Jennifer Cardy. Jennifer was nine years old when she was abducted on 12 August 1981 from the roadside around a mile from her home in the village of Lower Ballinderry, County Antrim. Her body was found ten miles away six days later in the local mill pond known as McKee's Dam just outside Hillsborough.

As a child I had always been warned not to talk or go with strangers, and the Soham case and the case of the abduction and killing of little Sarah Payne in Sussex two years earlier in 2000, made me realise why I had been warned of the dangers.

The Soham murders really brought home to me, a young teenager at the time, the dangers that children could face in life, that there were bad people out there who had the potential to take children away from their loved ones and do them great harm.

In August 2002 during the search for the missing Soham schoolgirls Holly Wells and Jessica Chapman, I asked my mother if she remembered anything of this awfulness happening in Northern Ireland, where we lived, as was happening in England. She mentioned that the only case that stuck out in her memory was the murder of Jennifer Cardy and as she told me the basic details that she could remember about the case I listened horrified. As a young woman my mother was living in the County Armagh town of Lurgan at the time of Jennifer's abduction – not that far away from where Jennifer lived in the village of Ballinderry. My mother had a younger sister who was about the same age as Jennifer and she remembers the police going around her estate with a megaphone and 'Missing' posters of Jennifer on the police cars and in the shops in Lurgan, appealing for any information. She also remembers the sadness and fear expressed by the community when Jennifer was found murdered six days later.

I then asked my mother if they had ever caught the killer. She told me that they had not but that suspicion was on a convicted child killer who had murdered little girls in England and Scotland and who was working as a van driver in Northern Ireland on the day that little Jennifer was snatched. Robert Black was first questioned by Northern Irish detectives over the murder of Jennifer Cardy in 1996, two years after he was convicted of three child murders in 1994.

That conversation with my mother was what led me to discovering and studying the crimes of Robert Black and the (at the time) unsolved murder of Jennifer Cardy.

Soon after Robert Black's 2011 trial for the Cardy murder and his conviction I began a correspondence with a former Norfolk Police intelligence officer named Chris Clark who like myself was carrying out his own research and investigations into Black's past. Like myself, he believes that Black was responsible for other unsolved crimes, including the attempted abduction of his now wife, Jeanne Clark (née Twigden) when she was a fifteen-year-old schoolgirl in the early summer of 1971 – of which more later.

INTRODUCTION AND BACKGROUND

This book is the tragic story of what happened to Jennifer, the investigations involved in bringing her killer to justice, his eventual trial, and the possibility of him having claimed other victims. It will also explore the other serious crimes Robert Black has been convicted of and the life he led from his early childhood to his death.

His little victims, like all children who die young, were angels. This book is a tribute to them and their memory, to their loved ones, friends and families, who still miss them every day and who suffered such an unfair tragedy.

This book is dedicated to my family and friends, whose encouragement and support is much appreciated.

It is also dedicated to the memory of the late great American true-crime writer Ann Rule. She was the author behind the book that inspired me to become a true-crime writer, *The Stranger Beside Me*, based on the crimes of the serial killer Ted Bundy. I would have loved Ann to have read this book but sadly she died in 2015.

Finally, I would also like to give a special thanks to my co-author and good friend Chris Clark and his wife Jeanne. Their friendship, encouragement and enthusiasm for this project has been inspirational to me and will forever be appreciated. Chris is a detective not only of intelligence but of bravery and perseverance, and it is these qualities that have those responsible for murders still unsolved, up and down the country, sleeping less easily at night.

ROBERT GILES

May 2017

INTRODUCTION
BY CHRIS CLARK

It was round about 2009 when I was researching material for my forthcoming police-force autobiography that my wife Jeanne confided to me the detail of her attempted abduction during the spring of 1971. This led me down the various paths I have trodden since.

In August 2012 the *Hackney Gazette* in London, the local paper to where Robert Black resided from 1968 to1990, ran an article on Jeanne's attempted abduction and appealed for information on Robert Black.

On 18 August that year I received an e-mail from twenty-four-year-old Robert Giles, our first contact of many, who introduced himself as a Criminology graduate from Northern Ireland and spoke of his interest and research into Robert Black, his background and suspected offences, all of which Robert Giles had been studying for several months, planning to eventually write a book on Black and his life and crimes.

I was immediately impressed with his enthusiasm, the depth of his knowledge and the amount of research that he was carrying out, similar to mine but worlds apart in terms of our professional backgrounds, expertise and age. I had been a police officer for almost thirty years with an intelligence-themed dedication, whereas Robert is an emerging criminologist who has to limit himself to part-time research when not working long night shifts as a carer, with the job's associated sleep deprivation, brain fatigue and little time off.

Since then I have received nearly a hundred e-mails from Robert about Black and other serial killers and unsolved murders, and we have had many long telephone conversations to the detriment of our family lives. I am an expert at doing other people's heads in with information overdrive; Robert does my head in with the volume and multi-diverse topics which he speaks about, without break; a mini computer mind.

Robert tells me that he has amassed over two hundred books about serial killers and all aspects of their crimes, solved and unsolved, as well as DVDs and other research material from the internet, and that his bedroom resembles my office – in Jeanne's words, a dump! – conjuring up the popular image of a coffee-/tea-swilling, chain-smoking armchair detective merrily typing away on endless manuscript projects, surrounded by bins full of screwed-up paper representing completed or discarded research (although neither Robert nor I are smokers).

In the years that I have come to know Robert, his enthusiastic and dedicated approach to many cold cases –

some of them murders committed long before he, and in some cases his parents, were born – combined with a strong empathy for the victims and their families, have not ceased to amaze me. Take for example, the 1981 murder of Jennifer Cardy: this occurred when I had served nearly sixteen years as a police officer, some seven years before Robert came into the world, and the 1990 arrest of Robert Black when Robert Giles was just a toddler and I was a Local Intelligence Officer with a long-service medal.

Robert has a natural ability when it comes to tackling unsolved crimes, a gift for research and the maturity of someone much older, and he has been very supportive to my own work throughout the time we have known each other, sometimes quietly suggesting from a different viewpoint a change in direction, as I come close to falling into the trap of blinkered thinking. We both continually bounce ideas off each other which helps to keep our minds focused and our eyes on the ball.

In this book Robert has captured the very essence that drove Black to kill time and time again, and placed him in various parts of the United Kingdom and on the Continent in locations of unsolved murders, as well as deducing Black's method, motive and opportunity in his acknowledged crimes.

For me this book is a fully absorbing true-crime read and I wish Robert Giles every future success as I believe this is the platform that will launch him into a career where he can make the most of his powers of deduction and analysis and his abilities as researcher. We need thinking detectives like those famous fictional ones – Inspector Morse, Barnaby of

THE FACE OF EVIL

Midsomer Murders, Lieutenant Columbo and Detective Inspector Frost – in Robert Giles you have that man who sorts fact from fiction.

My part of this work is dedicated to Jeanne, to her lucky escape, and to her continuing support.

And to the memory of April Fabb. Without both, my story would not have been told.

CHRIS CLARK

May 2017

PART ONE

TEARS BY THE
LAY-BY

1

WHAT HAPPENED TO JENNIFER?

Northern Ireland was not by any stretch of the imagination a safe place in August 1981. The hunger strikes by Republican prisoners in the Maze prison in an effort to attain status as political prisoners was on-going and making the news worldwide. As each prisoner died and UK Prime Minister Margaret Thatcher refused to give in to the demands of the hunger strikers, rioting and murder would follow as Republicans and Loyalists took part in campaigns of violence. The conflict that had been raging since 1969 in Northern Ireland between Irish Republicans and Ulster Loyalists, known simply as the 'Troubles', was experiencing one of its most turbulent and troubling years. The security situation across the province was very tense indeed. However, despite the Troubles, Northern Ireland was one of the safest places to live in the United Kingdom, with a very low rate of non-politically motivated crime. Murders unconnected with the Troubles were rare, the murder of a child was rarer yet.

Across the six counties of Northern Ireland are many villages. These villages contain many God-fearing close-knit communities made up of hard-working families. The heads of these families did their best to get on with their lives during the Troubles and provide as normal a way of life as possible for themselves and their children despite the political carnage going on around them.

In August 1981, one such family was the Cardy family who lived on the Crumlin Road in the rural village of Ballinderry, County Antrim. Ballinderry is actually the name of the townland and civil parish of the area. The area itself is made up of two villages, Lower Ballinderry to the west and Upper Ballinderry to the east. It is around ten miles west of the city of Lisburn.

The Cardys lived on the Crumlin Road in Upper Ballinderry. Andrew Cardy, his wife Patricia and their four children: Mark the eldest, followed by nine-year-old Jennifer, Philip and baby Victoria the youngest.

Wednesday, 12 August 1981 should have been just another normal summer day for the Cardy family. It started out as one but by the end of that day, the events that would take place would ensure that it was anything but a normal day.

The older children were enjoying their summer holidays like all children, making the most of the good weather and the activities each day brought until school would resume in September. That day while Andrew Cardy was at work at the company he co-owned, Richardson and Cardy Kitchens, in the nearby city of Lisburn, Jennifer and her brothers were with their mother Pat, and had just finished a lunch of poached eggs, Jennifer with her baby sister Victoria on her lap.

She had arranged to visit her friend Louise Major, whose mum ran the local post office and lived about a mile and a half away. Louise's house was on the Station Road in Ballinderry and Jennifer planned to use her new red bicycle to get there.

Jennifer and her mother Pat had travelled the same route previously together and Jennifer was eager to go and see her friend. Her new red bicycle had only been bought for her by her father two weeks before as she had outgrown her last one. It was her pride and joy.

Louise and Jennifer were good friends and just two weeks earlier they had sat together glued to the television, along with the rest of the world, watching the wedding of Charles, Prince of Wales and Diana Spencer.

Jennifer asked her mother to wind up her red watch to the correct time. She planned to leave her home at 1.40 p.m. so as to arrive at her friend's house around 2 p.m., and to return home in time to view a popular kids' TV programme, *Jackanory*, that she enjoyed.

Wearing her favourite T-shirt – white with a red border and a design of red strawberries on it –a white cardigan and red trousers, Jennifer set off on her bicycle, looking forward to seeing her friend and to the rest of the day.

It was when Pat Cardy realised that Jennifer had not returned home in time for *Jackanory*, which started at 4.30 p.m., that she became worried, but she couldn't go out far to look for Jennifer as her car had a puncture. When, shortly afterwards, Jennifer's father Andy came home and heard that Jennifer had not come home for her evening tea, he changed the punctured tyre and drove off to collect her. He reached the Majors' house to hear the worrying news that Jennifer had never arrived there..

A frantic search of the immediate area and local houses that her parents thought she might be in uncovered no sign of Jennifer. Andy Cardy contacted the local police services, the RUC (Royal Ulster Constabulary), at 9 p.m. The operation that ensued would escalate to unprecedented heights.

Police immediately began searching around the surrounding roads and word was spread of the missing child. Retired RUC Inspector Cyril Donnan recalled the search shortly after Robert Black's eventual conviction for Jennifer's murder.

Speaking years later to the *Daily Mirror* (28 October 2011), he said, 'I received a call from my colleague at 6 a.m. on Thursday. He had been on call on Wednesday when the report that Jennifer was missing came in. I normally went in at 8 o'clock but I went in early. I got my welly boots and went out. My colleague had then gathered up a handful of officers and did a sweep and found the bike in the field close to the road. They searched the scene.'

The discovery of Jennifer's bicycle at the time was an important development as police were still trying to discover what actually had happened that led to the child going missing. The red bicycle of which Jennifer was so proud had been thrown over the hedge that ran alongside the road about a mile from the home she had set off from that afternoon of Wednesday, 12 August.

WHAT HAPPENED TO JENNIFER?

One of the theories put forward was that Jennifer had been a victim of a hit-and-run accident and that the driver of the vehicle involved had thrown her bicycle over the hedge in a panic. This theory was quickly dismissed, however, as there were no reports of any accidents in the area. Besides which, the bicycle showed no signs of damage and neither did the part of the road or the hedge where the bicycle was thrown over. Worryingly, it quickly began to look as if Jennifer had been abducted. The examination of her bicycle did reveal one thing, however. The bike's stand had been pulled out, indicating that Jennifer had stopped her bike before being abducted.

Within hours of the little girl going missing local residents and volunteers organised by local police had begun searching or helping in any way that they could. Farmers and landowners were encouraged to check their outbuildings. Close to a hundred civilian volunteers helped police in the search. Due to the vastness of the local countryside surrounding the abduction point the search was initially focused within a five-mile radius. One of the policemen searching for Jennifer in the fields and roads around Ballinderry was a young uniformed constable by the name of Stephen Clarke, who would later reach the rank of Detective Chief Inspector before retiring. His in-depth knowledge of the case meant that he was able to provide valuable assistance to detectives of the PSNI (Police Service of Northern Ireland, successor to the RUC) re-investigating Robert Black over twenty years after Jennifer's murder.

'We thought at that early stage, and hoped, that she could have been alive but as days rolled on and there were no leads we thought, "This is going to be a body." We never ever thought something that dreadful,' Cyril Donnan told the *Daily Mirror*.

Extra back-up was soon drafted in the form of the Ulster Defence Regiment (UDR), the local British Army regiment, who assisted with the search. As word of the missing child spread, local people from the area, and further away as well, joined in the search.

Donnan continued: 'As search coordinator you worry: Has someone missed something? You are relying heavily on the public with eighty to ninety people searching – so it's not only the police eyes.'

At a time when Northern Ireland was so politically divided the people of the two communities came together, uniting as one to help search for the little girl, as roads and fields were walked through and searched around the Ballinderry and nearby Aghalee areas, the police concentrating on areas within a five-mile radius of where Jennifer's bicycle was found. Workers from Richardson and Cardy Kitchens also took part in the search on full pay. One of the other searchers at the time was future Social Democratic and Labour Party Deputy Leader and Member of the Legislative Assembly for nearby Upper Bann, Dolores Kelly. Dolores recalls taking part in the search and the feeling of dread knowing that a child was missing in the community.

Speaking on ITV *Live Tonight* following Black's conviction, she said, 'Well, I actually was, along with my sister, one of the search party; we had volunteered to go through the fields and the local areas; I was twenty-one at the time and I had younger sisters, you know, the same age as Jennifer, so everyone was very frightened; although there had been many children killed in bombs and children traumatised, the fact that a young girl had been abducted not that far from her home heading towards the local post office, which was just up the road from there. You know, it was a normal, everyday activity and this young girl just disappeared for days into thin air. There was a great fear and a dread.'

Jennifer's parents appealed for their daughter's safe return on BBC television. Pat Cardy said: 'Time goes on and you think every day without news means you have some hope left and yet every day without news seems to take some hope away so you try and face the inevitable and carry hope with you.'

Jennifer's father Andy told the media that he had warned his daughter on many occasions never to accept a lift in a car and that she had reassured him that she would not. Speaking to ITN on 13 August 1981, during the search for his daughter, he said, 'If she did get into a car she was forced into it – there is no way she would have got into it of her own accord.'

Police set up roadblocks and questioned local people as to whether they had witnessed anything suspicious or anything relevant, but they drew frustrating blanks in their quest for information – although people living on the Crumlin Road did report witnessing a blue van speeding through the area around the time of Jennifer's disappearance. It was later traced and eliminated – even so, this sighting would be brought up in court over thirty years later at the trial of the man accused of Jennifer's murder. There was also a sighting of a middle-aged man walking in the area whom police were keen to trace and speak to. Ultimately, however, it was to be a red herring.

'Missing' posters featuring a photograph of Jennifer and details of her physical appearance, her height, age and clothing, along with information about her disappearance, were distributed locally and further afield in an additional effort to receive information.

Nobody, however, had witnessed the abduction or heard a scream or cry for help. Whoever had forcibly taken little Jennifer had done so very quickly indeed on that quiet country road. Locally and regionally, the story continued to develop from the evening Jennifer had been reported missing and her bicycle being discovered shortly afterwards. It was only ever reported once on the British mainland that she was missing – in the *Daily Express* on Saturday, 15 August 1981, on page 5 – and nothing subsequently about her body being found and a murder hunt and after that nothing until 2002! This is very significant when one looks at the conversation Robert Black later had with a man called John (see Chapter 18) in a London pub in 1983, only two years after the incident.

As each day passed the chances of finding little Jennifer alive were decreasing. Yet, as in any case like this, there remained a ray of hope, a ray shared by the whole people of Northern Ireland, of finding Jennifer alive as they followed the day-by-day search. Then, sadly, it was extinguished on Tuesday, 18 August 1981.

McKee's Dam is a large pond just outside Hillsborough at the edge of the dual carriageway off the A1 between Belfast and Dublin. Despite being so close to the motorway and being on a busy road itself, it could be described as quiet and tranquil. It is accessible from the dual carriageway via a lay-by which is often used by members of the public, indeed the lay-by was known to have been used by drivers to stop over for a rest or a bite to eat, particularly those who drive long distances for a living, such as lorry or van drivers. It was this local fact that would become very interesting to police and prosecutors many years later whilst investigating who was responsible for Jennifer's death. The dam was also very popular with anglers as a fishing spot. On the early afternoon of 18 August 1981 two young duck hunters arrived at McKee's Dam; as they made their way to the edge of the pond they noticed something red floating in the water. The search for Jennifer Cardy was over.

Jennifer's body was found floating face-down in the water of the weed-infested pond. The two duck hunters, horrified at what they had discovered, made their way to Hillsborough RUC station and reported what they had found. It had been six days since Jennifer Cardy had disappeared, six days of searching, hoping and praying. The news that her body had been found was devastating for her family and also for all the people who searched for her as well as the people of Ulster who had followed the story in the news, hoping against hope that she would be found alive and well.

Where Jennifer's body was found was certainly a secluded spot, but its aura of peace and tranquillity was changed forever now it had served as a dumping ground by the killer of a kind young girl. Jennifer's body was found in around six inches of water; she was wearing her white cardigan and red trousers.

'The killer certainly wanted her to be found,' retired RUC Inspector Cyril Donnan said in the *Daily Mirror* on 28 October 2011. 'But the question at that stage was how long was she in the water? He wanted her remains to be found. There was no compassion in it. It was "I'm finished with this".' Cyril Donnan was certainly right about the lack of compassion shown by Jennifer's killer in the disposal of her body. It was undignified and without feeling, cold and calculating. The child's body was dumped in such a way that it was almost as if her killer was taunting the police, for while her body was not left in an open area it was left where it would be easily spotted by someone close to the dam.

There was a degree of cool arrogance displayed by the abductor and killer of Jennifer Cardy. At the height of the Troubles in Northern Ireland, the second wave of hunger strikes was in full course with all its attendant horrors – while in a quiet backwater just a short distance away, a random abductor and killer was committing a deeply callous crime. Road blocks and security alerts were common at the time due to the security situation, yet the killer left very little trace of himself. The crime committed, he remained calm and confident, making no effort to bury Jennifer's body, to cover it up or conceal it in any way.

Her body was callously dumped in McKee's Dam as if it were a bag of rubbish being thrown at the side of the road. Black's later, mainland-based victims would be disposed of in similar fashion and their bodies found in an equally undignified situation. To Black these little girls were not innocent children loved and cherished by many, they were not even considered as human beings but as objects of his depraved paedophiliac lust, to be discarded without any kind of dignity at all when he had finished his awful deeds, to the shock of the victims' families and the general public – a callous message of defiance to the police.

This confidence, arrogance or defiance, call it what you will, displayed by Jennifer's killer led to some uncomfortable questions being asked in August 1981. Had Jennifer's killer killed before? Had he experience of abducting children? Such questions about the possible other crimes of Robert Black pre-August 1981 are still being asked today.

The difficult task of identifying Jennifer's body fell to her father Andy at Craigavon Area Hospital where Jennifer's body had been taken after the police had removed it from McKee's Dam. A post-mortem revealed that Jennifer had died from drowning although police did not at the time reveal publicly how Jennifer had been killed. The further details of her post-mortem would provide evidence for the prosecution in its case against her killer.

Jennifer's funeral took place on 21August 1981 and was attended by many from the local community and from afar, including the leader of the Ulster Unionist Party (UUP) James Molineux, and the leader of the Democratic Unionist Party (DUP) Ian Paisley. As the hundreds of mourners both Protestant and Catholic, many of whom had helped in the search, lined the road beside the Cardy household, an outdoor service took place in the garden, where Jennifer's favourite hymns were sang. The minister thanked those who took part in the search in a cross-community effort. Pink carnations in the shape of a heart were wrapped around the small coffin of a much-loved little girl. Jennifer was buried in the Laa Lau graveyard in nearby Glenavy.

One of the speakers at Jennifer's funeral was the Reverend William Beattie, who, following Robert Black's conviction in October 2011, recalled to Northern Ireland's BBC *Newsline* the sadness and grief felt by the Cardy family at the time.

'They were devastated. They were showing signs of shock and devastation from the beginning, but when they heard what happened, that she had been found in water, in a dam face down, there were all sorts of concerns as to what happened.'

The police still had their hands full with events surrounding the hunger strikes at the Maze Prison and the public disorder each striker's death brought to certain areas of Northern Ireland, but they did widen their search for the killer. As the murder hunt intensified, they initially suspected that the killer was a local man.

'My view, because of where the body was, was the killer could have been local,' said the retired RUC inspector Cyril Donnan in the *Daily Mirror* on 28 October 2011, explaining, 'At the time I only lived three or four miles away from where she was found and I never knew a dam to be there. But at the time it was totally overgrown. There was no connection between Hillsborough and Aghalee.'

However, the fact that the nearby lay-by that adjoined the dam was known to be used by lorry drivers and van drivers made police revise that viewpoint. 'There was a lay-by where lorries could have pulled up, and potentially if you were in a cab in a lorry or van you would have been able to see the dam,' continued Cyril Donnan. 'I thought she had been picked up in a vehicle of the size to take a bicycle.'

WHAT HAPPENED TO JENNIFER?

The police realised there was really no reason for anyone to be in these rural surroundings unless they lived locally or (as was to prove to be the case) they were delivery drivers.

The police began checking with companies in the area to see if any deliveries had recently been made; one of these was Hicklands Cycles (where two weeks before, Jennifer had gone with her father to pick up her new red bicycle), based on the Glenavy road towards the nearby city of Lisburn, but it led to nothing.

Ultimately, they were right that Jennifer's killer was a delivery driver but he was not delivering bicycles but advertising posters – something that, over thirty years later, Robert Black would be confronted with in Armagh Crown Court.

While parents across Northern Ireland, as well as the police, were haunted by the thought that Jennifer's killer could strike again – which tragically would prove to be the case – they could have been forgiven for never imagining a serial killer was at work. Child murder in Northern Ireland, and indeed on the whole island of Ireland, was a rare thing, and child murder committed by a stranger rarer yet. In mainland Great Britain, however, child murder was unfortunately a less rare occurrence, as former RUC inspector Cyril Donnan remarked in the *Daily Mirror* interview: 'It never crossed your mind it was going to be a serial killer. That was something you read about in papers such as the Moors Murders in England, not in Northern Ireland.'

Detectives in the RUC and the local media did note the similarities between the abduction and murder of Jennifer Cardy and another similar crime, the disappearance of thirteen-year-old Genette Tate who had gone missing as she delivered newspapers in her home village of Aylesbeare in Devon almost three years previously. These similarities included the facts that both girls were travelling on bicycles near their homes in rural villages when they were abducted; that they were of a similar age and abducted during the hot summer month of August at a similar time of day, and that they lived in villages near motorways. At the time, though, there was nothing to establish a firm evidential link between the two cases. Detectives from East Devon hunting for missing Genette certainly noticed the similarities between the two cases and contacted the RUC at an early stage of the Jennifer Cardy investigation, yet whilst they did compare notes between the cases there remained no suspect in 1981 to tie the two cases together. That would all change and the similarities would take on a greater significance after Robert Black's first murder convictions in 1994.

* * *

Beginning in the early 1970s and into the 1980s, the United States of America had experienced a serial murder epidemic with a frightening number of sexually motivated serial killers striking fear into major American cities. The killers included such as Ted Bundy, who murdered at least thirty young women and girls, and possibly many more; John Wayne Gacy, who murdered thirty-three young men and boys; Richard Ramirez, the Los Angeles 'Night Stalker'; and Jeffrey Dahmer, to name but a few who between them claimed possibly a hundred victims.

WHAT HAPPENED TO JENNIFER?

In 1981convicted and confirmed serial killers in the UK were comparatively rare. Earlier that year thirty-four-year-old Peter Sutcliffe had been arrested and subsequently confessed to being the notorious 'Yorkshire Ripper', the depraved killer who murdered thirteen women and almost killed another seven over a five-and-a-half-year period across the north of England. In 1976 Bradford man Donald Neilson was sentenced to life imprisonment for four murders, two attempted murders and the kidnapping of seventeen-year-old heiress Lesley Whittle, whose death was one of the murders he was convicted for. Neilson, whose crimes were all for financial gain, was named 'The Black Panther' for his speed as he committed his crimes and because he dressed entirely in black during his violent crime spree.

Serial child murder was deemed rare despite the infamous Moors Murders, which saw partners Ian Brady and Myra Hindley murder five children from the early to mid-1960s in and around the Greater Manchester area in a case that still makes the headlines today, over fifty years after their first killing. The murder of Jennifer Cardy gave nobody in 1981 any indication of the other young lives that would be snuffed out by the same man over the years that followed, or indeed the years that went before. We will perhaps never know what little girl became the first ever to have her life cruelly ended by his murderous actions. There is a good chance that when Jennifer Cardy and Black encountered each other on that quiet country road in Ballinderry Black was already an experienced child killer. We will explore this possibility at a later point.

By October 2011 and Black's conviction for killing Jennifer Cardy, the number of confirmed and convicted serial killers in the United Kingdom had increased and Black's name is now amongst the very worst of examples.

★ ★ ★

On 19 August 1981 – the day after Jennifer's body was found – the police staged an already planned reconstruction of Jennifer's last movements in an effort to jog someone's memory. The part of Jennifer was played by a twelve-year-old girl from the nearby village of Agahallon. As she cycled the route Jennifer had taken, wearing similar clothes to Jennifer's and on Jennifer's bicycle, the police blocked the roads and set up a large noticeboard asking local people, passing motorists, and those who watched the reconstruction on television, three important questions.

1. Were you in this area on Wednesday last?
2. Did you see a child like this?
3. Can you help?

Police then revealed to the media that they thought that it may have started raining that day shortly after 2 p.m., after Jennifer had set off to visit her friend. The onset of rain, they believed, may have meant Jennifer stopped beneath a tree on the side of the road where her bicycle was found thrown over the hedge to remove her cardigan from the carrier bag on the bicycle. It was as she was putting on the cardigan, the police believed, that Jennifer was abducted. The police ended by reiterating the warning to parents not to let their children out alone.

In the months following Jennifer's murder, the investigating team, led by Detective Superintendent David McNeill, continued to appeal for information from the general public while they sifted through witness statements, possible suspects and persons of interest. While determined to catch the cruel killer of this young child, they would continue to be frustrated as days turned to weeks, weeks turned into months and months into years, in their efforts to find Jennifer's abductor and killer; as the murderous conflict known as the Troubles continued to rage, police would find themselves stretched, yet the investigation remained open and they continued to do as much as they could.

In 1984 people's hopes were raised when a man seemed to confess to the murder – but it later emerged that he suffered from mental health issues and had a history of confessing to crimes he had not committed.

In 1992, the investigation into the murder received a blow when a Provisional IRA bomb destroyed the forensic laboratories in Belfast. The laboratories contained the clothing that Jennifer was wearing the day she was abducted and murdered: not a shred survived the bomb blast. With the advancement of forensic science and forensic analysis in recent years and the important part it can play in solving cold cases, this is particularly galling as it means that no physical evidence can ever be recovered from Jennifer's clothing.

In terms of child murder in Northern Ireland that of Jennifer Cardy stood alone as a horrific yet solitary case. Whilst there were other child murders in Northern Ireland, none bore any similarities to the Cardy killing; in the years prior to 1981, and in the years since, no other child has been abducted and murdered in Northern Ireland in an even remotely similar way. When put in context of the life and crimes of Robert Black after his conviction in October 2011 for Jennifer's murder, however, it took on a familiar aspect of a depressing and deadly pattern of offending .

As the years passed, people continued to wonder who was responsible. Rumours and reports in the media by the mid-1990s began to focus attention on a possible suspect that the police were looking at in connection with Jennifer's murder – a recently convicted serial killer of young girls on mainland UK. It was to take over fifteen years, however, before the suspect was confirmed and convicted in a court of law as the man responsible.

But who was this man who had struck fear into the hearts of Ulster folk in the summer of 1981? What other fear would this man strike into other hearts before he was finally caught?

Who was Robert Black?

2

WHO WAS
ROBERT BLACK?

It was on Monday, 21 April 1947 that Jessie Hunter Black, an unmarried twenty-four-year-old factory worker, gave birth to her firstborn son at Falkirk's Royal Infirmary. He was christened Robert. Jessie lived in the nearby Grangemouth Docks area and was the daughter of a railway worker.

Robert Black was never to know the identity of his biological father or come to know his natural birth mother, who refused to put the name of his father on the birth certificate. Having a child out of wedlock carried with it a certain social stigma back in the 1940s and for many years afterwards. As a low-paid factory worker and unmarried, Jessie felt she was in a poor position to raise an illegitimate child. During the weeks following Robert Black's birth the possibility of adoption was explored but never acted upon. Instead, at six months old, Robert Black was fostered. For her part, Jessie was to emigrate to Australia, where she died in 1987. Within a year of Robert Black's birth she married a local man, Francis Hall, with whom she went on to have four children – none were told about their half-brother.

Jack and Margaret – or 'Betty' as she was also known – Tulip were a couple in their mid-fifties who had experience of fostering children, having already fostered several other children. Jack was originally from England and Betty was Scottish, originally from Motherwell. They lived in the Highland village of Kinlochleven in Argyllshire, on the eastern edge of Loch Leven, not far from Glencoe, the site of an historic massacre in 1692.

The Tulips had experience of looking after badly behaved or difficult children and it was soon clear that the young Robert Black was to be no different. From an early age he displayed signs of both anti-social behaviour and an aggressive temper, particularly towards other young children.

When Black was aged five, his foster father died. Jack Tulip was the closest thing Robert Black ever had to a father figure, but Black had no clear memory of Jack Tulip despite the fact he was five when Jack died. As a criminologist, I have wondered whether Robert Black repressed this particular part of his early childhood due to the way he may have been treated physically by his foster father. Did the trauma of any possible physical abuse block out this part of his memory?

When he was old enough, Black started attending the primary school situated in Kinlochleven village. Whilst his foster mother did her best to keep the young Robert looking well-groomed and dressed, the other primary school children could be cruel in their jibes and taunted the young boy with 'Smelly Robbie Tulip!'. While this could be put down generally to children being hurtful and insensitive to other children, it is interesting that such a description would follow Robert Black well into his adult and working life, where he was generally regarded by those that knew him either through work or social activities as having a body odour problem and being of generally rough and scruffy appearance and dress.

At primary school Robert Black quickly began to earn himself another reputation however – that of an aggressive bully. He was not afraid to use his fists on his fellow pupils and in the school playground had younger children hanging around him in your typical playground gang. He would often bully or beat up those children younger, smaller, or generally weaker than himself. Black even once dished out a ferocious beating to a disabled boy who had an artificial leg. The beating was unprovoked.

Punishment for this bullying and aggressive behaviour was usually carried out by Betty Tulip, who would lock Robert inside the house or pull down his trousers and underpants and slap his bottom with a belt. Although a local policeman by the name of Sandy Williams, quoted in Anna Gekoski's 1998 book, *Murder by Numbers: British Serial Sex Killers Since 1950*, remembers Black as a 'wild wee laddie' who 'didn't give a damn – no respect for authority' and 'needed a smack round the ear to keep him in line', the boy was perhaps rather more vulnerable than he seemed. At night he would sometimes have a recurring nightmare of a large hairy monster under his bed waiting to get him, sometimes this monstrous figure would be imagined to be in a cellar full of water. When awakened from this bad dream Black would find that he had wet the bed, and that meant another beating from his foster mother would follow.

As well as the anti-social and the aggressive nature of the character of the young Robert Black, he was worryingly beginning to display abnormal behaviour and attitudes towards sex. At the age of five he and a little girl who lived locally compared genitalia and whilst this can be looked upon as little more than childish experimentation of the doctors-and-nurses variety between two curious young children, Black soon began to display more abnormal signs of his sexuality. At the age of eight he was looking after a neighbour's young baby, wheeling her around in her pushchair, and took the baby girl into his house. He told sex crimes expert Ray Wyre, who interviewed him following his arrest for child abduction in 1990, what followed: 'I took her home . . . And I looked at her privates.' (From *The Murder of Childhood* by Ray Wyre and Tim Tate, 1995.)

Around this time young Robert Black was sent to Highland dancing classes, but he seemed to be more interested in lying on the floor and looking up the skirts of his female class mates rather than learning traditional Scottish folk dance.

Also at about that age Black began to experiment with self-abuse. He would insert items into his anus in a crude and bizarre way to see how much he could fit in it. The first of these items, he recalled, was a small piece of metal. He also had a strange fantasy of defecating into his hands then rubbing the faeces into his body; however, he admitted he never acted this particular fantasy out. This early form of self-abuse and self-penetration and exploration would be best described as an obsession with the orifices of the human body. When police raided Black's flat after his arrest in 1990 they found several crude Polaroid pictures that showed him inserting a variety of objects into his anus – these included a wine bottle, a telephone handset and the end of a table leg. Black also confessed to Ray Wyre that he liked to dress up in little girls' clothing – in some of the photos he was dressed in a little girl's swimsuit.

Black continued to be obsessed with orifices of the human body, not just his own rectum, but the vaginal and anal areas of little girls. He was fixated on thoughts of how much he would be able to fit into them, a depraved form of gynaecology which would follow him into adulthood and into his life as a sexual predator and criminal offender. His early and continued practice of rectal self-abuse was in no way an indication of any kind of homosexual ambitions he may have harboured, but rather, it was rather his way of making up for the fact that he did not have a vagina. He commented to Ray Wyre that he disliked male genitalia and in my opinion he may have wished he had been born a girl – this might be backed up by the female children's clothing that he used in acts of transvestism later in his life. Black always denied any interest in homosexuality and all of his confirmed and known victims and the targets of his depraved perversions have been female.

In 1958, at the age of eleven, Robert Black once again lost someone close to him. Although only foster parents, the

Tulips were the only family he had had any experience of at that point, but Jack Tulip had died when Black was only five years old, and now, six years after her husband, Margaret 'Betty' Tulip, the only maternal figure in his young life, also died. For the young Robert Black the parental loss in his only short life must have been shattering: Whatever emotional bonds might or might not have existed, the Tulips had provided some stability and a home environment. In hindsight it is hard not to feel sorry for the young Robert Black as he had had far from the best start in life, and may, as the years went by, have experienced feelings of abandonment and rejection when looking back at his early beginnings and his childhood and lack of normal family life. The absence of love and affection that he probably experienced as a young boy cannot for one minute be seen as an excuse for his later monstrous actions of abduction, abuse and murder. There are many others who have suffered similar, and in some cases worse, starts in life and have gone on to lead perfectly normal lives, but it can help us perhaps understand the lack of empathy and sympathy he had for the childhoods of his later child victims, which he destroyed forever through his deeds. One episode from his childhood might serve to illustrate the kind of deprived and affectionless childhood that Black may have felt he had had. In Ray Wyre and Tim Tate's brilliant 1995 book on Black and his crimes *The Murder of Childhood*, Black talks about one Christmas when he was about eight or nine when he received no gifts from Father Christmas or his family, because, Betty Tulip told him, he had been bad that year and would not be getting any presents. He did at least receive one gift – of a football from a woman who was possibly a neighbour or friend of the Tulips, which he eventually lost. He could not remember any verbal or physical affection from his foster mother. Both verbal and physical affection are vitally important for the healthy emotional development of any child. Black it seems received little of either.

Following the death of Betty Tulip, a decision had to be made about where the young Robert Black went next. A local couple who were friendly with the Tulips, the Taylors, whom Robert knew as Uncle John and Auntie Flo, offered to take the young orphan in, but as they already had four children of their own the local Social Services decided it was not a good idea.

Soon the eleven-year-old Robert Black found himself placed in an establishment known as Redding House in Stirlingshire. The children's home catered for children both male and female, from young babies up to thirteen years of age.

In November 2012 I travelled to Dungannon Crown Court in my home county of County Tyrone, Northern Ireland to have a chat with a Mr Bill Nichol, an officer at the court. Bill had for six months shared a bedroom with Black at Redding House all those years ago. When I contacted him and asked if we could have a chat about the time he spent with Black as a young boy, Bill said he'd be happy to talk to me and answer any questions I had. I started off by asking him what Black was like as a boy.

'Strange but he initially appeared to be fairly normal. I shared a room with him, had a bed next to his in the six months I was there. Some of the female staff, or children's nurses as they were called, he would make very weird sexual remarks about them, he displayed an over-active interest in the pursuit of young girls both younger and older than him.'

Bill's life could not have gone in a more different direction than Robert Black's did. Whilst Black was travelling the length and breadth of the country stalking, abducting and killing young girls, Bill had undertaken a twenty-five-year-long career in the Scots Guards with his experiences taking him to the Falklands War and an award for exceptional bravery.

Bill recalled waking up one night to see a little girl of around six in her night clothes standing next to Robert Black's bed. Bill remembered a nurse then walked in and took the little girl out of the room. Bill saw nothing to suggest Black had touched the little girl but the next day Bill remembered Black being summoned to the see the Matron. Not long after, Black was gone from Redding House. From Bill's point of view Redding House was a fantastic place, a safe and clean environment where the staff broke their backs to make sure the children were well looked after. Bill believes the care system was not to blame for the horrendous future path Robert Black would begin to walk down.

'It was drilled into us, the difference between right and wrong,' said Bill. 'But something interrupted that sense in Black. No one should have any pity for this evil degenerate.'

After he left Redding House in Falkirk, the powers that be decided that an all-male environment would be best for Robert Black. That environment was Red House, an all-boys home based in the East Lothian town of Musselburgh about six miles east of Edinburgh. He would spend four years of his life at this establishment. From 1958 when he was aged eleven to the summer of 1962 when he was fifteen, Black was a resident here and was given a number like the other boys who stayed there. Black was boy number 28. His sleeping quarters were in the attic room of the tall building, which he shared with several other young boys resident at the home. Whilst this placement was intended to be a fresh start for the young Robert Black it would be anything but. Robert Black found himself in a role rather different from what he was used to previously in his short life; for while Black had already shown abusive tendencies, had been a predator in the past as he would be again in the future, he was now in the role of victim, the prey for another predator. For at least one of the years he spent in Musselburgh, perhaps even two, Black was routinely sexually abused by a male member of staff, now dead. The man's routine was to target a young boy to abuse and when in due course that boy moved on, as was normal in children's homes, he was made to suggest another boy in the home to take his place. Robert Black had the misfortune of being named by the man's previous victim when that boy left the home. Later, after his final arrest in 1990, Black was to tell sex-crimes expert Ray Wyre of the cycle or routine that the abuse would take. 'He would make me put his penis in my mouth, touch him, you know. He did try to bugger me once, but he couldn't get an erection.'

For Robert Black this period of abuse would reinforce the wrong, dark and dangerous ideas, attitudes and feelings that he already had and would have for the rest of his life as a predator in regard to sex. Sex to the young Black was to take what he wanted when he wanted it, it was about domination over another person – during his period of being abused he identified with his abuser rather than his own victims. A fighting bully and a molester of little girls, while at Red House, aged only twelve, Black, along with two other boys, attempted to rape a young girl in a field but they could not get erections. Even then he showed how little he cared about his victims and the wrong he had done them; he had no sympathy, no remorse of any kind for the damage he had done to them. His own abuse by an adult male had confirmed in his dark mind that his victims, past and future, were not people, they were merely objects, playthings for his own sexual gratification.

Whilst at Red House, Black attended the local Musselburgh Grammar School, where despite his early setbacks as a child and his less than favourable start in life, he was on the higher side of average in terms of academic ability. His real talent and passion in terms of schooling was sport. He enjoyed football and was goalkeeper for Red House's own football team; athletics was another favourite and he was good at both. Table tennis and billiards he also enjoyed, and as an adult he liked to practise weight-lifting in order to obtain a stronger upper body. His real passion sportswise, however, was swimming, which he enjoyed thoroughly. He would often walk from Musselburgh to the nearby Portobello swimming baths were he would swim; even gaining a lifesavers' badge for his ability as a young swimmer. Black's visits to Portobello had a darker side, however, as he would spend time watching the little girls in their swimwear splashing about in the pool.

WHO WAS ROBERT BLACK?

In April of 1962, Robert Black would turn fifteen. By the summer of that year he was to leave Red House in Musselburgh and also leave school.

On the move again, this time free from school and care-home environments, the young Robert Black would take his first steps into employment and young adulthood. It should again have been a fresh start, a move away from his past experiences, but in spite of the changed circumstances Black's sexual perversions would continue to fester, grow and come to the surface as Robert Black the sexual predator of children was never far away. No matter where Black moved to, his dark, paedophiliac attacking instinct was forever with him like a shadow.

The local child welfare authorities and agencies had a responsibility to set Black up in new lodgings with a job opportunity. Across the United Kingdom, most young men who came from poorer backgrounds and who left full-time education in the 1960s at the age of fifteen, went into full-time employment to earn money – perhaps in a local factory, as a farm labourer or an apprentice. Robert Black would become an apprentice to a butcher and work as a delivery boy in the western Scottish town of Greenock, lodging in a boys' hostel in the town.

Greenock is located within the central western lowlands of Scotland around twenty miles away from Port Glasgow, which lies to its east side. Following the Second World War it had a heavy industrial presence within the town and it was during this boom that young Robert Black got employment. He quickly saw its possibilities and started using – not for the last time either – his job as a means to approach and sexually abuse young girls. Whilst on his delivery rounds for the butcher he worked for, Black would regularly seek out little girls to molest at every opportunity that happened to come his way. The exact numbers may never be known but Black would later confess to Ray Wyre that the number could be anything from thirty to forty girls; sadly, the true number could be much higher as, Black conceded, he was only going on his memory of the attacks.

'If there was a girl on her own in the flats where I was delivering,' he told Wyre, 'I'd, like, sit down and talk to her for a few minutes, like, you know, and try and touch her: sometimes succeeded, sometimes not.'

It is extremely difficult to believe that Robert Black got away with all of this, that none of these assaults were reported to the authorities, or, if any of these attacks or attempted attacks came to the knowledge of the local law, that he was lucky enough never to have been connected to them. It is particularly hard to believe when you consider the sheer number of victims or potential victims. Even if he had vastly inflated the number of victims – and it is impossible to know either way – Black was now by his own admission a serial molester of children. At the age of just sixteen.

There was an incident, he recalled when speaking to Ray Wyre, during his early days in Greenock. He described how he, another young boy and a young girl, together went into a sort of hut, similar to a deserted old henhouse, in a field. There, the girl agreed for Black to look at her privates in exchange for a cigarette. Black cannot remember if he touched her or not, but clearly remembers the girl being in what he considered to be a position of control in regard to her telling him when they should stop, and then smoking the cigarette.

This incident serves to show how Black's obsession with orifices, and in particular the genitalia of little girls, was increasingly at the forefront of his sexual offending. Perhaps he was trying to paint a picture of a small group of children experimenting in an innocent doctors-and-nurses type of scenario with little damage to any of those involved, but in the light of what we know Black had done previously and would go on to do in the future, it is not a believable picture. In any case, he, and presumably the others, were somewhat too old for such explorations to be totally innocent.

It wouldn't take long for Black's offending to increase in brutality and cruelty. From voyeurism and molestations, Black soon went on to carry out an attack that would be both more sophisticated in its pre-meditation and horrific in the level of violence that he used. It would also result in his first court appearance for a sexual offence against a young female child.

It was an early summer afternoon in 1963 and Black had ventured into a local playground. There was a group of children playing on the swings. He bided his time as the children went home one by one until one little girl was left alone on the swings. He approached the little girl, who was aged only seven, and pushed her on the swings briefly. He knew where there were kittens, he told her, and offered to take the little girl to see them. As he and the little girl exited the park they passed a local policeman whom Black knew –

he was at the time attending a local youth club that was run by a local police sergeant.

Black took the little girl to a nearby abandoned air-raid shelter. As they entered it and encountered the darkness, the little girl grew frightened and, wanting to leave, started to cry. But rather than being in the company of a caring young person who would relieve her of her distress, she was in the company of a youth who was in a depraved sexual frenzy and would proceed to subject her to a terrifying ordeal. Black put one of his hands over the child's mouth to stop her from crying out and screaming, and then put the other hand around her throat, throttling her, and pushing her down to the ground. The little girl fell unconscious and Black proceeded to assault the defenceless child, lifting her skirt up, taking off her underwear and inserting his finger into her vagina. Black then masturbated and ejaculated onto the floor, following which he put her underpants back on the child and left the shelter, apparently unaware of the state of his victim – whether she was still alive or if he had killed her as he throttled her – and unconcerned. This disregard for the life and well-being of his victim is particularly distressing, and telling at the same time, considering what we know of the murderous offences Black would go on to commit in the future. Thankfully, his young victim survived and was later found walking the streets alone and distressed, tired, confused, crying and bleeding.

Black was arrested the very next day and charged with 'lewd and libidinous behaviour with a young girl'. In hindsight, however, and looking at the facts and details of the attack he should have been charged with attempted murder.

He received a twelve-month suspended sentence at Greenock Sheriff Court on 25 June 1963.

The sentence was little more than a telling-off, a slap on the wrist, a warning. No account of the incident was written up in any newspaper. A psychiatric report at the time concluded that the incident was isolated, a one-off that was unlikely to happen again. We now know that, sadly, nothing could have been further from the truth. Black was not offered or recommended for any kind of treatment although a report by the Probation Service released three weeks before his court admonishment suggested that he might need residential psychiatric care; it appears to have been ignored. It seemed luck was on Robert Black's side: the sixteen-year-old had already a disturbing criminal career of repeat molestations, an attempted rape, and now enticing, attempting to murder and indecently assaulting a young girl, and was still not served a custodial sentence. He had got away with an awful lot of offending.

Following his admonishment for the park attack, Black lost his job, and the local Social Services, taking a far more serious view of what he had done to the little girl in the park than did the psychiatrists or court, decided he should leave Greenock. Once again Black was on the move, this time back to more familiar territory in Grangemouth, near Falkirk, close to where he was born. If this was supposed to be another fresh start for Black again it failed miserably as his past behaviours simply followed him and eventually reappeared.

It is thought that, in 1964, at the age of seventeen, Robert Black got his first job as a delivery driver with John Menzies, the newspaper and magazine distributors. This was reported in the 20 May 1994 edition of the *Daily Express* newspaper. Co-author of this book, retired Norfolk Police intelligence officer Chris Clark, contacted former Fleet Street journalists Ian McKerron and James Gryllis who told him it was their understanding that Black at this time worked first as a delivery driver for the Glasgow *Evening Times* and then John Menzies. Unbeknownst to his then employers, Black did not have a driving licence at the time – he did not pass his driving test until 1976 when he was twenty-seven, so this early driving work indicates, like many young men at that time, he was prepared to gain driving experience at the risk of not having a licence or the appropriate paperwork.

It is known that while in Grangemouth, Black worked for a while at a builders' supplies company as well as having the odd labouring job at other times. He lived with an elderly local couple in the Newlands Road area. They provided a homely setting that was the first Black had experienced for some years, having only known children's homes of one sort or another since leaving Kinlochleven, and his life came as close to 'normal' as it ever would. He attended a local youth club, and there he met a young woman, Pamela, with whom he struck up a relationship. It would be the only real consensual relationship he would have, and the only one with an adult female. For several months they dated and Black harboured hopes that they would one day marry. Whilst this relationship appears to have been fairly normal, there is little doubt that Robert Black's paedophiliac desires remained within him. He would later reveal to Ray Wyre that he and Pamela fell in love, had a normal sexual relationship and that things were good for period of time. It all came crashing down, however, when Black received a letter from Pamela telling him it was over. It is unclear as to why Pamela decided to end it. Was it his body odour and personal hygiene problem? Had she met someone else? Or had she heard of Black's past and reputation in regard to his sexual inclinations? Whatever the reason, the break-up devastated Black, who refused for a long time to accept that Pamela had left him. The theme of rejection by women was becoming as familiar to him as his deviant sexual offending. From being given up as a baby by his natural mother, to his foster mother dying when he was a young boy, to the constant teasing by his classmates and then his break-up with Pamela as a teenager; these events would no doubt have had a detrimental effect on Black as a person, and whilst none of it can condone or justify for one second his actions against young girls, it can help us understand his lack of feeling or compassion, his coldness and cruelty as an offender towards his victims and their loved ones.

An indication of how much Pamela's spurning of Black wounded him, and how he allowed the rejection to fester, is the comment he made in 1992, getting on for thirty years later, after being served with ten summonses by police for a number of very serious charges, including the murders of three little girls. As the police began to leave his cell, Black called out to them the words, 'Tell Pamela she's not responsible for this.' He clammed up when they asked him to explain further. That Black brought up Pamela's name without the police having even mentioned it, after being charged with three murders, implies that he was blaming her for the path he had taken after she had broken up with him. This attempt by Black to shift the blame for his actions (or, at that time, alleged actions) is of course ridiculous but it demonstrates how resentful Black was at Pamela's dumping of him, one more rejection by a female in his life.

After his break-up with Pamela, Black's life as a sexual predator came to the fore once again. In 1966 he was found to be regularly interfering with the young granddaughter of the couple he was staying with. He was immediately ordered to leave the house. The police were not called at the time as the family felt that the young girl had been through enough, although they did consider notifying them. The girl was aged nine or ten at the time. Many years later, when police interviewed the victim after Black's 1990 arrest, she told them he would regularly insert his fingers into her vagina.

So once again, it seemed, Black had luck on his side, at least when it came to any dealings with the law. Shortly after this he was called into the office of the builders' supplies company he was working for, and was told his employment there was ended. He later admitted that he lost many jobs through his inability to arrive at work on time.

Black was once again on the move, and soon he was back in the familiar territory of Kinlochleven, where he had once lived with the people who were the nearest he had ever had to parents, the Tulips. Here he found employment, taking on various labouring and driving jobs, and lodged in the Appin Road area with a married couple, the parents of one of whom had been friends with the Tulips.

The couple had a six-year-old daughter whom they

frequently trusted him to babysit. One night while Black was drinking in the local pub, police showed up and arrested him. At the police station he was charged with three counts of indecent assault. He had been abusing the little girl while he was supposed to be looking after her.

This time Black would not escape a prison sentence, and on 22 March 1967, a month short of his twentieth birthday, he was sentenced to one year in borstal. He was also convicted of the lesser charge of voyeurism: the village postwoman had caught him staring through a window at her young sister and had complained to the police.

A year later, in 1968, Black left borstal and stayed for a brief period in a probation hostel in Glasgow, where he again had a brief brush with the law when he was collared by local uniformed police for loitering outside a shop with the intention of stealing.

After this Black was once again on the move. This time, however, where he moved to would be his home until 1990. England's capital city was an attractive option for a young man like Black. Like many young Scots who travelled down south to the capital, he saw better job opportunities in London, a big city with a big population. He also recognised that London offered anonymity – most important to a repeat sex offender with a past and convictions – and the chance for a truly fresh start as, unlike people and police in Scotland, those in London were unaware of his past. Authorities made no attempt to keep track of him; he was a free man.

London was to be the next chapter of Robert Black's life; he would get a new home, a new job, a new circle of friends and at last a long-term period of stability, and would appear to be the most settled and happiest that he would be in his entire life. This however was to be no Dick Whittington-type story. Sadly, despite these new opportunities and stabilities, instead of turning his back on past paedophiliac tendencies and depraved behaviour, Robert Black would continue to develop as an increasingly dangerous and deadly sexually predatory criminal. So deadly in fact that by the next time he would be behind bars, over twenty years after he first arrived in London, he was no longer just a serial abuser of children, he was an abductor and serial killer of children.

3

HEADING
SOUTH

Robert Black arrived in London at some point between August and October 1968, a young man ready to seek out lodgings and employment. As a predatory paedophile arriving in a big city full of unsuspecting people he must have been aware of the opportunities to seek out victims. Although the capital can be a frightening place for a newcomer, given its size and general fast-paced way of life, the twenty-one-year-old Robert Black quickly began to integrate into London life despite its being a world of difference from the rural and tightknit Scottish towns and villages he was used to. Although he would never venture too far away from King's Cross, he would live at three different addresses in the Stamford Hill/ Stoke Newington area of North London. The first one was an attic bedsit at 24 Bergholt Crescent, a five-bedroom guest house, where Black lived for at least a year, moving in before

10 October 1968 (the cut-off point for the 1969 electoral register, which has Robert Black's name on it). During his stay at Bergholt Crescent a thirteen-year-old girl by the name of April Fabb disappeared as she cycled near her home in the Norfolk village of Metton, in April 1969.

Some months later, Black moved again, to another bedsit, at 47 Albion Road in Stoke Newington, only a couple of miles away from Bergholt Crescent. This was at some point between the 10 October 1969 and February 1970, and he would remain there until the autumn of 1971.

It was during Robert Black's time as a resident of 47 Albion Road that, in the spring of 1971, a fifteen-year-old girl called Jeanne Twigden had a lucky escape when an attempt was made to abduct her as she cycled home from an open-air pool near the village of Great Paxton, Cambridgeshire. Jeanne would later go on to become the wife of Chris Clark, co-author of this book. There will be more on April and Jeanne's cases and their connection to Robert Black later in the book.

★ ★ ★

During his early years in London, Robert Black had a variety of casual jobs, most of them poorly paid, but he was never heard to complain, seeming happy to supplement his wages with part-time work as pub barman. Indeed, pubs were to form a regular part of his social life as well, and Black would often be found drinking in various pubs of North London, a regular at a number of them. While he would take a drink he never drank heavily, preferring to stay in control, just sipping at a pint of lager or Bass shandy. He stood out as a fairly good darts player and played in several different pub teams on the amateur North London pub league darts circuit, winning several trophies along the way. One of the teams he played for was that of the Baring Arms pub on the Baring Road in Islington, just on the border of Hackney and just south of Albion Road in Stoke Newington, where he lived. He would be a regular at this pub for many years. One of the many darts players he played against on the amateur circuit was none other than future world darts champion Eric Bristow. Black's fondness for football would also re-emerge during his early years living in the capital as he was invited to play a trial match for a well-known non-League London football club, Enfield Town FC. However, any potential career in football was unlikely due to Black's poor eyesight and the trial did not result in Black being offered professional terms or a playing contract.

Whilst he would make acquaintances in his social activities at the local pubs near his home and in and around the Church Street/Stoke Newington areas and was accepted as a regular part of the neighbourhood and local drinking community, he never made any real friends, and one word that would continually come up when his former fellow pub regulars were asked for their thoughts on him was 'loner'. Black remained a loner throughout his life, a man whom people couldn't get close to, or maybe more precisely did not want to get close to, and he was never seen with a girlfriend when he went to the pubs, although he did enjoy annoying or winding up women with the occasional remarks and swear words.

In regard to his working life one of the jobs Black took

was that of a lifeguard at an indoor swimming pool (now long gone) on Clissold Road, which was only around a five-minute walk from his home on the Albion Road. He was put on a six-month trial but before he got the chance to be offered a permanent position he was sacked for being late for his early-morning shifts. Black would later tell the late Ray Wyre, who interviewed him in prison, that he found it hard to get up in the mornings and that as a result he lost a lot of jobs because of poor time keeping. It must have been a disappointment to lose the lifeguard job, which would have suited him well – he was good at swimming and he enjoyed it. Rather more sinisterly, the work gave him plenty of opportunity to watch little girls clad only in their swimming costumes, and the possibility of touching them while they were swimming. There was the added interest of a primary school in the close locality.

After taking on and then being sacked from a variety of jobs for his bad time-keeping, Black saw an advertisement for a job as pool attendant in an open-air pool for the whole of the summer season, which would have been from May to September. He applied for the job and got it. It is believed this was the Clissold Park Paddling Pool, again situated only half a mile from where he lived. Black worked there through the entire summer period, and when the pool closed at the end of the season he applied for a similar job with a different council and again he was successful. For the next couple of years he worked as swimming pool attendant at Hornsey Road Swimming Baths.

Robert Black was by no means the only young Scotsman to move down south to the English capital to look for work and a new life. Many others had moved south to other parts of the United Kingdom in search of work, and had integrated into local communities whilst retaining their Scottish identity. In autumn 1971 Robert Black met one such couple, Edward and Katherine Rayson, fellow Scots who had moved to London from north of the border. Edward and Katherine, or Eddie and Kathy as they were usually known, got into conversation with Black whilst he was playing darts at the Three Crowns pub in Stoke Newington. As they chatted, Black soon discovered that the Raysons were originally from Musselburgh, where Black himself had lived for between the ages of twelve and fifteen, at the Red House. In the course of their conversation Black confided to the Raysons that he was unhappy with his current accommodation at Albion Road, where he had been staying for anywhere from a year to two years, although he never explained why: had his landlord or landlady become concerned about Black's behaviour in the neighbourhood? Black then asked Eddie Rayson if he had a spare room he could rent off him. Eddie Rayson was reluctant to invite the young man whom he had met only briefly to stay at his house straight away but he talked to his wife Kathy about Black's proposal. Kathy was more open to the idea than her husband, and shortly afterwards Robert Black moved into what would be his third and last North London residence, the attic room of 7 West Bank, Stamford Hill, a four-storeyed Victorian property, with Eddie, Kathy and their seven children.

Black was to stay here until his arrest some nineteen years later, and the Raysons were to become the closest thing

Robert Black ever had to a family and a settled family life. After Black's first murder convictions in 1994, a shocked Eddie Rayson spoke to Ian McKerron of the. *Daily Express* (Friday, 20 May 1994).

'He was a perfect tenant. He always paid his rent on time and never caused any problems. He had the flat at the top of the house. We would go in occasionally for a game of cards or to listen to a record. He had masses of LPs, mainly Country and Western. And he spent a lot of money on hi-fi and video equipment.'

The Rayson family would have no idea that the man who shared their home for so long was a dangerous predator until Black's 1990 arrest for child abduction and sexual assault. To them Black was the hard-working fellow countryman who would eat his meals with the family, accompany the Rayson men to the pub for a game of darts and a pint of shandy, and play an occasional game of cards and listen to Country and Western records with them. When not working or at the pub playing darts he would amuse himself by watching television, solving crossword puzzles and lifting weights in a makeshift gym he had in his attic flat.

Black would attend the christenings of the Rayson grandchildren and other family events through the years and would give gifts to Kathy Rayson, who encouraged him to take regular showers and to keep himself fresh and clean – though it appears that personal hygiene and cleanliness were low on Robert Black's list of priorities, and the Rayson children would tease him over his body odour problem. They would never see him with women or see any evidence that he was interested in dating or pursuing a relationship. There was a possibility he may have used prostitutes but the Raysons only ever recalled him having a girl back to his flat once in the nearly twenty years he lived with them, and whoever this girl was she was gone in the morning and would never again be seen at Stamford Hill.

The Rayson family, like Black's work colleagues and associates from his early days in his native Scotland, were shocked and appalled when his crimes came to light

'This has been very upsetting for the family,' Eddie and Kathy's son Paul said to the *Daily Express* (20 May 1994). 'We never had a clue that he could be capable of such terrible crimes. How could we?'

They would jokingly refer to Black as David Bailey after the famous photographer. Black owned an expensive camera and, although he was not keen on having his own photograph taken, he enjoyed taking photos of other people. When, following Black's arrest in 1990, police searched his flat, they discovered videos and photos taken of children at playgrounds and by the seaside, so it appears his purchase of the expensive camera and video equipment had a more sinister purpose than at first appeared. (Black is similar in this respect to the American serial killer Rodney Alcala who took hundreds of photographs, mostly of young women and children whilst on a spree of savage murders in the 1970s.) Police also found in Black's flat a photograph album containing photos of the Rayson children. There was never, however, any suggestion of anything untoward, and the family have roundly rejected such an idea – Black would by now have realised that any such action would ensure a repeat of what happened to him in Scotland: he would at the very least be banished from the household and forced to seek new lodgings or be would be put in prison and have to move to a new area to live after his release and find new employment. No, Robert Black had become settled in Stamford Hill and in North London generally and did not wish to jeopardise what had become the most settled part of his life. If victims of his sexual depravity were to be found it was to be elsewhere.

★ ★ ★

While Black was good at swimming and enjoyed it, his job at Hornsey Road Swimming Baths also brought him the advantage of doing different shifts on different weeks, one week he did early shifts, the next week he did later shifts, which gave him the chance to lie in. And although pool-attendant pay was poor, he worked in the evenings at various pubs to boost his income.

It was not long, however, before Black's perversions would come into his work at the pool, and would ultimately cost him his job. At the start his lust for kicks was satisfied by behaviour such as going underneath the pool and removing the lights so that he could watch from below, unseen, young girls as they swam round. Another distasteful activity he would indulge in during his period as pool attendant was to break into the swimming pool at night and swim lengths with a broom handle inserted in his rectum. Before long, the inevitable happened and Black once again found himself in trouble over an incident with a child. A ten-year-old girl complained that he had indecently touched her while they were both in the pool. Black was arrested and taken to the local police station where he protested his innocence, stating that there were several kids of both sexes in the pool at the time and if he had touched her it was accidental not intentional. However, when the police became aware of his previous convictions he was ordered to hand in his notice to the pool. The police advised management to accept his resignation or they would ensure Black was sacked. After a meeting with management they accepted his decision to quit. This incident occurred in the early part of 1976, and Robert Black was no longer to work in a swimming-pool environment again. His next job, whilst not involving working with children would provide him with employment for the next fourteen years and would regrettably also provide him with opportunities to abduct, abuse and kill children.

4

THE MIDLANDS
TRIANGLE

During his brief period of unemployment in 1976, Black must have found he had time to indulge in and enlarge his collection of child pornography, which he would continue to build up for the next fourteen years. Following his arrest in 1990, police searched his attic flat at Stamford Hill and discovered over a hundred child pornographic magazines and almost a dozen child pornographic films inside a blue suitcase. Black, in taped conversations with Ray Wyre later in prison, explained that he used to purchase the porn from a shop in the King's Cross area that sold ordinary books as a front but had an 'adult' section at the back of the premises. Initially, Black bought adult pornography, and then a chance enquiry about teenage sex magazines was met with material featuring children. Black claimed to Ray Wyre to have been embarrassed, taking the material and making a quick exit, but there can be no doubt that he had found a source of such obscene and depraved material and probably revisited the shop on several more occasions. He also disclosed that he obtained child pornography while on trips to Amsterdam and Copenhagen.

Black's spell of unemployment was a short one as he soon found a job that would provide him with a steady income and employment for the next fourteen years. As well as providing him with these, the natural requirements of any worker, this job would also unwittingly facilitate his unnatural needs.

Poster, Despatch and Storage, or PDS as it was generally called, was a company based in Goodwin Street, Hoxton, East London. Formed in the 1950s but now defunct, the company's business was sending out vans to deliver posters used in billboard campaigns at over a hundred locations around the United Kingdom and occasionally in Europe. The drivers would use a variety of different vans, often depending on the route they were taking and the load they were carrying. For Black, who had dishonestly gained driving experience working in the 1960s in Scotland delivering newspapers without a driving licence, it seemed a good choice of employment. There is evidence that he had access to several vehicles in London – indeed, he was arrested for an offence involving cars in 1972 (*see* p. 310) – and there is even a suggestion that by this time he had obtained a white Transit van for his own personal use and had already started working delivery jobs on an occasional basis. Full-time work in this field seemed a logical next step. He had no partner or family to spend time with and for a young man with no ties a job with long hours travelling away from home did not present a problem. One problem however was his lack of a driving licence – he needed one, and soon, in order to get the job of courier with PDS. His years of driving experience served him well, though, and he seems to have passed his driving test with no hitch. Once he had his full driving licence he became a PDS employee.

PDS directed its drivers to make deliveries and stops at a variety of different runs and routes up and down and across the United Kingdom. Robert Black would at one point or another work all of them. The five main runs were:

1. The South Coast Run. This was one of the longer delivery routes for the PDS drivers and could involve runs or deliveries from London on to Gloucester, then Cardiff and Swansea or, after Gloucester, on to Bristol, then Taunton, Exeter, Plymouth, or then on to Southampton, Portsmouth, Eastbourne, and then on to Hounslow in London. In August 1978 a thirteen-year-old girl called Genette Tate would disappear from an area within the points of this particular delivery route.

2. The Scottish/Northern Run. This delivery run was also long in terms of distance and time, and was not favoured by many of the PDS drivers, especially those with wives and families, and usually because it was a weekend run. It took in stops from London to the southern towns of Luton and Northampton, then went on to the Midlands cities such as Coventry and Nottingham, on to Yorkshire cities like Sheffield and Hull, then through

the Border areas of Scotland and on to the cities of Edinburgh, Dundee and Glasgow. The return leg of this route would follow the west coast of England via the M1 motorway. Black was willing to do this route the majority of times, usually having nothing to do over weekends. On this route over a four-year period in the 1980s three young girls would disappear and later be found murdered, their bodies dumped in a triangular area of the East Midlands.

3. The East Coast Run. This was a shorter route for the PDS drivers in terms of the number of drop-off points and the shorter distances and times undertaken to complete the journey; it therefore offered smaller bonuses. The stops on this route took the driver from London to Northampton, on to Norwich, as far as Lowestoft, then back south through Ipswich and past Chelmsford and back to the capital.

4. The Midlands Run. This included stops in the West Midlands cities of Birmingham and Coventry before sometimes going further into the north-west to Liverpool and Manchester, before returning south via Peterborough and Northampton. Interestingly, the Midlands run also included, when required, a trip to Northern Ireland, where PDS drivers would mostly make deliveries in and around Belfast and then go on to the County Down city of Newry and sometimes as far west as the town of Enniskillen and the County Fermanagh border. It was whilst making this work trip that, on 12 August 1981, Black would abduct Jennifer Cardy from the village of

Ballinderry, not far from the main motorway linking the cities of Belfast and Newry, and murder her.

5. The European Run. There was also the occasional work trip into the central part of the continent, and Black would make deliveries for PDS in parts of northern France and to Germany during the mid and late 1980s. A number of murders of little girls would occur in those areas, during these periods . . .

To his work colleagues Black was someone whom they could never get really close to and from the comments after his arrest had no real desire to as his body odour problem followed him into further adulthood and his new long-term employers and fellow workers would often complain to each other about his smell and personal hygiene. They obviously had no idea how dangerous and cold a man Black was and the monstrous crimes he would go on to commit while working for the company, but they did have their suspicions that Black was a pervert and that he had a liking for younger girls. On one occasion a young woman in her late teens or early twenties passed by where the drivers were gathered in the company's yard, and, as many men can do, they remarked on how pretty this young woman was. One driver, however, then turned to Black and commented that she was too old for him. These are words that Black would have not taken well as he would have been desperate to keep his paedophilia a secret. One incident in particular may have led to the remark and to the suspicion amongst his colleagues that Black was perverted. One Christmas Day he was invited to a work colleague's house to spend the day with him and his family. During his stay Black was playing with his workmate's children but whilst many adults love children and play innocently with them, Black's type of play was viewed as anything but innocent by the children's father. When later asked by another PDS employee how he got on with Black on Christmas Day, the father replied that whilst 'playing' with his children Black would repeatedly put his hand on his daughter's genital area during what he was obviously trying to portray as innocent horseplay. To the father, it certainly was not innocent, and Black, he said, would never again be welcome in his home. No repeat invitation was forthcoming.

Despite these later suspicions and worries about Black's character to many at the company he was generally viewed as a hard-working driver who never complained when asked to do any of the less desirable trips and who was willing to help out other drivers who couldn't make particular routes on any given day for a particular reason. Many workplaces in all fields have workers who although maybe not personally popular are popular in their work ethic and reliability for helping out their employers in certain areas. Robert Black could be considered one such person. He was a fast and sometimes reckless driver and would often cost the company a lot of money in insurance claims, due to a number of road traffic accidents and scrapes throughout the years, which eventually resulted in his dismissal in 1986. The company was bought out in 1987 by two employees and Black was re-hired with the proviso that he bought his own vehicle and insured it himself, with PDS merely supplying him with the posters and instructions on where to deliver them. Black readily accepted this new arrangement and by 1989 he was a freelance delivery driver and thus became self-employed.

Because the early-morning traffic in London was often nightmarish in its busy and time-consuming flow, the company introduced the practice of having their drivers leaving the yard at night, thus beating the early-morning traffic not only in London but also on the motorways up and down the country, which saved time and improved efficiency. It also meant that Black and the other drivers were issued with a set of keys so that they could leave the posters at the required location should the delivery take place out of hours. The drivers would have to sign a document, a delivery log or book, giving their name, detailing the precise time of delivery and what they had delivered. This practice would help bring about Black's eventual arrest, when the police began investigating him in connection with a number of child murders as it would prove when and where he was when making certain deliveries.

Another procedure that would later provide the police with irrefutable documented evidence in building a case against Black was to be the petrol agency cards PDS issued each driver with when they set off on a work journey. These cards would be used to pay for fuel for the work vans and also served to record the time, date and location the cards had been used.

Robert Black would drive a number of vans for PDS during his employment with them, from 1976 when he began working for the company. These included:

Mercedes vans (1976)
VW LT vans (1976)
Fiat Dailys (1980s)
Ford Transits (1980s to 1989)
Nissan/Datsun (usually used for the smaller runs and the
Northern Ireland trip)

These vans would vary in colour but were usually white or a dark/navy shade of blue. Some of the Transits might also have been fire-engine red.

To Black his van would eventually become a lot more than just his work vehicle – his workmates, if he gave them a lift, for example, would complain and wonder about the smell and the rubbish strewn inside with the mattress in the back after he had used it for a delivery run. It would become his home away from home, the centre of his secret depraved world and an important part of his offending pattern. The dark, stinking and frightening back of his van was his secret lair, the physical manifestation of the fantasy world in which Black was the king. It was in his van that his deviant thoughts become a reality. The van not only transported him and his load of posters for work purposes, but transported him in thought and action away from the normal world he had been living in with the Raysons at his attic home in North London. The quiet man who chatted pleasantly over a pint in the pub, or played darts, the hard-working van driver for whom no trip was too small or too long and who helped his fellow drivers out from time to time, as he stepped into his van, stepped, too, into the secret world in which he would abduct, abuse and kill children. Previous to this the only type of regular paedophiliac indulgence he had was in the privacy of his attic flat where he would view his child-pornography films and leaf through his child-pornography magazines. Additionally, his van was important in that it enabled him to carry out attacks on children well away from his home territory or base, which is one reason why there was never any question that Black had attacked or interfered with any of the Rayson children. As was commented after his first murder convictions in 1994 he likely did not wish to mess on his own doorstep, and after having had to flee across Scotland for doing just that, he had no ambition to once again be on the move looking for a new home or, worse, face prison. The job of delivery driver unwittingly gave him the opportunity to explore the length and breadth of the United Kingdom, abducting and killing a number of young girls before returning home to North London as if nothing had happened, slipping back into the normal reality of the world he had cultivated around him. Just an ordinary bloke who enjoyed a pint of shandy and playing darts in pubs and listening to country music when not working hard travelling such long distances.

The geographical mobility his job gave him would provide a cover for Black to carry out his crimes, making him the very dangerous 'travelling offender' type. A travelling offender is much more difficult to pinpoint and track down than the offender who carries out his crimes within the community in which he lives. By the 1980s police were just beginning to understand this dangerous type of offender, particularly the ones that used their job and the geographical mobility that came with it as a tool or weapon to help them commit and conceal their crimes.

5

THE MIDLANDS MURDERS

THE MURDER OF SUSAN MAXWELL

The village of Cornhill-on-Tweed in the county of Northumberland lies just on the English side of the border with Scotland. A beautiful rural civil parish with fields and farming families within it, a proud community not dissimilar to that of Ballinderry in County Antrim. The vast River Tweed runs through the village and the nearest significant-sized town is Berwick-upon-Tweed, over a dozen miles away. A mile to the east lies the smaller town of Coldstream.

Eleven-year-old Susan Maxwell was enjoying her summer holidays when she went missing. The daughter of journalist Elizabeth Maxwell and journalist-farmer Fordyce, Susan Claire Maxwell lived on Cramond Hill Farm in Cornhill-on-Tweed with her parents, sister Jacqueline and brother Tom. On the early afternoon of Friday, 30 July Susan arranged to meet up with her friend Alison Raeburn who lived just over the border with Scotland, in nearby Coldstream. It was a lovely hot day and the two school friends agreed to meet in Coldstream for a game of tennis at the tennis club Susan had joined the previous week. Susan had originally planned to cycle into Coldstream but her mother thought it was not a good idea so she decided to walk into the town; in the end she did not have to, however, as one of the workers on the farm gave her a lift. Susan arrived early in Coldstream and went to the local post office in the Tweed Garage to buy some stamps before meeting her friend. Susan and Alison played tennis for an hour with Susan emerging the victor, winning the set six games to five. The two girls left the tennis club together to walk home, and parted at Lennell Mount in Coldstream, a short walk from the River Tweed, agreeing to see each other at a carnival in Coldstream the next week. Susan, who was wearing a bright yellow T-shirt with a palm tree motif on the front, a pair of yellow shorts and white ankle socks, walked on towards Cramond Hill Farm. As she approached the Coldstream Bridge over the Tweed she would have had no idea of the imminent danger she would face. It was about 4.15 p.m. As she came to the bridge, she was spotted by a van driver passing her on the opposite side of the road heading in the direction of Coldstream town centre. Susan began to walk over the bridge while the driver, who had already turned his vehicle round, was now driving, in a southerly direction, back the way he had come, again passing Susan, only this time on the same side of the road as her. Black passed Susan and made his way over the bridge and soon came across an empty entrance to a field just off the road. There was no gate at the entrance and he was able to reverse his van into it where the vehicle would not have been visible to anyone until they actually came upon and passed the field's entrance. Black knew it was the perfect place to park his van and he knew this was another opportunity to abduct another child. Knowing that Susan was walking across the bridge and would be imminently walking past his van, Black waited for a minute and then exited his vehicle as the child approached. Susan was then, in a matter of seconds, abducted.

Liz Maxwell, meanwhile, thinking her daughter might be rather tired to walk home after playing tennis in the summer heat, decided to put Susan's younger siblings in the car and go surprise her by meeting and giving her a lift home. But when she arrived at the tennis club the place was empty and locked up. Considering it strange that she hadn't seen Susan on her way into Coldstream and that the child wasn't at the tennis courts either, she returned to Cramond Hill Farm and telephoned Alison Raeburn, who told her that she had last seen Susan on the outskirts of Coldstream, walking in the direction of her home. Panicked and worried, the Maxwells quickly phoned 999 and told the police their daughter was missing.

Local police based both at Cornhill-on-Tweed under the Northumbria force, and at Coldstream under the branch of Lothian and Borders Police immediately began searching the general area where Susan was last seen, which was just over the Coldstream Bridge; they made house-to-house enquiries, and urgently traced and contacted possible witnesses who might have seen Susan, such as motorists who could have passed her on the road, in the hope they had seen anything of relevance.

The Maxwell family were positive that Susan would not have readily accepted a lift from a stranger. Detectives working on the case almost immediately began to fear the worst – that Susan Maxwell had been abducted.

The police were quickly able to establish that there had been a number of witnesses who had seen Susan walking home that afternoon carrying her tennis racket, walking towards, and then across, Coldstream Bridge. A number of motorists had seen her walking along the bridge, which is on the main road linking the northern English city of Newcastle to Coldstream, containing the actual border line between England and Scotland; just past the bridge is a small white monument that displays the red cross of St George, marking the entrance into England from Scotland. As it was a busy road full of drivers on holiday or business trips as well as drivers who lived locally, it was not surprising that there were a number of sightings of Susan as she made her way across the bridge, but there was a small gap between the last sighting made by a motorist (a Yorkshire businessman) of the child making her way over the bridge and, two minutes later, when another motorist passed. The second motorist had seen no sign of Susan, which indicates that she had disappeared during the two-minute gap between these two motorists driving by. There was also a woman who worked in a nearby garage based in Cornhill and a lorry driver who stopped on the English side of the Coldstream Bridge for a break in the minutes after Susan had left Alison Raeburn to walk home; both of them were adamant that Susan had not passed them. This confirmation from various motorists who had crossed the Coldstream Bridge at that time of the afternoon passing both ways quickly strengthened the fears of the police that Susan had been abducted. There had been sightings of her walking towards a certain point of the road just off the end of the bridge at a certain time and after that time there had been no further sightings. In less than two minutes she had been abducted. Frustratingly for police, a local farmer who would normally have been in a particular nearby field at that time of the afternoon was elsewhere so he didn't see Susan making her journey home. Interestingly, however, there were sightings of something else from witnesses around the time of Susan's disappearance: it was a vehicle, to be precise it was a white van. The vehicle was at one point seen parked in a field gateway near to the point where Susan Maxwell was last seen alive walking, just across the Coldstream Bridge on the English side. Police could never positively trace the van or the driver due to the fact that whilst several people had seen the van in the nearby vicinity they could only offer a general description of its colour and type.

This is understandable considering how many vehicles there are to be seen every day, being driven or stationary by the side of a road, and indeed considering how similar most everyday vehicles are to one another. Unless there is something very unusual in the appearance of a vehicle, in its location, or in the way it is being handled, drivers and pedestrians will be aware of it but not give it a second glance, never mind noting its make or registration. The sightings of this white van, however, would take on a much greater significance during the investigation, trial and conviction of Susan's killer some twelve years later.

The next day saw a full-scale search undertaken for the missing girl, with scenes very similar to those the previous August, with the Royal Ulster Constabulary and local volunteers searching for Jennifer Cardy in rural Ulster, although at the time nobody imagined the two cases were connected and the same killer was responsible. Fordyce Maxwell, Susan's father, joined the army of volunteers who under the direction of Northumbria Police, working in tandem with Lothian and Borders Police, combed through areas stretching across some fifty miles of mostly rural terrain. Specialist police diving teams from the North-East of England were drafted in to search the River Tweed, while from its banks to the forests and fields, searchers, including police with specially trained tracker dogs, systematically scoured the land in the hope that little Susan would be found safe and well. But while that flame of hope flickered on, with each hour and day that passed it was getting dimmer.

As the Maxwell family, like Andrew and Patricia Cardy had done the year previously, spoke to the media, giving interviews and making pleas for Susan's safe return on television and in newspapers, the police in Northumbria were carrying out investigative actions similar to those their counterparts in Northern Ireland had undertaken the previous summer. A reconstruction was staged with a little girl who looked similar to Susan filmed walking in similar clothing across the Coldstream Bridge. This was done, like all reconstructions, in a bid to reach potential witnesses who had not come forward or to trigger the possibility of new information coming in to police. One plea made by detectives was for three youths who had been seen having a picnic on the English side of the Coldstream Bridge between 4.30 p.m. and 4.45 p.m. that afternoon. They had been travelling in an old purple-coloured Mini-Traveller. The vehicle and the young men were later traced, interviewed and subsequently eliminated. That Sunday, the second full day of the search, prayers were said for the Maxwell family and Susan's safe return in the nearby church.

As the days passed and the following week was upon the team of detectives searching for Susan, the Maxwells, both respected journalists, used their knowledge of the media and the way it worked to their advantage knowing that the more Susan's face and description was on television and in the papers the better the chance she would be found. Liz would normally be the one at home speaking to journalists and surrounded by friends and family who were there to support her whilst she was there for her two younger children, three-year-old Tom and five-year-old Jacqueline. Fordyce was spending every hour he could with the search teams desperately looking for his little girl.

'At least it kept me doing something,' he said. 'It kept my mind occupied and stopped me sitting round thinking too much.' (Quoted in *Fear the Stranger: Susan Maxwell, Caroline Hogg and Sarah Harper* by Hector Clark and David Johnston, 1994.)

Fordyce was questioned by police about his movements the day of Susan's disappearance and his relationship with her – this is normal police routine investigation and Fordyce was quickly eliminated as having had nothing to do with Susan's disappearance, but it would have no doubt added to their pain. That Tuesday was Jacqueline's birthday and in an effort to maintain a level of normality for her two other children in the midst of such a worrying time for the Maxwell family a little birthday party was held with presents for little Jacqueline from her big sister Susan, as photographers from the newspapers snapped her cutting her birthday cake, all in attendance aware that keeping Susan's story in the public eye was the priority via whatever necessary means.

That same day police held a meeting in the packed local village hall where Chief Inspector Fred Stephenson from Northumbria Police addressed those in attendance specifically focusing on Susan's last journey over the Coldstream Bridge and appealing for witnesses to Susan on this her last known walk to come forward with any information. Also in attendance was the Chief Constable of Northumbria Police Stanley Bailey who announced to the residents of Cornhill village that he wished them to agree to every house being searched so that the village could be eliminated. The possibility of nearby Coldstream also having every house within it searched was also raised with Lothian and Borders Police helping in that task, which would undoubtedly be a bigger one but police were eager for both areas and their residents to be eliminated from the enquiry. Whilst this ultimately meant a request for police to search every home, outhouse and private property of the local people there were no objections from anyone local such was the eagerness to find a little girl from their own community who was missing. Parents attending the meeting no doubt would also have been conscious of the possibility it could have been one of their own children who had been abducted. In a two-day search every property, business, house and shed, in Cornhill-on-Tweed was searched by police with the agreement, and support of local residents. Nothing of significance, however, was found.

Liz Maxwell herself had a feeling about what had happened to her daughter and it was in the end proved to be the correct analysis of the situation.

'The only thing I can suggest is that somebody stopped and asked her directions – and grabbed her,' Liz Maxwell said during the search for her daughter (quoted in *The Murder of Childhood*).

One week after Susan's disappearance detectives depressingly had to admit they hadn't one single strong lead in the investigation and the little girl's whereabouts were still unknown. By the following Friday, 13 August, which marked the second week since Susan went missing, her fate was to become known, in a horrific and distressing way.

Susan Maxwell's body was discovered in a ditch beside a lay-by on the A518 road at Loxley near Uttoxeter in the county of Staffordshire in the West Midlands of England – over 250 miles south from where she had disappeared. The warm weather of that 1982 summer had taken its toll on Susan's remains, so much so she could only be identified by her dental records. The Maxwells had just made a plea on the popular BBC Radio 2 programme *The Jimmy Young Show*, which reached an audience of millions, for information on their missing child. The police arrived at the local radio station to collect the Maxwells and brought them home to a detective waiting to deliver the news that every parent of a missing child dreads to receive. In breaking the news to the Maxwells, the officer told them that a girl had been found but he could not bring himself to say the girl was dead, telling them instead that she had been 'found not alive'. The search for a missing child had ended, but a new search, the search for her abductor and killer had just begun.

Susan's body was discovered by a gentleman by the name of Arthur Meadows. Mr Meadows lived in nearby Uttoxeter and was a lorry driver. He had stopped in the lay-by to take a shortcut on to a friend's house when he looked to his left and saw a pair of white socks in the ditch; he felt uneasy but tried to convince himself that what he'd seen was a tailor's dummy that someone had dumped. He went to his friend's house, then travelled on to Scotland with his work, all the while trying to convince himself that he hadn't seen anything untoward in that lay-by ditch and that it was something entirely innocent. Doubt got the better of him however and he confided in a work colleague about what he thought he may have discovered. His colleague advised him to call the police, which Mr Meadows did when he arrived home in Uttoxeter.

When the police arrived at the scene they were certain they were looking at the body of a young child and whilst the clothing was similar in description to what Susan was wearing when she went missing, a comparison of dental records and fingerprints removed any doubt that it was Susan's body.

The pathologist who examined Susan's body was unable to confirm her cause of death or if she had been sexually assaulted due to the state of decomposition her remains were in when she was discovered, though he was able to determine from them that Susan had been dumped in the lay-by shortly after she was abducted.

There was a clue, however, that pointed Staffordshire Police – who had taken over the Maxwell murder investigation as her body had been found in Uttoxeter, which was in their force area – in the direction of looking at a sexual motivation behind the killing. Whilst Susan was found in the clothing she had been wearing the day of her disappearance two weeks previously, her shoes were found beside the body and, more tellingly, her underpants had been removed and folded up neatly underneath her head. Her shorts had then been put back on her after her underpants had been removed. This discovery reinforced fears that Susan had been abducted and killed by a paedophile.

Staffordshire Police started the murder investigation by releasing a large poster displaying a picture of Susan Maxwell in her bright yellow outfit, detailing the date and location she was last seen and the date and location of where her dead body was found, and then crucially asking the following question 'Did you see her between those dates?'

They also cordoned off the wood that was adjacent to the lay-by ditch where Susan's body was found but, despite the fact the wood was used sometimes to dump items of rubbish and resembled an unofficial tip, nothing of note or significance was found during the forensic examination. Following this, Staffordshire Police interviewed people living in Uttoxeter and the surrounding areas, as well as those staying in caravans and hotels, in case the perpetrator had been holidaying in Scotland before returning south to his home or was a tourist. There were a number of possible reasons as to why Susan's abductor would transport her body and dispose of it so far away. Others who were interviewed were men who worked for firms that required them to travel between Staffordshire and Scotland, the police reasoning that this would explain the distance of some 250 miles between Susan's abduction point and the location where her body was discarded. The killer could perhaps be a travelling salesman or lorry driver . . . or van driver?

The man who had killed Susan Maxwell was indeed someone who travelled between the Midlands and Scotland and back again as part of his job, the job of a van driver – but his name never entered the investigation and neither was it at any point put forward to detectives as a possible suspect or person of interest.

Black would have been aware of the hunt for Susan Maxwell and the murder investigation that started two weeks later with the discovery of her body. He would have been watching the news in his attic room in Stamford Hill watching the desperate pleas of a frantic mother seeking news of her child; he would have read the national papers detailing Susan's disappearance whilst eating in a roadside café during a break as he continued working delivering posters up and down the country. He could have phoned the police and let them and the Maxwell family know what he had done at any time and brought their suffering to an end much sooner but he chose not to. He had a similar opportunity to do the same thing for the Cardy family twelve months earlier, when he abducted and murdered their daughter. Again he chose not to. Instead he continued his life, separating his public and private worlds – publicly the hard-working, darts-loving, foul-smelling van driver who would sip a pint of shandy in the pub, and privately the sadistic paedophile who had abducted and killed two innocent little girls, and more than likely, as we will look at later, had killed more. Black by now, his thirty-fifth birthday having passed a few months previously, was firmly on the road of serial child abduction and murder, and showed no sign of stopping or slowing down. If anything, the carnage was just beginning.

As Susan Maxwell's little body was laid to rest in the graveyard after a memorial service in the village church that only two weeks previously had said prayers hoping for her safe return, the Maxwells stood dignified as they said goodbye to their child. The congregation sang Susan's favourite hymn 'All Things Bright and Beautiful' during the funeral service. As the newspaper photographers and television cameramen filmed the service and subsequent burial many would have been forgiven for momentarily turning their thoughts to the individual behind this tragedy. The man responsible. Who was he? How could he have done something so cruel? Perhaps however most chillingly was the question would he do it again? Almost one year later, he would answer that question in the worst way possible.

THE MURDER OF CAROLINE HOGG

Friday, 8 July 1983 was the day the inquest into the death of Susan Claire Maxwell was held at Uttoxeter, Staffordshire.

The enquiry into her murder had been wound down and was almost entirely based in Staffordshire, although there was still a high number of detectives working on the case. Ironically, that was also the day that Robert Black would abduct another young victim. Just as he had done, almost a year before, on the day he abducted and killed Susan Maxwell, Black left his East London work base with a van full of posters to be delivered. Posters that, just like on the day that Susan Maxwell was abducted, had to be delivered to areas of Scotland. He left on the morning of Thursday, 7 July and travelled north, making a delivery in Gateshead near Newcastle that night before pulling his van up for a few hours' sleep. The next morning he was up and continued his journey, leaving the North-East of England and using the A1 to travel over the border into Scotland. His next delivery was due at the Mills and Allen depot in Portobello, an eastern coastal suburb of Edinburgh. To reach it he had to drive through Musselburgh, a place of which he had bad memories and flashbacks due to the unhappy time he spent there in his youth. After making his delivery he travelled down the Portobello road, on to the promenade where he parked his van and got out of it. His next delivery drop was due to be at another Mills and Allen depot, this one in Glasgow. But rather than continue on his work journey straight away Black decided to go for a stroll along the promenade and stretch his legs.

Sadly, going for a walk and stretching his legs was soon to be the furthest thing from Black's mind. It was a nice, warm, sunny and calm July evening and the promenade was full of people, young and old, male and female, both local and holiday-makers from outside the area. The beaches were full of people relaxing, building sandcastles, or venturing into the sea for a paddle. Also on the promenade were numerous amusement arcades and an amusement park full of children and young people enjoying their school holidays. Black walked through these buildings as he tried to normalise his presence in the crowds but even in a place full of people he stood out on account of his shabby, scruffy and generally unkempt appearance. He was an unappealing-looking figure and yet drew no real attention to himself as he strolled along the promenade taking in all the fun and activities in his sight. He rolled himself a cigarette and leaned against the railings of a children's playground to smoke it. There was a small group of children there, playing on the slides and the swings, Black watched them until he fixed his sights on one little girl in particular. Soon the little girl was on her own. Just like back in Scotland in June 1963, and, more recently, the summer days when he had spotted Jennifer Cardy and Susan Maxwell – a child, alone. Black saw his opportunity and began to draw in. The fears of everyone connected with the Susan Maxwell murder a year previously were about to be confirmed, this opportunistic predator was to strike again.

Five-year-old Caroline Hogg like so many children in the United Kingdom that day was enjoying the summer holidays. That Friday in the warm sunshine her day had been packed with activity and fun. She had spent most of the day at her friend's birthday party playing party games and enjoying party food with the other children there. The little girl with long blonde hair was pretty as a picture and in fact a now heart-breaking photograph of the little girl was taken at that very party, the last ever photograph to be taken of the child, wearing a lilac and white dress with white ankle socks and her special shoes for the party. Her mother collected her around 4 p.m. and they returned the short distance home to 25 Beach Lane, Portobello where Caroline and her brother Stuart lived with their mother Annette and their father John. As she went through the door of her home she was pleased to see her grandmother there but quickly went outside once more for more adventure, staying close to her home, however, as her parents had strictly warned her not to venture past a certain point from the family house. Normally Caroline would ride her little bicycle but it was broken at the time and few of her wee friends who lived locally were about. Soon it was tea time but Caroline was not hungry and would have preferred to continue playing. After tea she accompanied her mother to drop her granny off at the bus stop.

Once they had returned to 25 Beach Lane little Caroline, still full of exuberance and energy, begged to be let out once more for a few more minutes' play before bedtime. It was 7 p.m. and still a nice bright evening. Caroline's parents agreed that she could go out for just five minutes as long as she changed out of her good party shoes and promised not to venture out of the playground, which faced the sea. Caroline had often been forbidden to go onto the promenade, near the sea, beach or to any of the arcades or funfair without the company of an adult. The little girl changed into a pair of pink trainers and went out for a few minutes' fun, passing the local primary school Towerbank, which she attended, on her way. After a little while in the playground Caroline, as many little children do, forgot her promises and ventured onto the promenade towards the bright lights of the funfair and amusements despite her parents' warnings. As she made her way along the seafront a man was following her. A teenage girl who knew Caroline would later come forward to say she had seen Caroline at the start of the promenade walking along, with a man walking just behind her. A number of people were to see Caroline with this man that evening, and came forward after she was reported missing as witnesses, to say they had seen her in the company of a man whom they all gave the same general physical description of a scruffy, overweight individual with glasses.

As Caroline sat down on the wall of the promenade the day's activities were starting to take their toll. The little girl was tired and was probably thinking of going home when this scruffy glasses-wearing man engaged her in conversation. The next thing witnesses reported seeing was Caroline walking hand in hand with the scruffy stranger towards the funfair, which was called Fun City. There was nothing immediately worrying or sinister about the sight – many children were on the promenade that night, some alone or in the company of other children playing happily on the beach or at the amusements and funfair. Many were with their parents or grandparents, aunts or uncles, just as in any coastal suburb in the United Kingdom during the summer holidays. So to see a little girl smiling and seemingly happy as she walked along, holding the hand of a man who could have been her father, uncle or family friend into the funfair was nothing unusual. As they walked into Fun City the stranger paid 15p for Caroline to go on a children's roundabout ride, watching and waving to her as she sat on the little carousel's bus. After the ride was over Caroline was then seen once again walking hand in hand with the scruffy-looking spectacled man, only this time walking together in the direction of the back exit of Fun City. Little Caroline, like so many children, had innocently put her trust in an adult, and that adult would go on to break that trust in the most devastating and cruel fashion.

At 7.15 p.m., Caroline's mother Annette, wondering where her daughter was, looked outside and called her name. There was no reply, and she stepped outside her house and found her eleven-year-old son Stuart playing football with friends; she asked him if he had seen his sister, for it was approaching her bedtime. Stuart, however, had not seen Caroline. With a sense of dread Annette informed her husband John and soon the whole family were searching the immediate area around Beach Lane and the local playground and then through the hundreds of people thronging the promenade. It was 7.30 p.m.

This was also the time of the last reported sighting of Caroline: she was last seen by a seventeen-year-old boy who worked at Fun City, and was indeed none other than the attendant for the roundabout ride Caroline had been given money to go on by the scruffy man. The youth had seen them leave towards the back exit of Fun City hand in hand.

By this time the Hogg family, neighbours and friends were out searching for Caroline and word spread that a child was missing. The very sad possibility remains that those searching for Caroline had entered the Fun City amusement park at the front entrance at the same time Caroline and her abductor were leaving at the back entrance, or if not at the same time, then within a matter of minutes, frustratingly just missing each other. This thought was reinforced by a little boy who had seen Caroline hand in hand with a scruffy man with a stubble-type beard and thick-lensed spectacles that had black frames with no bottoms; the young boy was quite insistent that Caroline was not laughing and happy-looking as other witnesses had described seeing her earlier on the promenade. On the contrary, he described Caroline as frightened-looking. His grandmother lived near Caroline and they knew each other well but when he called out a greeting to her, Caroline did not reply, the little girl afraid and no doubt confused. The funfair ride was over, now where were they going?

At 7.50 p.m. with a situation that was becoming increasingly serious the police were called. Immediately Edinburgh police mobilised search parties and by that Sunday the local area had been thoroughly searched by several hundred volunteers under the direction of the police, but all to no avail. A week later at Portobello Town Hall thousands of people crammed in for a police briefing as volunteers came from far and wide to help look for the little girl whose smiling face was soon on every newspaper and news bulletin, just as Susan Maxwell's face had been almost twelve months previously. The search widened across the city of Edinburgh with army regiments drafted in, and the coasts and hills beyond, but again no trace of the little girl was found. A mobile police caravan was also set up in Fun City.

Caroline's parents John and Annette Hogg attended a press conference as the search for their daughter went on, with John Hogg making an appeal to Caroline's abductor 'Just give her back, whoever has her.'

In the midst of all this and as they organised search parties, the police were also taking witness statements from those who had seen Caroline just before she had disappeared. Almost thirty people had seen her, and half that number reported seeing her on the promenade and in Fun City with the stranger, giving a similar description of the man each time – the word 'scruffy' continually coming up. Adults and children had noticed the man both in Caroline's company and beforehand on his own. Some thought he looked like a tramp, others thought he was under the influence of alcohol. Some had seen him roll and smoke a cigarette whilst staring at a group of children. Two witnesses who although they had only seen the man for a few seconds gave police enough to go on, and an artist's impression of the scruffy stranger was drawn up. The police, however, decided to hold it back from public release, on the grounds that doing so could be counterproductive, choosing to save it for a later stage in their hunt. It was indeed to be very useful in the conviction of Robert Black for Caroline's murder.

John and Annette Hogg were certain that Caroline would never have gone to Fun City on her own as she had been repeatedly warned never to venture that far onto the promenade – on one occasion when she did make it that far on her own she was punished. The little girl, her parents were sure, had to have been enticed there and those witnesses who saw Caroline in Fun City with the scruffy-looking stranger confirmed this is what happened.

Caroline's body was found on 18 July 1983, and, like the remains of Susan Maxwell, found in an unlikely place. Ten days after her disappearance her decomposed body was found by a motorist who had pulled into a lay-by in Twycross in Leicestershire to answer a call of nature. The lay-by was located just off the A444 connecting Northampton and Coventry. Just as in Susan's case the hot weather had had an effect and because of the state of decomposition a cause of death could not be established. Caroline was identified from the little baubles that held her hair and a locket around her neck. Police were also certain that Caroline's murder was sexually motivated – the little's girl's body had been found without a stitch of clothing. The detective who arrived at the scene was Detective Chief Superintendent David Baker, head of Leicestershire CID. David Baker as well as being involved in the hunt for Robert Black is also the detective who caught Colin Pitchfork, a serial flasher who abducted and murdered two teenage girls in villages in Leicestershire in the mid-1980s, that particular case being of note as it was the first murder conviction secured by the help of the now world-renowned but at the time just-discovered genetic fingerprinting or, as it is commonly known, DNA evidence.

Over thirty years after Caroline's murder David Baker recalled the horrific crime, as reported in Scotland's *Daily Record and Sunday Mail* on 12 April 2015:

'It was extremely difficult because the body was badly decomposed and it was my job to go to Portobello to see

Caroline's parents. I had to get them to try to identify her by what we found. We had a couple of little trinkets.'

The location point of disposal was over 300 miles from Caroline's point of abduction yet only 24 miles away from where the body of Susan Maxwell had been discovered in a ditch off a lay-by in Uttoxeter the previous August. Had Susan's killer struck again? Was the same man involved in both child killings?

The similarities between the cases were noted by the detectives from four respective police forces now involved in the two murder investigations. Both little girls were pre-pubescent and wearing white ankle socks when abducted on a warm Friday in July twelve months apart after enjoying outdoor activities near their homes, one on the border between Scotland and England, the other a suburb in Scotland's capital. Both were abducted and taken away in some kind of vehicle and transported hundreds of miles south, with their bodies both found dumped in lay-bys in the English Midlands 24 miles apart. Both killings were sexually motivated.

The four police forces now involved were the Northumbria and Staffordshire forces, with regard to the Maxwell case, and Lothian and Peebles Edinburgh Division (from where Caroline was abducted) and the Leicestershire Constabulary (from where Caroline's body was found). All agreed that, given the strong similarities between the two murders, one man was responsible. The four Chief Constables also agreed that a joint enquiry with one senior investigating officer overall overseeing things was the best way to go.

The man chosen for the job was Hector Clark from the

north-east of England and serving Deputy Chief Constable of Northumbria Police. He was viewed as a wise choice on account of his vast experience and his success rate in murder investigations – for which he was known as 'El Supremo'. This nickname was quickly picked up by some of the media upon his appointment to catch this evil child killer already being compared to the infamous Moors Murderers Ian Brady and Myra Hindley of some twenty years before. His first day on the job was the 22 July 1983.

Clark had already been involved in the Susan Maxwell investigation, recommending to investigating officers that all lay-bys 100 miles north and south of Coldstream be searched in the hunt for Susan, as they subsequently were. Now Hector Clark had the task of overseeing and directing the overall joint enquiry into the abduction and murders of Susan Maxwell and Caroline Hogg.

The last murder investigation the United Kingdom had seen that was similar in scale to the Maxwell/Hogg investigation was that of the hunt for the Yorkshire Ripper, Peter Sutcliffe, a few short years previously. To ensure the mistakes that were made during the Ripper investigation – where significant clues and connections were lost in the sheer volume of paperwork – were not repeated here, Hector Clark began to look at the investigative advantages provided by computerising all data and information. All information that stemmed from the Maxwell case had already been recorded by hand on index cards, but Clark decided that the data and information from the Caroline Hogg investigation should be entered into a computerised system. As he explained at the time to the press: 'What we had in the past is a paper manual index of vehicles and people, and they're subject to misplacement, misfiling and loss. Now the computer just does not allow this. We shouldn't overlook something that perhaps has happened during previous enquiries.'

To ensure that time was not wasted in transferring the vast number of indexes from the Maxwell enquiry it was kept in the form of a manual paper index.

A reconstruction of Caroline's last movements in Fun City was enacted and shown. House-to-house enquiries in Portobello were undertaken and those witnesses on the promenade and in Fun City that night were traced and interviewed.

Holidaymakers, including those from the other side of the world, were asked to send in their holiday snaps and video film in an effort to find any photographs or film footage of Caroline or her abductor or both of them together, but sadly and frustratingly nothing of note was photographed or recorded. Parking tickets in Edinburgh were examined whilst police in Leicestershire sat close to the A444 road noting the registration of every vehicle that during the next couple of days passed by close to the lay-by where Caroline's body was found, in case her killer used the road regularly and a vehicle registration was spotted more than once and a link or connection could be established at some point in the enquiry.

The forensic pathologist who examined Caroline's decomposing body was tasked with finding out for the police when and how she died. There are perfectly routine questions a detective will ask a pathologist in the aftermath of a post-mortem of a murder victim as the answers to such questions often aid the police in catching a murderer: a time of death helps establish what happened between the abduction of a victim and their body being discovered, and a cause of death can help establish a modus operandi or MO (method of operation) that an offender, particularly a serial offender, uses and can help build a psychological profile of a suspect.

The doctors informed the police that Caroline had not been strangled as there were no markings on her neck or skin or injuries to that particular area, but while strangulation was ruled out, a cause of death could not be established. On the time of death, the police gained from the help of scientists and entomologists who studied the cycle of insects that, as little Caroline's body lay out in the open, in warm weather, laid eggs that hatched in her body. It was their professional opinion, although admittedly it was an estimate at best, that the body had lain in the lay-by ditch anything from four to six days. So Caroline's body had been left in the lay-by at some point between 12 and 14 July, and was in the possession of her abductor and killer anything from four to six days beforehand. The difference in time between Caroline's abduction and the earliest point of her body being disposed is distressing to think about.

A couple by the name of Mr and Mrs Flynn came forward to say they had witnessed a scared-looking young girl with a man driving a blue Ford Cortina. Whilst initially this looked a promising lead it eventually proved to be unconnected with the abduction and murder of Caroline Hogg, but not until after 20,000 blue Ford Cortinas were traced and their drivers interviewed and eliminated. This in hindsight was similar to a possible lead that cropped up during the investigation into Susan Maxwell's murder the year before, when a psychiatric nurse named Mark Ball came forward to say that on the day Susan Maxwell was abducted he had witnessed a girl matching Susan's description hitting out with a tennis racket at a maroon Triumph 2000. As with the later Flynn sighting, this had initially seemed promising but was ultimately ruled out – again only after the drivers of nearly 20,000 maroon Triumph 2000s were traced, interviewed and eliminated.

By the summer of 1984, one year later, a television documentary had already been made and broadcast on the unsolved murders of Susan Maxwell and Caroline Hogg consisting mostly of reconstructions of the girls' abductions, based on evidence and hypothesis, news footage, photographs and interviews with the families and detectives involved. It was broadcast in the hope that one of its viewers would recognise something in the programme and come forward with a clue or information that would bring the investigation forward. It would also have been broadcast in the hope of reassuring the public that the investigation was still open and on-going and even though the killer was still at large all effort was being undertaken to find him and bring him to justice.

Despite this the reality was that the police were aware of the lack of real leads or real suspects in the case. There was little to go on despite the near half a million index cards containing information on the Susan Maxwell enquiry and the computerised system brought into force in connection with the murder of Caroline Hogg. Intelligence officers with every force in the country were asked to send in lists of possible persons of interest but these too had failed to come up with a strong suspect.

Because the killer had struck twice in the summer warmth of the month of July police wondered again about the possibility that he was someone who took advantage of children being off on school summer holidays and being outside more in the hot weather; they also speculated that he might holiday in Scotland before travelling south through the north of England on to the Midlands where he would dispose of the little girls' bodies; and they once more pondered the high probability that he was someone who used a vehicle and could travel great distances for his work, and again the questions were raised: was he a travelling salesman, a lorry driver or, as turned out to be the case, a delivery driver using a van?

So the police, media and general public could have been forgiven for being nervous that summer of 1984 as they wondered if the scruffy-looking stranger would strike again as the summer months rolled by.

Black was no doubt aware of the media frenzy that followed his abduction and murder of Caroline Hogg in July 1983. He would also have been aware, just from watching the television and reading the newspapers, of the renewed efforts of the police to find him as the four constabularies came together in a joint enquiry to hunt him down. He would have read and listened to the words of the man in charge 'El Supremo' Hector Clark, and must have known that the police would never slow down in their bid to catch him. Part of him must have been waiting for a knock on the door of his

Stamford Hill flat – after all, a lot of people had seen him on the promenade in Portobello smoking his cigarette, watching the children and walking hand in hand with Caroline Hogg as he led her away like a lamb to the slaughter. The police were bound to come to his door and arrest him, someone must have recognised him or the description of him or put his name forward to the enquiry. But luck, it seems, was at that point on Robert Black's side, for no knock on the door would ever come.

★ ★ ★

By the summer of 1984, we now know, Black had abducted and murdered at least three young girls over the previous three years, all during the months of July and August, all when he was on work trips in his van delivering posters for PDS.

That year, however, during the summer or at any other time, no murders of children were recorded that match Black's modus operandi. It is highly likely that he stalked children during this period and very possible that he tried, maybe even several times, to abduct a child, but if he did so it never came to police or public attention. It seems that 1984 was a gap year for Robert Black's serial killing. This is not unusual even with the most prolific of serial killers: there is usually in the timeline of an offender's murderous activities a break or gap in their offending. This gap can be anything from a couple of months to a year or even several years. The reasons for this stop in killing can vary – the offender may have experienced a change in their personal or professional life that has in some way and for one reason or another brought about a stop to the killing, or they may have been imprisoned for other offences. In Black's case he simply seems to have carried on that year watching his child pornography in the privacy of his attic flat, drinking the odd pint of shandy, playing darts in pubs, as well as attending family get-togethers with the Raysons, whom he lodged with. Work continued, travelling all over. Hard worker, that Robbie Black, people remarked, never complained and helped his workmates out if they couldn't make a trip and a replacement driver was needed. The mask that covered the face of a serial killer was well and truly on.

Black simply kept his head low during the year of 1984. He would have wanted the fury of public and police reaction following the Maxwell and Hogg killings to have calmed down and any further killings that year would surely have given the police fresh impetus or information which in turn would have aided them in catching him.

By the summer of 1985 Black was still at large. He confided to sex crimes expert Ray Wyre in prison following his 1990 arrest that in June 1985 in Carlisle he lured two young girls into his van, but, he said, once they were in his van he changed his mind and let them get out, unharmed, to go on their way. And in the following August, he later admitted, he had approached a girl who looked around ten in an alleyway in South London; the girl had screamed at his approach and had run away, while Black in a panic had jumped in his van and sped off. These incidents or, rather, attempted abductions were never reported to the police and would probably have remained unknown if it wasn't for Black's own admissions. It is impossible to know if he was telling the truth about these attacks, or even if they had ever actually happened. He claimed that having got two young girls into his van, he then let them out just like that . . . He claimed that when a young girl screamed he fled . . . We might wonder if those reactions were likely, considering Black had already killed at least three young girls. My gut feeling, however, is that he was telling the truth, for while he was undoubtedly a determined paedophile, abductor and killer, even Black would have had his reasons not to take abduction opportunities, not just necessarily because he didn't want to on that particular day but because there may have been external factors at play that presented the risk of his being detected.

At first glance no child murders took place in the United Kingdom in 1985 so it would appear Black's break from killing was extended. Or was it? In the summer of that year a ten-year-old girl called Silke Garben was abducted and murdered in Germany, of which more later.

Of the three confirmed murders Black was responsible for by 1985 all had been committed during the summer months. Jennifer Cardy had been murdered in August 1981 and the now jointly investigated Susan Maxwell and Caroline Hogg murders occurred in July 1982 and July 1983 respectively. Does this suggest a summer theme or reasoning to his murderous activities? A more likely answer would be that children during the summer months are off school and in the warm weather are often found outside gaining some independence, having fun playing, or walking or cycling just as Black's victims all were. It is a time of year when prey is more easily accessible for a predator and opportunities for abduction present themselves more often. Having said this, the summer periods may also have been a time of year when Black, himself a fan of summer and outdoor activities such as swimming and football, found his paedophiliac desires more often than not at the front of his mind while he was making his deliveries in the hot and sunny weather. It is therefore somewhat ironic that the next little girl he murdered in the United Kingdom was abducted on a very wet, miserable night in March 1986.

THE MURDER OF SARAH HARPER

Robert Black had just signed the delivery log book on an assignment of posters, it was the evening and night was approaching fast. With no one at the location in Morley where he dropped off his load he signed his name, indicating an out-of-hours delivery, confident the posters would be discovered the next morning. He had done this before; it was common practice for after-hours deliveries. As he walked towards his white Transit van with his work done he must have been very aware of the wet weather as the dark of the night came upon him in a mixture of rain and cold. As he sat in his van preparing to set off back to London, he caught sight of a small figure heading up a nearby road.

★ ★ ★

It was a wet, dark and miserable Wednesday night on 26 March 1986 when ten-year-old Sarah Harper disappeared. She lived with her mother Jackie, sister Claire and brother David in a terraced house in Brunswick Place, Morley, a suburb of Leeds in West Yorkshire. After finishing her evening tea Sarah was asked by her mother if she would pop to the local shop to buy a loaf of bread. The little girl agreed, picked up a couple of empty lemonade bottles to return, and put on her anorak coat to make the short journey to the local shop, which was just along Peel Street on the corner. Sarah lived at Number 1 Brunswick Place, an end-of-terrace house that latched onto Peel Street. The corner shop in question was K and M Stores, owned and run by a Mr and Mrs Champaneri. When Sarah entered the shop she handed over the empty lemonade bottles, purchased the loaf of bread and with the returned deposits on the bottles bought two bags of crisps. Shortly after she had stepped in, another customer entered the shop – except the man was not a customer. He walked about the shop, had a quick look around, then left without buying anything or asking for anything. He was in the shop for too short a time to be genuinely browsing and left the shop before Sarah did. It was about 8.05 when Sarah left the corner shop, and as she set off home two young girls saw her make her way down an alleyway known as 'The Snicket', which was used by local people as a short cut and would have shortened Sarah's walk home on that very wet and cold evening. It was to be the last time anyone, other than the man who would abduct and kill her, saw Sarah Harper alive. As she made her way through the alley Sarah was forcibly seized and taken away in a vehicle. Robert Black had struck again.

The minutes ticked by. Jackie Harper was aware that Sarah's journey should have taken no more than ten minutes, but perhaps she was chatting to somebody she knew in the shop or had met someone to play with or talk to on the way home. As the time approached 8.30, Jackie asked her other daughter Claire to go out and fetch her sister. But Claire returned saying she'd not seen Sarah. Getting concerned, Jackie instructed Claire to stay with her brother David while she went out to look for Sarah. She put on her anorak and setting off in the heavy downpour, she made her way along the street to the shop looking for Sarah. Mrs Champaneri told Jackie that Sarah had indeed been in the shop and bought some items but had left shortly after 8 p.m. As the search for Sarah continued it was fast approaching an hour since Sarah was last seen. The police were called at 9 p.m.

While searches went under way in the local vicinity of Morley, and house-to-house enquiries were undertaken, there was nothing solid coming to the police that pointed to where Sarah could have been taken. In a public appeal on television a desperate Jackie Harper said that the family just wanted Sarah home. As the reservoirs, railways and parks of Leeds were searched by police and volunteers, Detective Superintendent John Stainthorpe from West Yorkshire Police, who was in charge of the investigation, told a press conference that whilst he remained hopeful of Sarah being found safe and well, the possibility of abduction could not be ruled out.

Sarah's body was found three and a half weeks later, on 19 April 1986. It was discovered by a man called David Moult who was out walking his dog along the bank of the River Trent in Nottingham. As he strolled alongside the river he noticed something floating on the surface of the water. Initially he thought it was something commonplace like a piece of clothing or a sack, but he took a closer look and as the pace of the river turned it around he saw to his horror it was the body of a child. Quickly he found a stick and managed to guide the body to the side of the river. Once he had dragged it to the bank, he contacted the police.

It fell to Sarah Harper's father Terry to identify the dead body as that of his daughter. Jennifer Cardy's father Andrew had had to do the same task five years earlier when his daughter was murdered. This was not to be the only thing, however, that linked these two murders, five years apart and right across the United Kingdom, over nearly 400 miles of land and sea.

Sarah's post-mortem made for some horrifying reading. The pathologist had concluded that Sarah had died from drowning, and that, significantly, she had been alive when submerged in the river, although in all likelihood she had been unconscious. Police worked out that Sarah would have been put into the River Trent at junction 24 off the M1. The pathologist also noted that Sarah had suffered heavy injuries to her vaginal and anal areas, indicating she had been subjected to a serious prolonged and violent sexual assault. Her anorak, skirt and shoes had been removed and have never been found, in spite of appeals on television and the official appeal poster from West Yorkshire Police on Sarah's murder.

At this early stage of the Sarah Harper murder investigation the police had to make a decision regarding the future direction of the enquiry. The similarities to the killings of Susan Maxwell and Caroline Hogg had not escaped them, but they were not convinced of a link at that stage. The question was, should they combine their investigation with the joint Maxwell/Hogg enquiry, which was already engaging four police forces; and take the number of forces involved to six?

Hector Clark, who was the overall chief in charge of the Maxwell/Hogg enquiry weighed up the similarities and differences between the two enquiries and decided at least initially to keep the two investigations separate but keep an open line of communication on what the other was doing. John Stainthorpe, who was running the West Yorkshire end of the enquiry, at first believed that the answer to who killed Sarah was to be found in Morley itself where she was abducted, rather than that it was linked to the other two murders.

There certainly were differences between the 1986 murder of Sarah Harper and the murders of Susan Maxwell and Caroline Hogg, four and three years previously. The differences included:

1. Susan and Caroline were abducted on hot summer Fridays in July whilst Sarah Harper was abducted on a wet, dark and miserable Wednesday evening in March.
2. Susan and Caroline were both dressed in customary summer attire for children, which would have made them both recognisable and attractive to a watching, passing predator, whilst Sarah was wrapped up in an anorak that covered her hair; her face would also have been barely visible on that dark, wet evening and she would therefore not have been instantly identified as a girl.
3. Susan and Caroline were abducted from areas that had a lot of people either travelling through them or visiting

them as a main route from England to Scotland (in Susan's case) or holiday resort (in Caroline's case), whereas Morley, where Sarah was abducted from, was the type of location that you would have to have had a specific reason to be there– it was not the sort of place that attracted random strangers, it was a tight-knit local community not uncommon across the north of England.

4. Susan and Caroline were abducted not particularly far from each other; Susan on the England/Scotland border and Caroline on the edge of Edinburgh, still deep in the southern half of Scotland, while Sarah was abducted from a suburb of West Yorkshire in England.

5. Susan and Caroline were each found in waste ground adjacent to lay-bys whilst Sarah's body was dumped in a river.

6. Susan's and Caroline's remains when examined showed no visible physical injuries to the body whilst Sarah Harper showed that she had been victim of a violent physical assault and a sexual attack.

In hindsight, it does appear that if the police had decided to conduct all three murders as one investigation – perhaps as a result of pressure, both internal and public – while they were not one hundred per cent sure the same man was involved in all three cases, it could have jeopardised both investigations and produced more problems than results in catching the killer.

But what was the open line of communication between the two investigations? What was the purpose of it? The reason for these two enquiries being run both separately and yet in parallel, comparing and contrasting information on tactics, suspects etc., and regularly and openly communicating was because while Hector Clark and the other senior police involved were not certain the same killer was responsible, they also were far from sure the same killer was not. To sum up, they kept an open mind and did not rule out either possibility. For there were similarities binding the three cases together despite the on-the-surface differences:

1. All three were pre-pubescent little girls abducted near their homes in public places and on all three occasions a vehicle was certainly used in the abduction.
2. All three victims were taken south from Scotland or northern England many miles from their abduction points and all were left in the Midlands: Susan in Uttoxeter, West Midlands; Caroline in Twycross, East Midlands, and Sarah was found in the River Trent in Nottinghamshire, East Midlands. On a map the locations of the three bodies make a triangle within a radius of twenty-six miles – hence the killings being later referred to as the Midlands Triangle murders.
3. All murders were sexually motivated, with Susan Maxwell's underwear removed, Caroline Hogg being found naked, and Sarah Harper the victim of a vicious sexual assault and with her skirt, anorak and shoes removed.

The differing sexual elements in all three murders, with the sexual emphasis of the murder becoming more recognisable or stronger from one killing to the next, would have pointed to a serial killer plunging to new depths of depravity and cruelty, a worrying factor to consider for all involved in the investigations.

The possibility of the three murders being omitted by a serial killer was aired in the April 1986 edition of the television series *Crimewatch*. The aim of the programme, presented at that time by Nick Ross and Sue Cook, was to bring unsolved crimes to the greater public attention, in the hopes of getting information from viewers that would help solve the crimes; using contributions from police officers in charge of the featured cases and reconstructions, it was a useful tool and still is to this day. The edition of the programme that was shown a few weeks after Sarah's killing featured the murders of Susan Maxwell and Caroline Hogg, with the murder of Sarah Harper featuring just briefly at the end of the programme as it was still an open and live investigation in its early stages. One has to wonder if Black watched the broadcast and whether he was concerned that any leads from it would bring the police to his flat door; unfortunately, however, he didn't have to worry. Black's name was not put forward to the detectives taking calls in the studio nor would it at any point be known until his 1990 arrest.

In the meantime West Yorkshire Police, along with their counterparts in the Nottinghamshire Constabulary, were undertaking other forms of investigation, rapping on front doors of houses in Morley, tracing and interviewing potential witnesses, stopping and questioning drivers, and contacting local intelligence officers from neighbouring forces for the details of possible suspects – in other words, men with 'form' in regard to crimes of a sexual nature – who were subsequently interviewed and traced. Nottinghamshire police also searched along the banks of the Trent for possible clues and appealed for fishermen or regular walkers by the river in get in touch if they had any information or had seen anything suspicious around the times between Sarah's disappearance and the discovery of her dead body in the river. Motorway users on the M1 between Morley and Nottingham were stopped at service stations by police and asked if they had travelled along that route on the evening of 26 March and, if so, whether they had seen anything at all that could be relevant to the investigation.

Police in West Yorkshire did glean some useful statements from witnesses in Morley on the night Sarah Harper disappeared. A few witnesses stated that they had seen a white Transit van parked out Sarah's house ten minutes before she disappeared. Neither the van nor its driver were ever traced and the man never came forward despite public appeals for him to do so. Another question that West Yorkshire police asked was who was the man with receding hair, heavy-set and wearing steel-rimmed spectacles, who came into the shop after Sarah Harper had entered and left before she did, without buying or saying anything. Too brief surely to be a genuine browser, and he was in the shop too short a time to be someone seeking shelter from the rain of that night; an artist's impression was drawn up and released, and appeals were made for the man to come forward as he could have been a witness; however, he never came forward, arousing police suspicions that he was implicated in Sarah's murder.

A man of similar description was also seen walking in Peel Street – was it the same man? Nobody locally who had seen him recognised him, but why would he not come forward? He could have been a witness . . . or maybe the killer.

The artist's impression, drawn from the Champaneris' description of the man in the shop, would later be seen to bear a striking resemblance to Black as he would have looked in 1986 – as police discovered when, following his 1990 arrest, they found a number of photographs of him taken during the 1980s.

Black also was driving a white Transit van at this point in 1986 and was working that night in Morley – he made a recorded delivery of posters to a depot 150 yards from where Sarah lived with her family. All this would be explained in detail to the jury by the prosecution during Black's trial for the murder of Sarah Harper eight years later.

In July that year Sarah was eventually laid to rest. Her family and school friends, many in their uniforms of the Salvation Army, of which Sarah was a member, sobbed as they said goodbye to another little girl who was simply in the wrong place at the wrong time.

By the end of 1986 Sarah's killer was still at large and enjoying his freedom when he should have been behind bars. To Black as the months ticked by it must surely have looked as though he had once again got away with a brutal child murder. By now he had claimed at least four murder victims in different parts of the United Kingdom, but the number might well be higher.

The end of 1986 also saw a change in the direction of the

THE MIDLANDS MURDERS

Sarah Harper enquiry as a decision was made to officially include Sarah's murder in the investigation of the murders of Susan Maxwell and Caroline Hogg, and it was agreed that the information relating to all three murders was to be entered into a computer system, for the similarities in all three cases were too striking to ignore. The computer system in question to be used was HOLMES, standing for Home Office Large Major Enquiry System, a suitable name and acronym for the task involved as well as a nod to the legendary fictional detective. The police could only hope that, as in the books of Sir Arthur Conan Doyle, HOLMES, the computerised version, would get the killer and justice would be served.

The HOLMES system was introduced to ensure that mistakes like those made in the Yorkshire Ripper investigation by West Yorkshire Police several years previously were not repeated. On that occasion, errors were made and connections were not made, largely due to the mass of paperwork all on handwritten index cards that contained the details of thirteen murders and several attempted murders. The police were simply overloaded with a paper trail of information so vast that there was not time nor space nor manpower to sift through it all and valuable clues and links were hidden – and so Peter Sutcliffe, the so-called Yorkshire Ripper, managed to stay at large and continue killing until he was caught almost in the act by a chance arrest in 1981.

The Midlands Triangle killings were fast becoming the largest and most expensive police investigation in Britain since the Yorkshire Ripper case so it was vital that all that could be done in terms of new technology was to be tried in an effort to catch the killer, and HOLMES was the prime example of this new technology.

The information on the Susan Maxwell murder enquiry was still all recorded on card indexes, and the Caroline Hogg investigation, whilst computerised, was on an older, different system from HOLMES and could not be transferred. As a result the backlog of details relating to the Maxwell/Hogg killings had to be fed into HOLMES as Sarah Harper's had been. The entire process took three years, and the single database was completed in 1990; long as it would take, however, the police were hopeful that, given the vast information fed into the system, it was worth it as a connection could be made, or a statement compared, or details on a suspect produced, at the click of a button on a computer keyboard.

With the end of 1986 and the beginning of 1987, questions surrounding this serial killer were continually being asked. Apart from the obvious one of his identity, police speculated as to his actions during the three-year gap between the murder of Caroline Hogg in 1983 and that of Sarah Harper in 1986. As the years passed after Caroline's death, people wondered if the child killer had been convicted of an unrelated offence and was therefore in prison, or if he had died. Or had he taken his offending elsewhere? Sadly, the latter remains a possibility but now with the murder of Sarah Harper police knew he had struck again and were concerned at the very real prospect of him claiming yet another victim.

When Prime Minister Margaret Thatcher, who was entering her third term of office, visited the headquarters of Lothian and Borders Police in Edinburgh with her husband

THE MIDLANDS MURDERS

Denis, she met and talked with Hector Clark, no doubt about the progress of the investigation that was both shocking and frightening the public. This was September 1987, a year and a half after Sarah's murder and preying on everyone's minds was again the dreaded question of whether he would strike again before the police caught him.

Eighteen months had passed and no child had been abducted and killed by this dangerous serial killer who was stalking the children of the kingdom. Once again the possibilities were explored, perhaps he was in prison? Perhaps he was dead and buried? Maybe he had stopped once and for all this carnage and had learned to control his proclivity for abduction and murder?

But what nobody knew was that Robert Black in the early summer of 1987 had been to France for work purposes and during his time there, as when he made his trip to Germany in June 1985, little girls were abducted and murdered. Was it a coincidence? Or had he taken his crimes elsewhere due to the intense police investigation after Sarah Harper's murder? These possibilities will be explored later.

Either way, Black had not finished his attacks at home. As the spring of 1988 approached he once again attempted to abduct a young girl. This time, however, his attempt would be unsuccessful. Yet it would not result in his capture.

6

A LUCKY
ESCAPE

The body of Sarah Harper had been found in the fast-flowing River Trent near Nottingham. Two years after the discovery of her body and whilst the hunt for her killer continued, Black was once again in Nottingham.

It was a hot Sunday evening, 24 April 1988, and fifteen-year-old Teresa Thornhill had been to a local park with a group of friends. When the evening came to an end, Teresa began to walk home with one of her friends, a boy called Andrew Beeson. Teresa and Andrew eventually went their separate ways and as Teresa made her way down Norton Street she heard a voice call out to her. 'Oi, can you fix engines?' A well-built man in a stained white T-shirt was peering through his glasses under the bonnet of his blue van. Replying that she could not, Teresa continued on her journey. She had barely walked a few steps when the man came up behind her and grabbed her, lifted her from the ground and walked with her towards his van. As he tried to contain her in a strong bear hug, Teresa screamed for help and struggled frantically with her attacker, knocking his glasses to the ground and grabbing him between the legs, which made him call her by a derogatory term and yell at her to get into the van. She continued struggling, and as he tried to bundle her into the vehicle Teresa, screaming for help all the while, managed to stick her feet against the van, on either side of the rear door of the vehicle in an effort to keep her attacker from pushing her in. At that point a timely intervention brought the abduction attempt to an immediate halt. Andrew Beeson, who had not gone far after he and Teresa had parted company at the end of the road, heard her screams and ran to where they were coming from, witnessing to his horror Black's attempt to abduct his friend. He ran towards them, shouting at Black, 'Get off her, you fat fucking bastard!' As Andrew drew close, Black let go of Teresa and quickly jumped in his van and drove away from the scene. Andrew helped a frightened and shaken Teresa to her feet and the two teenagers quickly ran to Teresa's home. There they told Teresa's parents who phoned the police at once. In the meantime, Black, apprehensive about being identified through the glasses Teresa had knocked from his face during the struggle, swerved his van round back to the scene of crime to pick them up before they could be found by someone else.

The Nottingham police took the incident seriously – Teresa had had a lucky escape from an abduction – and they immediately began searching for her attacker. Teresa and

Andrew had provided good descriptions of Black and had noted that his van was blue – but blue Transit vans were common throughout the United Kingdom, and in the chaos of the situation they didn't get to take note of the van's registration number. A CCTV camera managed to film the incident but unfortunately it too was unable to record the registration number. The police put an appeal out via local media in an attempt to catch the perpetrator, showed Teresa photos of possible suspects, and asked her to attend an identity parade. But all was to no avail and the case went cold, to remain stalled until Black's arrest over two years later.

As Black hurriedly drove his way out of Nottingham that evening, down south to London he would undoubtedly have been deeply anxious. He would have worried that Teresa and Andrew might have provided enough information in their description of him and his vehicle that somebody would recognise him, or that his van would be traced and, through it, he would be. But in the end once again he had no need to worry as his name never got put forward.

One of the strange things to come about in the aftermath of this very serious incident was the failure to link the attack to the Midlands Triangle murders. In fact a link was not made or brought to the attention of Hector Clark and his team until Black's arrest in the Scottish Borders over two years later, in 1990. It is puzzling as to why the two cases were not connected; on the surface they may appear slightly different, with Teresa at fifteen being older than the three other girls, but it is worth noting that Teresa was petite and looked much younger than her actual age – more like eleven or twelve, which fitted in with the ages of Black's other victims, rather than fifteen.

Teresa was a young girl almost abducted not far from her home in an urban street – remarkably similar in circumstances to the abduction of Sarah Harper, also in a street near her home in a suburb of Leeds. Considering the fact that Nottinghamshire Police were also involved in the Harper murder investigation as Sarah's body had been discovered in the River Trent on the outskirts of Nottingham just two years previously, the lack of connection seems even stranger. It was a serious abduction attempt only foiled by Teresa's strength, courage and determination, and the timely intervention of her friend. The description given of Black and the presence of a Ford Transit van should also have provided a link, given the similarity in the descriptions of the suspect in the Caroline Hogg and Sarah Harper cases, and the sighting of a Ford Transit in those two cases; not to mention the suspicion that the serial killer drove long distances regularly, perhaps for a living, something which should have pointed to a possible connection. In hindsight, it is easy to criticise, but at the time – perhaps because the outcome was, happily, so different – no link was observed.

The connection was firmly made after Black's 1990 arrest as police discovered evidence he was in Nottingham an hour before Teresa was almost abducted. They also found a newspaper article from the *Nottingham Evening Post* in Black's West Bank attic room after his arrest, which detailed the attempted abduction of Teresa Thornhill and contained a police appeal for information on her attacker. A forensic examination revealed semen stains on the newspaper article, which Black probably bought when he was on his next trip to the city just a few days after the abduction attempt. It was no doubt kept as a ghoulish souvenir: serial offenders often collect items as 'trophies' or reminders of their crimes.

If the connection had been made in 1988 between the attempted abduction of Teresa Thornhill and the three child murders, would it, we have to ask ourselves, have made a difference? Would Black have been apprehended any sooner? If a connection had been made then, the available details about Teresa's attacker, such as his description and that of his vehicle, would have reached far more people all over the country in a national appeal as part of the Midlands Triangle killings coverage, which went nationwide, rather than an appeal in the local Nottingham newspaper. But in spite of this, there is no way of knowing for certain if this larger amount of coverage, awareness and publicity would have led to Black's name being put forward to the team of detectives still hunting him down.

What is clear, however, is that this failed abduction attempt was followed by a lull in Black's offending for over two years. Still nervous about the chances of being apprehended, he went about his work life as usual, and there is no record of any other child murders, sex attacks or abduction attempts that could be attributed to him for the rest of 1988 and 1989. That is not to say that he did not carry out crimes during this period; he may well have done but if he did they have not come to light, or if they did come to public attention then they were never connected to him.

When Ray Wyre later interviewed Black, after his 1990 arrest, his statement speaks volumes about his build-up to an abduction. 'I don't know what possessed me in Nottingham, like, you know, in broad daylight in the middle of the day . . . She was with a boy. I thought she looked about eleven or twelve . . . I turned up a side street, and as it happened the girl turned up the side street as well. I pulled up and stopped just inside the street and I got out and lifted the bonnet. I asked her if she would do me a favour and asked her to help . . . As I came back round her she went to go away. I grabbed her and tried to get her into the vehicle. She struggled and then, I don't know, the boy must have come round the block because he was coming down towards us shouting and I let her go.'

When Wyre asked what he had been going to do Black replied, 'Well, get her into the van, like, and then drive somewhere, a lay-by somewhere . . . Assault her.'

It would appear that Black was not put off by aborted abduction attempts to go by his response to further questioning by Ray Wyre. '. . . When was Nottingham? 'Eighty-eight? I'd say that it wouldn't have mattered if the next day I'd seen a nice little girl of ten or nine or something like that. If she had been in a short skirt with socks up to here or something like that, I'd probably have thought, Cor! Good lassie, that.'

The lull did not last long, and the hot summer of 1990 would see Black return to his predatory habits. This time, however, not only would the victim, thankfully, survive, but he would be caught. Caught and arrested in the act, and this time there would be no release, no chance to resume his murderous depravities. This time it was over for good. The cycle of opportunity had ended.

7

STOPPED IN STOW

The village of Stow of Wedale lies in the Scottish Borders. A place with a population of several hundred people, it is a stunningly pretty and picturesque area. This beautiful landscape is where Robert Black's run of luck would at long last come to an end when he was caught red-handed in the act of abducting a child, after unknowingly being spotted by a well-placed and sharp-eyed witness who quickly alerted the police.

Until then, luck, so unfair and so cruel, had, as we have seen, been on his side. He had been lucky not to have been identified following the attempted abduction of schoolgirl Teresa Thornhill in Nottingham in 1988. He was lucky before that attack to still be working as a van driver: he had been sacked by PDS because of the high number of scrapes and collisions with other vehicles he had had, which had cost the company a great deal in insurance claims over the ten years he had worked for them. But, as mentioned earlier, when two PDS employees bought the company out, they rehired Black – on condition that he bought his own van and insured it himself. It is hard to doubt that as the 1980s came to a close, Robert Black must have been revelling in his luck: he still had his very convenient job, and over some ten years he had committed at least four murders, yet somehow had always managed to stay one step ahead of the law. Until, finally, justice did catch up with him.

The day was 14 July 1990, a warm and bright day in Stow as elsewhere, with everyone been going about their business, work or pleasure, both adults and children, enjoying the fine summer weather. Black had been working in his van from the early morning of that Saturday making deliveries to Edinburgh amongst other places and was on his way down south to England and home. He had just one more drop of posters to do. His route took him through Stow, a village where he had stopped off a number of times in the past to catch a bite to eat, and he knew it well. It was a hot weekend, children were playing barelegged in the sun, there was just the one delivery left to make – to Galashiels, only several miles down the road. As he headed south towards the border, Black had plenty of time – time to go looking for a victim. He must have known this would inevitably lead to another little girl being discovered in the English Midlands and a renewed hunt to catch him, but he had always got away with it . . . .

As he entered the village, a girl immediately caught his eye, a young girl called Mandy Wilson walking her dog, whom he later described to Ray Wyre in prison interviews as looking around twelve years of age. He watched her in his rear-view mirror until she was out of sight, then drove out of the village and found a place to turn the van round to see if there was any chance of a pick-up. He looked up the side streets and saw the girl again. He pulled his van alongside her as she walked along the pavement and got out. Positioning himself near the passenger door of the vehicle, he asked the girl if there was a café in the village and she gave him directions. Clearly this girl was his intended victim that day but he quickly backed out of any abduction attempt when her golden retriever started barking erratically and loudly, which put Black off as he certainly did not want to attract attention to himself. But there was something other than a large canine making a lot of noise that stopped him from carrying out his intention – he had momentarily noticed, whilst the child was telling the dog to be quiet, that there was a man further up the road, working on his car: a potential witness who could get him caught. He changed his mind, thanked the girl, got back in the van and thought, as he later put it, 'no chance there', and casually drove away from the girl, who certainly had had a lucky escape, unaware as she was of the danger she was in.

In his later interview with Ray Wyre he said, 'Too many houses about, people about and this fellow back up the road working on his car.' Clearly he had taken all of this in, like a leopard stalking its prey until it was safe and the right time to strike.

Frustrated, Black drove around a bit more, then stopped off at the village café located in Townfoot Road, that he had eaten at several times before. As he finished his meal and gazed out of the window, his thoughts were dominated by the urge to abduct a child as he watched another little girl walk along the pavement near the café. His earlier, failed, attempt would not thwart him – this village was no different from Ballinderry or Coldstream, from where he had successfully abducted little girls. And even though by staying in the village for hours with no valid reason, he could have begun arousing suspicion, he just had to be patient, and the right opportunity would surely come along.

The right opportunity seemed to come shortly after he got back into his van and resumed driving round the village. He noticed a pretty, blonde-haired little girl walking past him in the opposite direction along the main A7 road and turning right towards the north of the village. Black continued on in the same direction until he came to a lay-by where he turned around and headed back towards where the child – six-year-old Laura Turner (not her real name) – was. Or should have been – for, unbeknown to him, she had popped briefly into a friend's house. His frustration growing, Black headed on into the village streets again, looking for her, before executing a three-point turn and heading back once again in the direction where he had first seen her. As he did so, Laura suddenly came out from the lane to her friend's house, to continue walking along the pavement, again in Black's view. Black drove past the little girl and pulled his van up onto the pavement on her side of the road as she approached his van to walk past it. Black had positioned the vehicle perfectly for his purpose, as the only way that Laura could continue her journey was either to squeeze herself between the van and the stone wall, thus passing the passenger door, or to walk around the van on the road, which would have taken her past the driver's door. Either way Black instantly knew he had a perfect opportunity to abduct the child; she would be very near to him and he knew that, with his strength and size and the child being so young and small, the whole operation would be completed in a matter of seconds, not minutes. Black opened the passenger door to block her way and quickly jumped through it onto the pavement as the little girl walked slowly but steadily towards him. Then with just one arm he lifted her off the ground and bundled her into the passenger seat of the van. Laura screamed in terror only to be warned with a scowl to be quiet as Black pushed her little body down to the vehicle floor under the dashboard. He then hastily ran round to the driver's side of the van, jumped in and drove away at speed. No dogs or potential witnesses to stop him in his latest abduction of a little girl.

But he was wrong. There was a witness, and although Black failed to notice him, he certainly noticed Black and indeed had witnessed the entire incident. What is more, he had the presence of mind to realise what it was that he had seen, and to get help. The man in question was a neighbour of Laura's, David Herkes, who at the time happened to be out mowing his lawn, which was below road level so that he was hidden from view. He saw Laura walking out of her friend's driveway and making her way along the pavement; he also saw the van pull up in front of her. Black was unaware of him and there was no tell-tale sound of mowing as something had caused the lawnmower blades to snag. Mr Herkes was down on his knees fixing the stuck blades and was low enough to see below the van to the pavement on the other side. There were two pairs of feet, Laura's and those of the driver. But when he again glanced towards the van a couple of seconds later, there was one pair of feet, the driver's. Those of the child had vanished. As Mr Herkes stood up he could see the van driver apparently pushing something through the passenger door before quickly running round to the other side of his vehicle, jumping in and driving away. There was no sign of Laura. Mr Herkes wondered where her feet had gone; he knew he had not seen her walk along the other side of the van. What must have happened was at once clear to him. Quick-thinking, he made sure to take note of the van's registration number and then hastily ran the short distance to Laura's house where he told her mother what he had just seen. Mrs Turner immediately telephoned the police and within minutes policemen and cars had swamped the village. The police in Scotland were only too aware of the abductions and murders of Susan Maxwell and Caroline Hogg some years previously, and police cars in the area were straightaway radioed the details of the incident and the description of the abductor's van.

★ ★ ★

Once he had seized the child, Black headed out of the village back towards Edinburgh, effectively in the wrong direction. While there are those who suggest that this error demonstrates the severity of the depraved sexual frenzy Black was in at the time, Black himself would later explain to Ray Wyre his reasons for doing so, and while he may have added or omitted a few details, the explanation is both plausible and supported by circumstantial evidence.

There was still one more delivery to make, Black explained, but with the child huddled in the footwell on the passenger side, it was too risky for him to go straight to the delivery point in Galashiels. Somebody could have gone up to the van to collect the delivery off him and seen her. Or even before then she just might have managed to attract another driver's attention as they travelled south towards Galashiels. But he knew of a lay-by a couple of miles away on the road to Edinburgh. So he headed back in that direction and stopped in the lay-by. There, unseen, he took the little girl out of the front of the van and into the back, where he had what might be called his home-made abduction kit.

Once they were confined in the back of the van, Black told Wyre, he asked Laura her name and then proceeded to tie her hands behind her back. Tearing a length of sticking plaster off a roll, he put it across the child's lips, asking her if she could breathe okay through her nose. He took her socks and shoes off and put a cushion cover over her head like a hood, and then sexually assaulted her before bundling her into a sleeping bag and returning to the front of the van and turning it round in order to carry on with his journey to Galashiels. The whole episode lasted just under fifteen minutes.

To get to Galashiels he had to head back into Stow. As he made his way into the village he must have been somewhat alarmed by the number of police vehicles about, and the unusual number of people milling around. But perhaps he felt safe in the knowledge that his abduction of the little girl had not been witnessed, or so he thought . . .

★ ★ ★

David Herkes, standing by the roadside giving police officers – one of them the child's father – as much detail as he could about what he had witnessed, was more than a little startled when he saw the blue van heading back towards him. 'That's him! That's the van! That's the same van!' Black, as he drove along the road was suddenly forced to brake sharply and swerve to avoid hitting a police officer who had leapt out into the centre of the road, shouting for him to stop. He brought the van to a halt.

Black was taken from his vehicle and immediately handcuffed, while Constable Ian Turner hurried to open the back of the hot, stinking van, calling his daughter's name. At first, disturbingly, there was no answer, then he glimpsed slight movement coming from what looked like a pile of bedding in the far corner of the van. Frightened at what he might find, he pulled at it and saw it was a sleeping bag, which he dragged out and hurriedly opened. Ripping off the cushion cover that was encasing the head of the small figure in the sleeping bag, he was overcome with relief to see that the little girl was alive – gagged, terrified, red-faced from the heat and lack of air, but, apparently, physically unharmed (it was not known at this point that she had been sexually assaulted).

As the policeman untied his daughter's hands and took the plaster off her lips, that relief quickly turned to fury as paternal nature kicked in, and he turned to Black and shouted at him, 'That's my daughter! What have you done to her, you bastard?' Black did not react in any way, he did not speak or give any indication of what he was feeling emotionally. He remained cold, quiet and distant.

* * *

In a BBC Northern Ireland *Spotlight* programme broadcast in February 2016 retired PC Ian Turner was interviewed about the circumstances surrounding the day his daughter was abducted. In the programme Mr Turner stated that he immediately recognised Black as being someone he had seen before, the spitting image of a sketch that he had seen some seven years earlier, in 1983, when Caroline Hogg was abducted from a funfair in Edinburgh.

It was this hitherto publicly restricted identification of Black that led directly to him being investigated for the abduction and murders of Susan Maxwell, Caroline Hogg and Sarah Harper.

This was to prove the end of the road for the criminal activities of Robert Black. He would never again be a free man, but regarding the details of those crimes and the growing number of them coming to light and public attention it was only to be the beginning.

* * *

As he was being taken to Selkirk Police Station, some fourteen miles away, Black spoke openly to officers, remarking that it should have been the day before, Friday the 13th, as he had been having an unlucky day, what with an earlier road traffic collision in Edinburgh and now his arrest for child abduction. He went on to offer an explanation for his actions, saying that he had 'always been interested in young girls since I was a lad', claiming to a police sergeant, 'It must have been a sudden rush of blood to the head.' Black went on to say he had only touched her 'a little' and that he wanted, after he finished his delivery, to take her somewhere 'like Blackpool' so that he could spend some time with her.

Black readily admitted the abduction and sexual assault of Laura Turner – he had been caught red-handed so he could do nothing else. His strategy here was undoubtedly to appear as open and honest as possible regarding the crime, and he co-operated with the arresting and interviewing officers as well as with the psychiatrists who were to be used in his upcoming trial for both prosecution and defence, explaining the nature of the sexual assaults he would have carried out on the child. His ultimate aim was to be seen as a man who had given in to an abnormal fantasy in a 'sudden rush of blood to the head', be given treatment, serve his time in prison and then be released back into society. Despite the fact that Laura, bound, gagged and stuffed into the sleeping bag like a discarded bit of clothing, had come close to dying from suffocation, Black insisted if she had it would have been 'accidental'!

There is no doubt that he had had no intention whatsoever of taking his latest little victim to Blackpool or anywhere else like that; the likelihood is that she would have ended up another little body dumped in the Midlands as he made his way back to his home in London. Thanks to the sharp eye and quick thinking of David Herkes, who sadly passed away in 2012 at the age of seventy-eight, that never happened. His swift actions that day undoubtedly led to Black's immediate arrest and it is impossible to know how many young lives were potentially saved by him and his quick thinking.

Detective Superintendent Andrew Watt, as the weekend senior officer on duty in Lothian and Borders, had been notified of Black's arrest and he soon spotted the similarities between the circumstances of the abduction in Stow and the Midlands Triangle murders and quickly notified Hector Clark of the arrest and the details surrounding it. Clark and his team began to ask themselves if this could be the man they had been hunting for almost a decade. Coupled with PC Turner's seeing in the man he had arrested a strong similarity to the 1983 artist's impression of Caroline Hogg's abductor, this certainly seemed likely.

Shortly before Black was due to appear at Selkirk Sheriff Court on the Monday morning, Hector Clark arrived at Selkirk Police Station to meet him. He had previously stated that he believed that the killer he had been hunting would eventually 'slip up' and that this slip-up would lead to an arrest. As he left the police cell, having asked Black a few brief questions, to which he had received even briefer replies, he was sure that he had just been in the presence of the man they had been after for so long. The tough work would now really have to begin as instinct and feeling are not enough in a court of law – now they had to prove it.

After his initial court appearance that Monday, 16 July, Robert Black was remanded in custody at Edinburgh's

Saughton Prison until his trial. On Friday 10 August he pleaded guilty in the High Court, hoping that by pleading guilty and therefore not making any witnesses take the stand in what was clearly a distressing case for all involved, he would get a lenient sentence. He was, however, to be disappointed, for he was sentenced to life imprisonment with the condition set by the judge that he would not be considered for release until it was safe to do so. Whilst Black's defence counsel had stated to the court that the abduction had been an isolated crime and that he had never acted upon any previous temptation and that the child would not have been killed, the psychiatric reports assembled by two prominent psychiatrists painted a very different picture. They painted a picture of man who was and would continue to be a grave danger to young children, and there is no doubt this was accurate.

As Black's legal team went to work on an appeal, Hector Clark and his team were already working hard to build a case to prove that the man who abducted and sexually assaulted a six-year-old girl in Stow, leaving her twenty minutes from suffocating to death, was the man who was responsible for the Midland's Triangle killings of Susan Maxwell, Caroline Hogg and Sarah Harper. It was to be a long, challenging and complicated investigation.

Black's appeal against his life sentence was lodged in September 1990, but it was dropped two months later, in November 1990, after the evaluation of Black, at the behest of his legal team, by the eminent sex-crimes expert Ray Wyre (referenced several times in this book) provided nothing to disagree with earlier psychiatric reports. Ray Wyre would interview Black twice in Saughton Prison in Edinburgh and would continue to interview him even after Black dropped his appeal. The book, co-written with Tim Tate, that he published in 1995, *The Murder of Childhood,* is based on these interviews and his thoughts of the Black case. Ray Wyre died in 2008 but there is no doubt he got closer to discovering the reasoning behind Black's actions, and what else he may have done, than anyone else did. He like David Herkes is an unsung hero in the Robert Black saga.

8

THE FIRST MURDER TRIAL

After Black's arrest, a search of his impounded Transit van revealed a number of items used as restraints, among them assorted ropes, sticking plaster and hoods. In addition, investigators discovered many articles of girls' clothing – none of which, they subsequently discovered, belonged to any of the victims – a mattress, a **Polaroid camera**, and a selection of so-called sexual aids. When asked to account for these items Black explained that on his long-distance deliveries he would often pull into a lay-by, dress in the children's clothing and masturbate. He would not give a plausible explanation for the sexual aids that had been found. These, it was later ascertained, had been kept, along with the mattress and restraining devices, in readiness for use upon his victims.

The Scottish police contacted London's **Metropolitan Police, who at their request** carried out a search of Black's

Stamford Hill lodgings in search of any incriminating evidence. Their search, as mentioned earlier, uncovered a large collection of child pornography in the form of magazines, books, photographs and videos, including fifty-eight videos and films depicting graphic child sexual abuse, which Black later said he had purchased in continental Europe. The police also found several items of children's clothing, a copy of a Nottingham newspaper with an account of the attempted abduction of Teresa Thornhill in 1988, and a variety of purpose-designed sex aids. All of this was impounded and sent to Edinburgh to assist the team there in their investigation.

Two weeks after Black's trial for the abduction of Laura Turner, Hector Clark again travelled to the police station in Edinburgh to conduct a second, and recorded, interview with Black. On this occasion he was accompanied by two colleagues, Andrew Watt and Roger Orr, whom he had appointed to conduct the actual interview, with specific instructions that they were to inform Black at the start that they would in no way be judgemental of him, whatever he might choose to divulge.

In this six-hour interview Black readily spoke of his early sexual experiences, his exploration of self-abuse, and his liking for wearing young girl's clothing; he also told the detectives how he was attracted to young children; and he admitted to having sexually assaulted over thirty young girls between the 1960s and 1980s.But when the questions became more specific, even when they pertained only loosely to any unsolved child murders and disappearances, Black became evasive. He did, however, volunteer that, in Carlisle in 1985, he had successfully enticed two young girls into his van on the pretext of asking for directions and had not much later allowed them to leave.

As the interview progressed the two detectives began to turn their questioning to the subject of child abduction and murder, at this stage focusing specifically on the murder of Caroline Hogg. They told him that police knew he had been in Portobello on the date of the little girl's disappearance, indicating that they had eyewitness accounts and petrol-station receipts that further proved his presence there at the time. Orr then brought out a facial **composite drawn from descriptions given by eyewitnesses** of the man who had been seen with Caroline. He placed this composite alongside photographs of Black that dated from the early 1980s and pointed out the similarities.

At this stage, Black became as terse and monosyllabic as he had been in Clark's interview on 16 July. The two detectives closed the six hours of interview with a direct appeal to him to confess in order to end the suffering of the families of his victims. Black said nothing. Although the information gleaned from this exhaustive interview would achieve little to actually advance the ongoing murder enquiry, it did serve to strengthen Hector Clark's conviction that Black was guilty. As the three police officers left, Clark commented to his two colleagues: 'That's our man. I'd bet my life on it.'

Combining their efforts, detectives from the six forces in the United Kingdom involved in the case (Northumbria Police, Lothian and Borders Police, Staffordshire Police, the Leicestershire Constabulary, West Yorkshire Police and the Nottinghamshire Constabulary) then embarked on an intense and painstaking hunt for sufficient evidence to satisfy the Crown Prosecution Service that it would be justified in instigating legal proceedings against Black with a reasonable chance of convicting him of the murders of Susan Maxwell, Caroline Hogg and Sarah Harper. Black himself clammed up and, as was his right by law, refused to co-operate with the detectives.

One of the first areas of focus for this joint investigation was the firm that had employed Black since 1976. Detectives contacted Poster, Despatch and Storage Ltd in the hopes that the company had travel records that could verify Black's whereabouts on specific dates crucial to the investigation. PDS staff confirmed that Black had always paid for petrol with credit cards and would then submit the receipts to the firm for reimbursement. The files containing them, along with several historical delivery schedules, were still in the company's archives. Searching through these archives, the investigators discovered that Black had made scheduled delivery runs to the counties where the abductions had occurred, and on dates that coincided with those of the abductions. While the precise times he had been in each locality were difficult to determine, petrol-station receipts confirmed that he had purchased petrol close to the location from where each girl had disappeared, and on the date of her disappearance. In the case of Sarah Harper, for instance, Black had been scheduled to make a series of deliveries across the Midlands and Northern England, with the two final deliveries being in the West Yorkshire towns of Brighouse and Morley. A petrol-station receipt showed that he had refuelled his van between these two towns shortly before Sarah had last been seen alive. His last delivery was to a firm located just 150 yards from the Harpers' home.

The investigators also discovered that on his journey back to London from his long-distance deliveries to Northern England or Scotland Black had often slept overnight at the house of his landlord's son John Rayson in the Midlands village of Donisthorpe. This village was in the so-called Midlands Triangle, close to where the three victims' bodies had been discovered. On his regular deliveries to Morley, the Leeds police discovered, Black often slept overnight in his van in the premises of the firm he delivered to, not so far from Sarah Harper's home.

Upon learning that Poster, Despatch and Storage had accounts with several oil companies, allowing their drivers to purchase fuel without cash changing hands, investigators approached the oil companies in question, who handed over seven million archived microfiche credit-card slips detailing fuel purchases made via this method at every one of their nationwide premises between 1982 and 1986. These were sent to the incident room in Newcastle upon Tyne, where a team of officers undertook the task of combing through them for Black's distinctive signature in order to identify exactly when, where and at what time he had refuelled his van. Although tedious, this endeavour did pay off: from October 1990 investigators began to unearth vital evidence of the precise times Black had paid for fuel at petrol stations close to the abduction sites. In every case, the time of purchase had been not long before or after each child had been taken. By December 1990 the enquiry team decided they had accumulated sufficient circumstantial evidence to persuade the Crown there existed a reasonable prospect of securing convictions against Black. Even though Clark harboured concerns that the enquiry had not discovered any actual forensic evidence to tie Black to the murders, all the accumulated evidence was submitted to the Crown in May 1991.

In March 1992 Crown lawyers decided that the sheer weight of this evidence was sufficient to warrant Black being tried for the three murders and the attempted abduction of Teresa Thornhill. Police held a news conference on 11 March in which Hector Clark told the press he was able to confirm that 'criminal proceedings have been issued on the authority of the Crown Prosecution Service against Robert Black'.

There were several pre-trial hearings held between July 1992 and March 1994; these hearings saw Black's defence team argue that their client should be tried on each count separately and that the prosecution should not be allowed to demonstrate any similarity between the modus operandi of each offence at the upcoming trial. In the penultimate pre-trial hearing, held in January 1994, Judge William Macpherson ruled against defence motions to try Black on each charge separately and also ruled in favour of the prosecution's request to tender similar fact evidence, a principle that is not always admissible as it has its flaws. In the case of Black's trial, the similar fact ruling allowed the prosecution to present the similarities between the cases and to introduce into evidence

Black's recent conviction for the abduction and sexual assault of Laura Turner. The prosecution was, however, prohibited from introducing into evidence the transcript of the interview of Black carried out by detectives Andrew Watt and Roger Orr in August 1990.

On 13 April 1994 Robert Black stood before Mr Justice William Macpherson at Moot Hall in Newcastle upon Tyne and, as the charges were read out, pleaded **not guilty** to each of the ten counts of kidnap, murder, **preventing the lawful burial of a body** and attempted kidnap. Throughout the entire trial, Black rarely displayed any notable interest, typically remaining expressionless, and speaking only when asked a direct question.

In his opening statement on behalf of the Crown, prosecutor Mr John Milford, QC called the case 'every parent's nightmare' as he set out the prosecution's contention that Robert Black had committed the three child murders and the attempted abduction as charged, highlighting the similarities between these offences and the 1990 abduction and sexual assault of the Stow schoolgirl for which Black was already serving a life sentence. Milford then outlined for the jury the circumstances of each abduction and murder one by one, asserting that each victim had remained alive in Black's van for several hours before her murder and that each had been killed at or close to where her body was later found. Upon hearing the details of the girls' kidnapping and murder, the victims' relatives present in court wept openly. Mr Milford cautioned the jury: 'It would be too easy to dwell on the suffering but we have to put that to one side, along with all our natural emotions and consider only this: is it proved by the evidence that this defendant, Robert Black, abducted and killed them.'

Referring to both Black's history of child sexual abuse, and to the **paraphernalia** discovered in his vehicle and at his London address, Mr Milford addressed the court: 'These three offences were so unusual, points of similarity so numerous and peculiar, that you can, members of the jury, safely conclude that they were all the work of one man. The Crown alleges that Robert Black kidnapped each of these children and did so for sexual gratification and then transported them and murdered them.' He closed his five-hour opening speech with the contention that the petrol-station receipts and travel records to be introduced into evidence would prove Black that had been at all the abduction, attempted abduction and body-recovery sites on the dates in question.

The second day of the trial saw the prosecution beginning to introduce witnesses, witness statements, circumstantial evidence, and forensic testimony. Each case was covered chronologically, with various witnesses describing the circumstances surrounding the abduction and the subsequent discovery of each victim, and investigators describing the evidence they had uncovered relating to Black's whereabouts on the relevant dates; the attempted abduction of Teresa Thornhill and the kidnapping and assault of Laura Turner were also covered. Statements made by the mother of each murder victim at the time of her child's abduction were also read to the court, followed by the testimony of the pathologists who had examined each body at the recovery location and also later conducted full autopsies upon each victim.

Black's appointed defence counsel Mr Ronald Thwaites, QC proceeded to cross-examine a number of the witnesses, focusing on matters such as minor discrepancies between times logged within record books at a firm to which Black had made a delivery on the date of Susan Maxwell's disappearance and those of petrol receipts introduced into evidence – which proved to be an **administrative error** – and the statements given by witnesses to police at the time. Thwaites also questioned the issue of memory accuracy, for many years had gone by, but most witnesses remained steadfast in their insistence as to the accuracy and honesty of their testimony.

The defence's cross-examination of the prosecution's witnesses continued into the third day of the trial. One of these witnesses was James Fraser of Lothian and Borders Police forensic laboratory, who had earlier testified as to the results of his forensic examination of more than 300 items recovered from Black's van and his London flat. Asked if he and his colleagues, having made over 1,800 microscopic comparisons, had uncovered evidence against Black, Fraser conceded that no forensic link had been established between Black and the three victims. In direct re-examination by the prosecutor Mr Milford, however, Fraser pointed out that the interval between the offences and Black's arrest – plus the fact Black had only bought the van in which he was arrested in 1986, later than at least two of the three murders in question – would make establishing a forensic link between the three murders highly unlikely.

The final prosecution witnesses testified on 29 April. Several detectives from the various police forces involved in the manhunt attested to the sheer scope of the investigation while Black had been at large and to the subsequent painstaking searches carried out to obtain the evidence required to prove his guilt – in all, over 20 tons of material had been collected for sifting through. The last detective to testify on this date was Hector Clark, who conceded Black's name had not been among those entered into the HOLMES database during the manhunt because he was not a known sex offender; his conviction for molesting his landlords' young daughter was in 1976 – a less serious offence and one that predated the timescale of those judged to warrant further investigation. Clark added that he could not recall any other cases where children had been abducted, killed and their bodies transported considerable distances. 'I don't believe there has been a bigger crime investigation in the United Kingdom, ever,' he stated.

On 4 May Ronald Thwaites presented his case in defence of Robert Black. He first reminded the court that the police had been unsuccessfully investigating the crimes for eight years before Blackhad been arrested for the Stow abduction in 1990 and subsequently convicted of it. The investigation, said Thwaites, 'reeked of failure, disappointment and frustration' and he went on to suggest that the investigators had seized the opportunity to make a **scapegoat** of his client to appease their feelings of failure and in an effort to restore broken reputations.

In describing the evidence presented before the court Thwaites claimed that although the paraphernalia introduced as evidence by the prosecution did indeed confirm his client's admitted obsession with procuring and viewing paedophiliac material, there was no direct evidence to prove Black had 'graduated from molester to murderer'. Thwaites had decided against permitting Black to testify in respect to the petrol receipts and travel records introduced into evidence, remarking to the jury that 'No man can be expected to remember the ordinary daily routine of his life going back many years.' He also reminded them that the fact that Black was not giving evidence was not a presumption of guilt.

'This case,' Thwaites added, 'has been determined using one incidence of abduction, which he [Black] admitted, as a substitute for evidence in all the other cases. Without it, there is no direct evidence against him,'

Witnesses for the defence were then called up to testify. To support Thwaites's contention that the three murders were not part of a series and had not been committed by Black, much of the testimony delivered by the defence witnesses referred to sightings of alternative suspects and suspicious vehicles seen in the vicinity of each abduction. Several people testified that on the date of Susan Maxwell's abduction they had observed a girl matching her description striking a maroon Triumph saloon with a tennis racket close to the site of Susan's abduction. This vehicle had contained at least two men. Yet others spoke of seeing red or dark-coloured cars in the vicinity. A fourteen-year-old girl who, eleven years previously had said she had seen a 'bad man' trying to take Caroline Hogg away, now only remembered that a child who used to play with her stopped being there to play with her. While these witnesses may have served to demonstrate the fragility of decade-old evidence, they did little to advance the case for the defence.

On 12 May the two counsels delivered their **closing arguments** to the jury. Prosecutor John Milford, QC spoke first, opening his final address to the jury with a description of the circumstances of Black's arrest in 1990, and then recapitulating the extensive circumstantial evidence presented throughout the trial. He was careful to refer to the total lack of physical evidence to link Black to the crimes, reminding the jury that this was because a considerable length of time had passed between the offences and Black's arrest. As to Black's close proximity to each of the abduction and body disposal sites on the dates in question being merely coincidence, Milford commented that this was 'an affront to common sense' – if this defence contention were true, it would be 'the coincidence to end all coincidences'. He closed by requesting the jury to reach a guilty verdict.

The counsel for defence Ronald Thwaites, QC then delivered his closing arguments. 'Where is the jury that will acquit a pervert of multiple murder?' he asked. He continued by representing his client as an individual against whom ample prejudice existed but no **hard evidence**, pressing upon the jury the need to differentiate between a child sex pervert and an alleged child killer. He attacked the credibility of several prosecution witnesses and ridiculed the nationwide manhunt: 'The police have become exhausted in not finding anyone; the public are clamouring for a result. What good are you if you can't catch a child killer? Is he their salvation, or a convenient expendable scapegoat?'

Mr Thwaites then reminded the jury of witness testimony that implied an individual or individuals other than Black had committed the three murders before concluding his statement.

Mr Justice Macpherson began his summing-up on 16 May, and finished on the 17th. He called on the jury not to be swayed by emotion, distaste for Black as a person, or for his proclivities; adjuring them not to be prejudiced by his record of sexual offences against children or his admission to and conviction of the 1990 kidnap of the young girl in Stow. The judge further directed the jurors to concentrate on the physical and circumstantial evidence in all the cases presented at the trial. 'The question is whether you are sure that the interlinking and similarities of these five cases drives you to the conclusion that this man, Robert Black, is guilty in the four sets of cases which are before you,' he said, adding that any conclusions of guilt on one charge should not automatically mean he must be guilty of all charges. The jury were then ushered out to begin their deliberations somewhere private, and reminded before they retired to consider their verdict that they were barred from speaking to anyone other than one another, from reading newspapers, watching television or making any telephone calls. Their deliberations would continue for two days.

On 19 May 1994 the jury returned their verdict. They found Black guilty of abducting and murdering Susan Maxwell, Caroline Hogg and Sarah Harper, and of preventing the lawful burial of their bodies, and of the attempted abduction of Teresa Thornhill – ten counts in all. For each of these, Mr Justice Macpherson sentenced him to a term of life imprisonment, and recommended that for each of the three counts of murder this 'extremely dangerous man' should serve a minimum of 35 years. The life sentences were to run concurrently.

The families of the victims were overcome with relief, long and harrowing as the trial had been, the verdict brought closure of a sort.

Black did not react on hearing the sentence, but as the judge dismissed him, he turned to the police officers present, who had been involved in the case, some from as early as 1982, and said, 'Tremendous. Well done, boys.' Mocking in tone, perhaps, but the words were seen as an admission of guilt, and tears of relief came to the eyes of some of those who had worked so long and tirelessly for this outcome. He was led away to start serving his sentence at HM Prison Wakefield, a high-security establishment for Category A prisoners (those considered a danger to the public).

Outside Moot Hall, a crowd of reporters had gathered, waiting to hear the verdict and for statements from the twenty-odd detectives from all the forces involved in the manhunt, who had attended the hearing. 'The tragedy,' commented Hector Clark, 'is these three beautiful children who should never have died. Black is the most evil of characters and I hope there is not now or ever another like him.'

★ ★ ★

Black's conviction marked the culmination of one of the longest, most exhaustive and costly British murder investigations of the twentieth century, with a dossier of evidence weighing some 22 tons and a total cost estimated at £12 million. But it was not over.

In the wake of Black's conviction, a meeting was arranged in Newcastle, attended by senior detectives from the police forces involved in the cases, and also officers from other forces in the UK that were grappling with unsolved missing-child or child-murder cases. At this conference, which was held in July 1994, all the evidence amassed by each force was considered in the light of Black's convictions. By then, his name had been linked to a number of further child murders and disappearances between 1969 and 1987, stretching from the Republic of Ireland, across the United Kingdom and into continental Europe. As he had been found guilty and given sentences that made it highly unlikely that he would ever be a free man, and he knew it, police hoped he might be persuaded to confess to several other child murders they believed he had been responsible for. Black, however, who had never admitted his culpability in any of the offences for which he was convicted, other than the abduction of Laura Turner, refused to cooperate with the investigators.

Indeed, Black actually chose to appeal his 1994 convictions, contending that he had been denied a fair trial because details of his 1990 abduction and sexual assault charges had been introduced as similar fact evidence – a ruling his defence counsel had objected to but been overruled on. In addition, Black argued, the final instructions delivered to the jury by Mr Justice Macpherson had been unbalanced. The appeal was heard before the Lord Chief Justice Lord Taylor at the

Court of Appeal on 23 February 1995; it had been expected to last three days, but at the end of the first day Lord Taylor ruled the verdicts had been safe and satisfactory and dismissed the appeal.

A few months later Black was attacked in his cell by two other inmates of Wakefield Prison who threw a mixture of boiling water and sugar over him in an attempt to 'rip his skin off', battered him with a table leg, and stabbed him in the back and neck with a homemade knife. The defence counsel for one of them said at their trial that Black was a 'particularly notorious prisoner' and attacked because of the nature of the offences for which he was serving his sentence.

Neither of these setbacks is likely to have helped persuade Black to open up to the detectives questioning him. Many years later, in October 2011, Roger Orr, one of his earliest interrogators, interviewed by the BBC, said of Black: 'He was a cooperative individual in a sense, but very closed and very controlled. There was a coldness in his empty eyes. In police interviews, any time we would close in on specific details, he would sit and stare at you for long periods of time, in complete silence.'

A fellow inmate of Wakefield Prison, confirmed this, as reported in Northumberland's *ChronicleLive* on 19 January 2015: 'He sits back, puts his hands behind his head and just smirks.'

According to Ray Wyre, the prime reason for Black's resistance both to cooperating with investigators and to admitting his culpability was an issue of control for him. In an interview granted not long before his death in 2008, Wyre

9

THE SECOND
MURDER TRIAL

The year was 2009 and Robert Black was sitting alone in his cell at Wakefield Prison in West Yorkshire. Christmas was fast approaching and as the Police Service of Northern Ireland officers entered his cell Black sat on his bed and looked at them. They were there to give him something but it wasn't a Christmas present – it was a summons charging him with another child murder, that of nine-year-old Jennifer Cardy in August 1981.

It was a cold Wednesday, 16 December 2009, when the news broke: news Andy and Pat Cardy had been expecting – that a man had been charged with their daughter's murder, and that the man in question was Robert Black. The Cardys had been aware since the mid-1990s, following Black's first murder convictions, that the Royal Ulster Constabulary (PSNI from 2001) were looking at Black as a strong suspect in their daughter's murder. They also knew that the police, having trawled through half a million petrol receipts, had found evidence that he had been in Ulster at the time of Jennifer's murder, in the form of a docket signed by Black. The investigators were to go on to find a wage book from Poster, Despatch and Storage that would add to the documented paper trail that put Black in Northern Ireland on that day. Due to the long and complicated nature of the investigation and the patient waiting and planning it entailed, it became known as 'Operation Perseverance'.

At the police conference in July 1994, two months after Robert Black had been convicted and given ten life sentences, officers representing police forces from across the British Isles and from Europe dusted off their cold-case files of missing and murdered children, some going back over twenty-five years, to see if there was anything that could link Black to them.

Just under twenty cases were looked at from different parts of England, Scotland, Northern Ireland, the Republic of Ireland, France, Germany and Holland. The media latched on to these and reported on them, naming the victims and citing the potential links to Black no matter how tenuous these links were.

At the end of the conference the numerous police forces involved took what they had learnt about Black and went back to the drawing board. In the years that followed, he could never be ruled effectively out of several of the cases but there was insufficient evidence to take the cases any further forward. For others he was completely ruled out and in some instances other men would later be charged and convicted of the murders in question.

But there was a small number of cases in which he certainly seemed a very serious suspect; so much so that the police forces involved knew there was further work to be done and intensified their investigations, focusing on whether they had a case against Black. One of those forces was the Royal Ulster Constabulary, who certainly had the strongest case to link Black with – the murder of Jennifer Cardy. In June 1996 the RUC and the Devon and Cornwall Police, who were investigating the disappearance of Genette Tate, went to Wakefield to interview Black at the police station. The information they gleaned from this interview was insufficient for them to press charges, but they continued to investigate him and over the years various police forces conducted further interviews with Black and with possible witnesses.

★ ★ ★

It was the morning of Friday, 22 January 2010 and the small public gallery at Lisburn Magistrates' Court in County Antrim was full. Murmurs spread through the seats of the public gallery as a prison van arrived carrying Robert Black, just flown in from Wakefield Prison in West Yorkshire. He was escorted from the van and into the court, handcuffed, wearing a blue jumper and navy jeans and glasses.

It was the first time he had been seen in public since his murder trial in 1994, almost sixteen years before. His hair and beard had gone from grey to white, he had put on weight and looked older and slower. But Robert Black was still the same man. A cold, calculating and remorseless paedophile and serial killer. Prison hadn't softened him in any way. He entered the dock and stood behind a glass wall; from there he confirmed his name and also that he understood the charges he was facing: the kidnapping and murder of Jennifer Cardy from a location only a few miles from the courthouse he was now in.

If the infamy of the prisoner was in doubt, the fact that, while the handcuffs were removed as he stood in the dock, four prison officers stood around him with another four just outside the dock, dispelling any doubt as to the enormity of the offence with which he was being charged. An even greater indicator of this would be Black's journey to Northern Ireland. This was no ordinary scheduled flight to Belfast – instead, the prisoner travelled with three prison officers in a private jet from Leeds Bradford Airport, a forty-minute journey during which he sat comfortably in his seat chatting to the guards and looking out of the window.

Black's defence counsel told the court that his client would be pleading innocent to the charges. The resident magistrate Rosemary Watters told him he would be remanded in custody in nearby HM Prison Maghaberry in County Antrim and would be arraigned at Craigavon Magistrates' Court in March.

★ ★ ★

The trial began on Thursday 22 September 2011 at Armagh Crown Court. The prosecutor was Mr Toby Hedworth, QC – who had been Mr Milford's junior at the 1994 trial, and was

Above: Robert Black's police mugshot following his arrest in Scotland for loitering with intent to steal, 12 August 1968. He was not convicted.

(from The Murder of Childhood *by Ray Wyre and Tim Tate, 1995; reproduced by kind permission of Tim Tate)*

Below: Thirteen-year-old April Fabb, who went missing while cycling near her home at Metton, near Cromer in Norfolk, on 8 April 1969. Although her bicycle was recovered, her body has never been found.

(left – © Sunday Post; right - © Norfolk Constabulary)

Above: In May 1971, fifteen-year-old Jeanne Twigden had a lucky escape when an attempt was made to abduct her as she cycled home from an open-air pool near the village of Great Paxton, Cambridgeshire.

Below left: On 21 May 1973, Christine Markham, aged nine, vanished while walking to school in Scunthorpe, Lincolnshire. Her body has never been found.

(© Sunday Post)

Below right: Aged just six, Mary Boyle disappeared on 18 March 1977 while on a family visit to her grandparents' home in Ballyshannon. Co. Donegal, Ireland. Black is known to have been just over the border in Northern Ireland at the time of her disappearance. Again, her body has never been found. *(© Sunday Post)*

Above left and below: On 19 August 1978, thirteen-year-old Genette Tate disappeared while delivering newspapers on Wilthen Lane in Aylesbeare, East Devon. Many years later, although reported by BBC News as the 'only suspect' in the case, Black died days before he could be charged with killing Genette.

(left – © Sunday Post*; below –*
Devon and Cornwall Police)

Left: Aged fourteen, Suzanne Lawrence did not return home with her younger sister after staying with a friend in Dagenham, Saturday, 28 July, 1979. During a senior police conference in Newcastle in July 1994, her name was added to the list of Black's possible victims.

(© Sunday Post)

On Wednesday, 12 August 1981, Jennifer Cardy rode to her friend's house on her new bike, but never arrived. The nine-year-old's red bicycle was found thrown over a hedge a mile down her road the next day; she herself was found dead six days later. *(above – © Sunday Post; below – © Royal Ulster Constabulary)*

Left: In the village of Cornhill-on-Tweed, in the Scottish Borders, eleven-year-old Susan Maxwell was abducted and murdered by Black when walking home after playing tennis with a friend, 30 July 1982. *(© Sunday Post)*

Below left: A year after murdering Susan Maxwell, Black abducted and murdered five-year-old Caroline Hogg in a similar manner, following her towards her local beach. She was found by a motorist ten days later in Twycross, Leicestershire. *(© Sunday Post)*

Below right: Sarah Harper, only ten years old, disappeared during the night of 26 March 1986 as she collected a loaf of bread from a local shop for her mother. Her body was found by a dog walker three and a half weeks later along the bank of the River Trent, Nottingham, 19 April 1986.

(© Sunday Post)

Right: On Saturday, 9 May 1987, ten-year-old Virginie Delmas did not return home after saying she had gone to play with friends; she never arrived. Her body was found five months later in an orchard in Mareuil-lès-Meaux, east of Paris, by a couple picking apples.

(© Sunday Post)

Left: On Wednesday, 3 June 1987, seven-year-old Perrine Vigneron was declared missing after not turning up for her pottery class. Her body was found three weeks later, three miles from the village from which Virginie Delmas had been abducted.

(© Sunday Post)

Right: Teresa Thornhill, aged fifteen, narrowly escaped Black's grasp by her screams for help, Nottingham, 23 April 1988. *(© Sunday Post)*

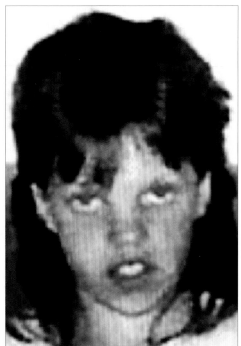

Left: In Germany on Thursday, 11 May 1989, Ramona Herling left her house to walk the short distance to her local open-air swimming complex. She was never seen again. *(© Sunday Post)*

Below: A Nissan/Datsun van similar to the vehicle Robert Black would have used for his delivery job, as well as for abducting Jennifer Cardy.

Robert Black, pictured after his arrest in 1990. He died from a heart attack in HMP Maghaberry, Northern Ireland, before he could face charges for further murders. *(© Sunday Post)*

therefore well acquainted with Black's iniquities. He laid the case out to the jury, informing them that police investigators had gone through more than half a million petrol receipts, old accounts and company records and in so doing had established that Black was in Northern Ireland at the time of Jennifer Cardy's murder.

He went on to detail the evidence as follows:

1. A salary ledger indicating that in August 1981 Black was paid a £50 bonus for the week in question– the bonus that was paid to drivers who did the Northern Ireland run.

2. The exclusion of all other drivers from Poster, Despatch and Storage (PDS) who did the route at that time.

3. A petrol receipt demonstrating that on the day after Jennifer's murder Black was driving the company's only white Datsun van. (This smaller vehicle was used only for short runs in nearby East Anglia and in and around London, and for the Northern Ireland run – for which it was the only vehicle used on account of the fact that it was small enough not to fall into the commercial-vehicle category, which meant that the cost of travelling on the ferry was considerably reduced.) The receipt, signed by Black, was from a Shell petrol station near Coventry on a southbound carriageway towards London from the West Midlands. This, Mr Hedworth said, showed that Black was returning from a Northern Ireland run after leaving the boat at Liverpool and heading south for home – and not working in London or East Anglia.

4. Order books from PDS indicating that a poster delivery to Northern Ireland was due around that time.

Black sat impassively in the dock wearing a grey jumper, white T-shirt and blue jeans; along with his glasses he wore a headset provided to him by the court due to his poor hearing so he could follow the proceedings better.

The first witness to take the stand was Jennifer's mother, Patricia Cardy, who recalled the last time she seen Jennifer. While her husband Andrew, Jennifer's father, and daughter Victoria, Jennifer's younger sister now aged thirty, watched from the gallery she began to speak about the day her older daughter disappeared. The plan that day had been for Jennifer to cycle to her best friend Louise Major's house, only a mile away, to spend a couple of hours with her.

Pat Cardy told the court how Jennifer had been holding her baby sister Victoria shortly before she set off from home on her shiny new red bicycle. She would never return from that journey. 'I can well remember what she was wearing,' Mrs Cardy recalled. 'It was her favourite T-shirt, a white T-shirt trimmed with red round the neck and on the T-shirt were red strawberries.'

Mrs Cardy went on to say how she had wound up her daughter's red watch before the little girl set off as Jennifer was punctual and didn't like to be late:

'She was a very thoughtful little girl and her time to leave was always 1.40 p.m. because she liked to get to her friend's house for about 2 p.m. Most importantly, she liked to be back in time for *Jackanory* and for that reason she always checked her watch. Just before she left she had given our baby Victoria to me. She made a cheeky little remark about her weight – that Victoria was a little heavy.'

The judge, Mr Justice Mr Ronald Weatherup, listened quietly as Mrs Cardy recalled how she became increasingly concerned when Jennifer had not returned by dinner time, and how, when she and Andy could not locate their daughter, the police were notified. As family, friends and neighbours began to search the vicinity, Jennifer's bicycle was found lying in a field half a mile away from her home, thrown over the hedge from the roadside.

Mr Hedsworth for the prosecution then recounted how, in her 1981 statement to the RUC, little Louise Major recalled that she and Jennifer had once watched a TV programme where someone was abducted when they got into a strange car. 'Jennifer said she would never do that,' Louise had said.

Alluding to the evidence he had put before the jury, Mr Hedworth, QC observed that, while Black travelled all over the UK for his job, every bit of the evidence pointed to him being in Northern Ireland on that day just over thirty years before.

'He was in fact on that Wednesday morning driving a poster delivery van off the Liverpool ferry at Belfast dock and commencing his drops at Belfast, then Dunmurry and finally at Newry, before returning to Belfast to catch the evening ferry back to England.'

He added: 'This would leave him – after completing his deliveries – with time on his hands in the general Lisburn area at exactly the time that little girl was plucked from the roadside in Ballinderry.' It was Mr Hedworth's opinion, moreover, that Black's return trip to the Belfast ferry would have taken him past the lay-by near which Jennifer's body was later found.

During 2005 interviews with the PSNI, Black had conceded he must have been in the area at that time – that he would have been in Ireland on 12 August 1981 as that was the day he made routine deliveries to firms in Belfast and Newry; he had also agreed that he used to use the A1 dual carriageway that ran between Lisburn and Newry when he was working in Ulster.

As the first day came to a close, Mr Hedworth concluded, 'Child murders in the UK are extremely rare, even rarer in Northern Ireland. That little girl never got to her friend's,' adding, in an echo of Mr Milford's words in 1994, 'Somewhere along the way, every parent's nightmare occurred. She was abducted, sexually assaulted and killed.'

The jury of nine women and three men were then left to ponder as he asked:

'Why would anyone take a young girl from the roadside and then, when they were done with her, discard her body?'

★ ★ ★

On the second day of the trial, Monday, 26 September, Black's defence team examined invoices from PDS that showed that Black was in Northern Ireland. The retired head of the London advertising agency Concord and Poster Link (CPL), which had commissioned PDS to deliver posters to Northern Ireland in August 1981, Alan Simmons, was brought to the witness stand, to answer questions from both prosecution and defence on the transactions between CPL and PDS.

The Crown's case relied heavily on Black's work documents proving he was in Northern Ireland on the day of the murder before getting the overnight ferry back to Liverpool. CPL had appointed PDS to deliver a large array of billboard posters to be used in nationwide campaigns to advertise the products of several major companies. As the advertising campaigns were scheduled to start on 1 September, Mr Simmons explained, 'I would expect PDS to take delivery early in the month before and distribute them around the middle of the month.'

He then stated that if the posters had not been delivered as commissioned he would have known as he had a regional employee who would check that deliveries had been made on time. This explanation was useful to the prosecution. The timing fitted – PDS would have taken delivery of the posters in early August, and they would have distributed the posters in the weeks after, around the middle of the month – which period included Wednesday, 12 August, the day Jennifer was murdered.

Black's defence team, headed up by Mr David Spens, QC, tried to show that there were no specific delivery dates recorded:

'There's no document that demonstrates on its face there was a delivery to Northern Ireland in the middle of August 1981?' Mr Spens asked.

In response Mr Simmons admitted that 'I can't give you a specific date, just a likely period during which it would have been delivered.'

David Spens then suggested that, rather than in the middle of August, PDS could have delivered the posters perhaps at the start of the month, or maybe even the end of the month – perhaps as late as only five days before the 1 September deadline.

'We didn't work to those sorts of short deadlines,' Mr Simmons replied.

The prosecution responded to this attempt by the defence to confuse things by pointing to the petrol receipt from the day after the murder, dated and signed by Black, which could not be wrong or confused as to when the petrol was purchased. They reiterated that the receipt showed he was driving the Datsun van used for runs only in Northern Ireland, East Anglia and in and around the London area. The fact that the petrol was obtained near Coventry ruled out the possibility he was working in East Anglia or London and pointed to him having bought the fuel from a garage as he travelled home to London after leaving the Liverpool ferry up north having completed his work in Ulster.

Next to enter the witness stand was retired Lothian and Borders police officer Thomas Bell who was one of the officers tasked with going through the thousands of petrol receipts located at Shell UK's company headquarters in Manchester in 1996 in an effort to locate Black's signature. He told the court that the police involved in the search had to comb through 304 boxes of microfiche film containing petrol receipts. While checking the signatures, they had found one of interest: 'Mr Black's was quite clear, it was quite distinctive.'

Mr Spens then asked if all the fuel purchases made by PDS

drivers had been traced, but Mr Bell explained that only Shell UK had the records from 1981 still intact; the records from BP filling stations had already been destroyed by 1996. There were no records of any sort for transactions at filling stations other than Shell, he said.

★ ★ ★

The next day of the trial would hear from a retired customer of PDS based in Newry, who recalled talking to Black in the early 1980s. George Hughes, who was the owner of billboard sites in the city of Newry, recalled Black mentioning that he sometimes used a petrol station in Hillsborough, County Down, near where the body of Jennifer Cardy was discovered. There was a petrol shortage at the time, Hughes recollected, and yet Black had driven over from England. He asked Black why, and 'He told me he had a card he could produce at Shell petrol stations and they would give him a fill-up and he told me he got a fill-up at a station in Hillsborough that morning.' This was a BP service station at the start of the A1 between Lisburn and Hillsborough.

This information, although it did not reinforce the Crown's claim that Black was in Ulster on that day, did indicate that Black would have been very familiar with the A1 dual carriageway between Belfast and Newry which runs past the lay-by and McKee's Dam where Jennifer's body was found.

The defence counsel, David Spens, proceeded to cross-examine Mr Hughes and asked him if he had company records that would show the exact day PDS delivered posters to him. Mr Hughes answered that he did not.

The Crown then brought up the subject of the £50 bonus paid to Robert Black two days after Jennifer was murdered, as shown on the PDS wage book, asserting that it was the bonus drivers received for doing the Ulster trip.

In 2003, police investigators had taken a statement from the co-owner of PDS, Mrs Valerie Staalem, and it was read to the court. She had been asked about a wage book that recorded Black's £50 bonus for the week in question. 'I would say on looking at it,' she had told them, 'that the Ireland run was done some time between the sixth and thirteenth of August 1981, and Robert Black did it as there was a £50 bonus paid to him.'

Mrs Staalem had died since then, but had she been alive and in court, David Spens defence QC informed the jury, he would have cross-examined her on whether or not an Ulster run actually did occur during these dates in August 1981.

Another witness, Raymond Baker, a former warehouse manager at PDS, revealed that Robert Black was only one of two PDS drivers who didn't mind travelling for work to Northern Ireland – the others were worried about the political troubles of the time.

On 13 August 1981, the day after Jennifer's murder, in addition to the Coventry petrol-station receipt, Black signed another receipt; this time it was later in the day, at a Greater Manchester filling station and he was using a different work vehicle, another type of van, and not the white Datsun.

When asked about this, Mr Baker said he thought Black had stopped in Coventry to refuel on his way back from Northern Ireland, returned to London, picked up more posters from the PDS depot in the east of the city and then made a delivery run to Manchester. 'A few times I could remember that Robbie [Black] has come from Ireland, possibly could've filled up in Coventry, and there was another load for him [at the depot] because he was a single chap who didn't worry about trips and he could have gone up and done another trip in the Fiat.'

The defence counsel in cross-examining Mr Baker asked him if he was absolutely certain that Black was in Northern Ireland the day before – that is, on the 12th – suggesting to him that Black might have simply driven to Coventry, made a delivery there, and returned to London.

'I can't be certain about anything at this stage, it's long after,' replied Mr Baker.

Mr Spens then turned his attention to the white Datsun van that Black had been driving and asked the next witness, another former PDS driver, John Radford, if the white Datsun van had been used in places other than Northern Ireland, London and East Anglia in the early 1980s as there were petrol receipts from then that indicated the vehicle had also been elsewhere in England, for instance Preston, which is north of Liverpool.

'The white Datsun van, although most of the time it was doing runs to East Anglia, London and Northern Ireland, it also made other runs, didn't it?' said Mr Spens.

'So it seems,' replied Mr Radford.

Mr Hedworth for the prosecution then asked Mr Radford if the white Datsun van could have refuelled at Preston as the Stranraer-to-Larne boat route had taken over from the

Liverpool-to-Belfast route in 1981. Mr Radford agreed that this was possible, which would have meant the white Datsun van could still have been Northern Ireland-bound.

When Mr Spens pointed out that Mr Radford had once been paid a £50 bonus for a working week that did not include a trip to Northern Ireland, Mr Radford explained that payments in the wage book did not have to mean a driver had undertaken a particular job, and bonuses could be paid to cover a combination of road tolls, routes and overtime work.

★ ★ ★

Wednesday 28 September, day four of the trial, heard from another former PDS driver, Michael Carder, who was unwavering in his conviction that Robert Black was in Northern Ireland the day Jennifer was abducted and murdered. He reiterated what had been said by the previous witnesses that the petrol-station receipt signed by Black outside Coventry suggested he was on his way south, having come off the Liverpool ferry; and this was reinforced by the fact that the vehicle used was the white Datsun van, which was utilised primarily for trips to Ulster, East Anglia and in and around London.

Mr Hedworth asked Mr Carder if he had any doubt Black was in Northern Ireland on 12 August 1981.

The answer was unhesitating: 'No.'

Mr Spens responded to this steadfast claim by Mr Carder by suggesting that his belief was based on the assumption that PDS had made a delivery on 12 August 1981 and that the white Datsun van had been used exclusively for the delivery runs mentioned. Mr Carder conceded the point, but maintained his belief that Black was in Ulster that day.

Another former PDS driver, a son of the proprietors, Mr Ian Staalem, who while he admitted he could not be certain Black had been in Northern Ireland that day, when he was asked what he made of the petrol–station receipt said, 'That would suggest to me that he was returning home to London. As it was the smaller van [the Datsun], it could have been from Liverpool, having done the Belfast run.'

The defence then presented evidence from a woman called Susan Marchant who had managed a London filling station in the early 1980s, and who revealed that dates on old fuel receipts could be wrong as the machine had to be manually wound on every morning.

Then David Spens QC once again suggested to the court that Robert Black could have been making a single delivery trip to and from Coventry on 13 August; the day he purchased the petrol. Toby Hedworth QC countered this by asking another former PDS driver, Mr Raymond Aldridge, if he remembered PDS drivers ever undertaking trips just to Coventry and back during his employment there. 'It never happened in my time,' Mr Aldridge answered firmly.

The prosecution then commented that Black would go off main routes and motorways on his delivery runs, and instead drive through smaller towns and villages – which would explain how he came to encounter little Jennifer Cardy on that quiet country road in Lower Ballinderry. This was indeed the case – Black would boast to his workmates of his almost encyclopaedic knowledge of the road network, explaining how he had come up with and travelled alternative routes between destinations using slip roads and the like rather than taking the more obvious route like a motorway. Those he talked to about this, as he showed them the routes he was referring to on maps, could never understand his enthusiasm for all this driving as such journeys took far longer. In hindsight it's easy to see why they appealed to someone like Black as it is virtually impossible on a busy dual carriageway or A road to stop and remain unseen, or to spot, target and abduct a little girl, while the quiet country roads that lay between towns and villages did provide such opportunities for a predatory paedophile like Black.

Michael Carder and another former PDS driver, Paul Scargill, both confirmed to the prosecution and court that Robert Black was well known for taking alternative roads off the main arterial routes.

★ ★ ★

The fifth day of the trial, Thursday 29 September, continued with the prosecution concentrating on the task of dispelling any doubt that Black was in Northern Ireland on the day of the murder.

In 2003, former PDS warehouse manager Albert Wells, who had since died, had provided police investigating the Cardy killing with a statement which Mr Hedworth read to the court:

'Robbie Black did the poster delivery runs to Ireland ninety-nine times out of a hundred. Other drivers did not like the ferry times and considered the bonus payment too small.'

Mr Spens told the jury that had he been able to cross-examine Mr Wells, he would have suggested to the court and to the witness that he was exaggerating. Mr Wells's statement, however, was supported by that of another witness, a former PDS accountant, John Thompson, who was not in court but had testified to the police,

The defence then returned to the validity of the dated petrol receipt obtained by Black in Coventry on 13 August 1981 and asked if human error could mean that the date on the receipt might in fact be wrong since the credit card machine that issued and printed the receipt had to be manually operated.

David Johnston, the owner of the Coventry Shell garage in question, where the petrol receipt was issued, told the court from the witness box that in his more than twelve years of working in the industry he had never been aware of any such mistake occurring.

'I can't recall any, no,' he asserted.

The defence team continued to attempt to confuse matters and plant seeds of doubt by claiming there was no real proof that Black was in Northern Ireland on the day of the murder despite the prosecution's claims to the contrary. The defence pointed to the statement made the day before by Susan Marchant in which she said that occasionally a member of her staff would forget to wind on the manual date settings on the card machine resulting in the wrong day being printed on dockets and asked Mr Johnston if his lack of recollection of such an incident meant it never occurred:

'I'm not saying that,' Mr Johnston replied, 'but I can't recall any [instances]. But it's a possibility.'

The prosecution after the first five days of the trial had made a solid start demonstrating to the jury that Black was in Northern Ireland on the day of Jennifer's murder and thus establishing he had the opportunity to carry out the crime. The next stage was to continue to emphasise to the jury how well Black knew the area where Jennifer's body was found, and demonstrate unequivocally that he had driven past the lay-by when on the Ulster delivery run, for which he travelled the A1 dual carriageway between Belfast and Newry.

* * *

On day six of the trial, Monday, 3 October, the court heard transcripts, read out by the prosecution junior counsel Donna McColgan and PSNI detective Patrick McAnespie, of an interview conducted with Robert Black in 1996 by the then Northern Irish police force, the Royal Ulster Constabulary (RUC), when they travelled to Wakefield in West Yorkshire to first interview him about the murder of Jennifer Cardy. During this interview, RUC detectives had asked Black how often he did the delivery run to Ireland for PDS.

'Often enough,' he had replied. 'Quite a few times actually, I couldn't put a number on it.' He added that only two or three PDS drivers did the run as the other drivers disliked it.

'I think they were a bit scared about the Troubles.'

In the interview Black went on to talk about how the typical Ulster work trip involved drop-offs of posters in Belfast, Dunmurry and finally Newry. He also admitted he had used the road where Jennifer's body was found outside Hillsborough, mentioning a BP service station where he filled his van regularly, located at the start of the A1. A crucial point was his admission that he used a lay-by to sleep in on the northbound side of the A1 dual carriageway between Newry and Lisburn. The RUC then proceeded to show Black a photograph of the lay-by on the A1 near to McKee's Dam, in which Jennifer's body was found. Black denied it was the lay-by he used, claiming he didn't recognise it. When, however, the RUC later provided Ordnance Survey maps from 1981 that clearly showed there was only one such lay-by on that stretch of the road at that time and that lay-by was adjacent to McKee's Dam, he conceded that it must have been the one he had used.

★ ★ ★

The seventh day of the trial heard tapes and transcripts from the 1996 interviews conducted in Wakefield, and also interviews from 2005, for which Black had been transported from Wakefield Prison to Antrim Police Station. The courtroom was deadly silent as the recordings began to play. In one of the tapes, Black was asked if he accepted he was in Northern Ireland on 12 August 1981, having been shown the petrol receipt he signed at Coventry on the morning after (the 13th) and the wage book that showed he was paid a bonus. When asked if the evidence showed he was in Ulster on 12 August 1981 Black replied calmly and coldly: 'That seems the most likely explanation.'

Pressed further as to if it could be the only explanation for the evidence, Black responded: 'I think the best I can give you is most likely, most probable – a high possibility.'

The detective described step by step the journey the police believed Black had taken from London to Belfast, and, his deliveries having been made, his route back to London. He then asked Black to give a firm answer as to whether he was in Northern Ireland on the day in question: 'You would have been in Ireland from the morning of the 12th of August until that evening – do you accept that?'

Black's response was a simple 'Yes.'

Crown lawyer Donna McColgan and DS Patrick McAnespie read the transcript from the next interview, during which Black agreed that he had used the road near which Jennifer's body was found on the day of the murder:

'Do you accept you would have been on the A1 road to Newry?' the interviewing detective had asked him.

'Yes,' replied Black.

During the 2005 police interviews, Black was not asked outright about Jennifer despite him fully knowing it was the reason for the PSNI interviewing him.

In 1996, however, the then RUC had attempted to take a direct approach with Black and Jennifer's killing. From the exchanges read to the jury, it would seem that such an approach tended to make Black less accommodating.

Interviewing officer: 'I'm saying to you, Robert, were you on that road, and did you lift Jennifer Cardy?'
Black: 'No.'
Interviewing officer: 'I want you to think about it.'

Black: 'I don't need to. It's something you would remember.'

The Crown's line of reasoning was that Black enjoyed going off motorways and exploring quiet country roads and villages in between or after finishing deliveries – which, said Mr Hedworth, was why he was in Ballinderry on 12 August.

There is no doubt that this was the case. In 1996 one of Black's RUC interviewers – in an unhappy choice of phrase – asked him if he was often left with 'time to kill' after he had finished his deliveries in Northern Ireland. Black had replied, apparently unconscious of the inadvertent double entendre – 'I would have all afternoon and early evening to kill.' He would have completed his assignment after his last drop-off in Newry, some time after midday. With several hours before he was due to board the ferry at Belfast he could have done what he did on some other occasions and gone to a pub near the docks where he would have had a pint or two of shandy and played a game of pool, or he might have gone swimming at a leisure centre he used off the Falls Road in West Belfast. That sunny afternoon, however, he decided against doing this and chose instead to go exploring in his van as he made his way from Newry towards Lisburn on the A1 dual carriageway. Sadly, as he made his way onto the rural Crumlin road on the outskirts of Ballinderry village he came upon a little girl on her new red bicycle on her way to play with her best friend. There and then, in a matter of seconds, he decided to abduct the child.

The prosecution had, in spite of attempts by the defence to prove otherwise, demonstrated that Black was in Northern Ireland on the day of Jennifer's murder through the signed petrol receipt and wage book with the bonus payment paid to him for doing the Ireland run, interpreted to mean just that by his former PDS colleagues and admitted to by Black himself. He clearly had the opportunity and the time to commit the crime. Black also agreed that he knew and had used the lay-by near where Jennifer's body was found in 1981, demonstrating that he knew the specific area. The next step was laying out the motive for him to abduct and kill Jennifer.

* * *

The ninth day of the trial, 7 October, was to be a pivotal day for all involved. During the previous eight days the women and men of the jury had, for legal considerations, been told nothing of Black's criminal past and convictions. Day nine changed all that as a shocked courtroom heard details from the Crown QC of what Black had done in the past and been found guilty of in a court of law. At the beginning of the day Mr Hedworth announced to the jury:

'The stage in the trial proceedings has been reached where I can tell you . . .' and he went on to tell the court how Black had been arrested in Stow in the Scottish borders in 1990 after abducting and sexually assaulting a six-year-old girl who was rescued from the back of his van, gagged, bound and without mercy bundled into a sleeping bag. He had pleaded guilty to this abduction and was jailed for life. The prosecution described to the jury how police had subsequently found evidence to charge him with the murder of three children – eleven-year-old Susan Maxwell in 1982, five-year-old Caroline Hogg in 1983 and ten-year-old Sarah Harper in 1986, all three of whom had been sexually assaulted – and with the attempted abduction of a fourth, fifteen-year-old Teresa Thornhill, in 1988. He had pleaded not guilty to all the charges but in 1994 was found guilty in Newcastle upon Tyne and was sentenced to ten terms of life imprisonment.

Toby Hedworth made it clear to the jury, however, that his other murders did not make him automatically guilty of Jennifer's.

'What you certainly must not do is say, "Well, he's done those other ones, he's a thoroughly bad man so we'll find him guilty in this case as well",' he cautioned. 'What you have to do is look at what he has been proved to have done in respect of those other girls and see whether it assists you in deciding whether you can be sure that it was Robert Black rather than some other individual who abducted and killed Jennifer Cardy. The prosecution will submit that the similarities between Jennifer's case and the other cases make it clear that they were in fact the work of the same man.'

* * *

Day ten of the trial, Monday, 10 October, was to focus on forensic evidence, specifically the initial pathologist's report, which had more recently been challenged by another pathologist who had different opinions on how Jennifer died and on whether or not she had been sexually assaulted before her death.

First up to speak for the Crown was former Northern Ireland state pathologist Professor Thomas Marshall, who had carried out the autopsy on Jennifer's body back in 1981. He stated that Jennifer's body demonstrated signs of neck compression, indicating pressure had been applied to her neck area. But he remained unwavering in his opinion that that was not the cause of death.

'I've always been certain that she died from drowning,' he said.

He also told the jury that he found no evidence that Jennifer was sexually assaulted: 'I did think about it and came to the conclusion there was no evidence of sexual activity.'

Professor Marshall repeated that he believed the cause of death was drowning as he had found fresh water in Jennifer's lungs.

David Spens, QC for the defence, then asked Professor Marshall if he was aware of the opinions of the other Crown witness Dr Nathaniel Cary. Dr Cary, a senior pathologist who had recently reviewed the case and looked over the findings, disagreed with Professor Marshall's findings, believing that Jennifer had died from strangulation and was the victim of a sexual assault. Professor Marshall confirmed he was aware of Dr Cary's report but he was still sticking to his views from 1981.

Andy and Pat Cardy left the courtroom for a short period as a black and white photograph from the 1981 autopsy was projected on to the courtroom wall. The photograph was of Jennifer's neck. Professor Marshall said that whilst her neck had been compressed; he was not sure how forcefully and he was adamant that it did not cause her death: 'I don't think death had been caused by whatever happened to her neck.'

When questioned by Toby Hedworth, QC for the prosecution, Professor Marshall conceded she could have been unconscious when she was dumped in McKee's Dam. 'She may,' he said, 'have been rendered unconscious by the pressure on her neck.'

Cross-examined again by Mr Spens, Professor Marshall reiterated that he had found no evidence of sexual interference.

The next witness to take the stand was an expert in forensic science, Mr David Scaysbrook, who reviewed the evidence from 1981 regarding Jennifer's clothing. When questioned about a stain found on Jennifer's underwear, Mr Scaysbrook was asked in his professional opinion if the stain was more likely to have been blood or bodily fluid that was released following Jennifer's death during the decomposition process. Mr Scaysbrook answered that, while he was not 100 per cent sure, he believed it was blood.

'If the stain was blood it would support the view that some form of sexual assault had taken place on the victim,' he added.

Mr Scaysbrook went on to criticise the 1981 forensic notes made on Jennifer's clothing, declaring that they were neither detailed nor comprehensive enough; he added they were of a poor standard even for their time, but he did concede that this could have been because the police and forensic services had had their hands full with the Troubles.

The court then learned that no forensic reviews or fresh tests could be carried out by police on Jennifer's clothes because they were lost forever, having been destroyed in 1992 in a Provisional IRA bombing of the forensic laboratories in Belfast where they were stored.

There were two other points of physical evidence, however, that also pointed to Jennifer having been a victim of sexual assault, both relating to the state of her clothing when she was removed from McKee's Dam. During the post-mortem it was noted that not only was the zip of the child's trousers down but her underwear was on inside out. This suggested that the bottom half of her clothing had been removed at one stage and then put on again, indicating a sexual motive for Jennifer's death.

Dr Richard Adams, former head of the Northern Ireland Forensic Laboratory, took the stand to discuss the significance of Jennifer's red Timex watch when her body was taken from the dam. The first day of the trial had heard from Pat Cardy, who said that she had wound up her daughter's watch for her just before Jennifer had left on her bicycle. The time was then 1.40 p.m. The time on the watch when Jennifer was taken from McKee's Dam was 5.40 p.m., four hours after the watch was set.

Dr Adams, who had gone to McKee's Dam when Jennifer's body was found, testified to having seen no signs of a struggle, although there were several buttons missing from Jennifer's cardigan and some blood on her clothing. He went on to explain that he had carried out a number of tests on the watch to observe the way it reacted when it came into contact with water and how long it ran for afterwards. He came to the conclusion that the 5.40 p.m. on the watch face was relevant to the day Jennifer was abducted: 'It stopped because water had entered the watch.'

This was significant in terms of Black's time frame: Jennifer entering the water on the day she was abducted at 5.40 p.m. meant that Black would certainly have had the opportunity and the time to carry out the crime as he was not due back on the boat to Liverpool until much later that evening.

* * *

The trial so far: by this stage it was clear how the case for the prosecution was progressing. The Crown had laid out a firm case that Black had had the opportunity to commit the murder, presenting documented evidence, such as the petrol receipt and wage book, as well as witness analysis of that evidence, to show that Robert Black was in Northern Ireland on the day of the murder and that he was in the general vicinity of Ballinderry at the time Jennifer was abducted. The prosecution also produced evidence in the form of police interviews in which Black conceded that he had used the lay-by adjacent to McKee's Dam where Jennifer's body was found, and therefore knew the area. Other evidence, too, such as timing – the time that Black finished his deliveries, the time of the ferries, the time he filled up in Coventry . . . and the time on Jennifer's watch – all helped to build up the case against him.

The prosecution then moved on by telling the court of Black's past crimes – the three child murders, the 1988 attempted abduction in Nottingham, and the 1990 Stow abduction that led to his capture – revealing that Black was a serial killer and committed paedophile. The emphasis at this stage, on how Jennifer died, and if she was a victim of sexual assault, was in order to bring in the third core point of the prosecution's case – the very strong similarity in MO, to the point of almost being identical, to the methods proved in a court of law to have been used by Robert Black previously, and so distinct that all crimes involved had to have been committed by the same man – and that man, the prosecution was convinced, was Robert Black.

10

THE TRIAL CONTINUES

The following day, day eleven of the trial, Tuesday, 11 October, heard from one of the topmost forensic pathologists in the whole of the United Kingdom. Dr Nathaniel Cary had in the ten years preceding this trial worked on some big murder cases, including the Ipswich serial murders of five prostitutes by Steve Wright, the 'Suffolk Strangler', and the case of the Soham murders of Holly Wells and Jessica Chapman. Dr Cary stated that Jennifer's murder was 'remarkably similar' to the 1986 murder of Sarah Harper; a killing Black was convicted of in 1994, and added: 'These cases are very rare. So if a rare thing has similar features that's an important point.'

Both Jennifer and Sarah's bodies were dumped in water (Jennifer in McKee's Dam and Sarah in the River Trent near Nottingham) and both girls were believed to have died by drowning, both thought to have been alive but unconscious when they entered the water. This in itself was a unique yet strong point of similarity.

The bodies had similar marks and injuries. With Sarah Harper there was no doubt that she had been victim of a violent sexual assault. And while there were no similar sexual injuries visible on Jennifer's body, the evidence of the blood stain on Jennifer's underpants, the zip of her trousers being down and her pants being inside out all indicated that she had been a victim of sexual assault.

It was not possible to determine if there were any such similarities between them and the two other victims Black was convicted of killing in 1994, Susan Maxwell and Caroline Hogg, due to the severe decomposition of both bodies in the summer heat by the time they had been discovered.

Dr Cary was asked in 2003 to review Professor Marshall's 1981 findings. Where he differed from Professor Marshall was in the matters of the cause of Jennifer's death and as to whether she was the victim of a sexual assault. Professor Marshall, as we have seen, stood by his 1981 conclusion that Jennifer had died from drowning and that she had not been sexually assaulted. When he took the witness stand the day before, day ten of the trial, he remarked that he had felt a sense of unease when in 2008 he had a meeting with prosecution lawyers to go over Dr Cary's review of his post-mortem conclusions. 'I think at that moment,' he said, 'there was a little pressure for me to alter the opinion I had given in 1981. I've a recollection of feeling I was being asked to say something which I didn't believe in.'

In response, Mr Hedworth asked him if his conclusions

ruled out sexual assault. Professor Marshall stated in response that they did not contradict the possibility of sexual assault but that there was no evidence of it found.

Regarding Jennifer's cause of death, Dr Cary did not rule out drowning but suggested three alternative possibilities as to what happened:

1. Jennifer was asphyxiated with the use of a ligature – possibly the sleeve of her cardigan.
2. Jennifer was strangled with the ligature to the point of unconsciousness and then thrown into the water where she drowned.
3. Jennifer managed to escape from the attack with the ligature around her neck and in the panic of escaping fell into the dam where she drowned.

Dr Cary, very reasonably, added that the third option was the least likely. The second option seems, to me, the most likely scenario given its similarity to Sarah Harper's death by drowning after being thrown unconscious into the water, and the conviction of Professor Marshall – who had, after all, conducted the post-mortem – that Jennifer had drowned. We must also take into account Black's attack when he was sixteen on the seven-year-old girl; whom he lured into an air-raid shelter, strangled to the point of unconsciousness, sexually interfered with, and abandoned there, apparently unconcerned as to whether she was alive or dead.

Whilst he conceded feeling 'uncomfortable' having to disagree with the findings of the respected and experienced

Professor Marshall, Dr Cary stressed that they were merely putting a different emphasis on what had happened, and he then put it into a wider perspective by stating: 'I actually don't think it matters, because if drowning took place it was clearly as a result of being abducted and dumped in water.'

Defence counsel David Spens then stepped forward to question Dr Cary, referring to Professor Marshall's view that there had been no sexual assault. Dr Cary stated that modern techniques in post-mortems make it much easier to identify injuries that result from sexual assault. He emphasised that he was not criticising Professor Marshall's analysis, commenting that the professor had not practised for nearly twenty years – 'I would not want to be judged in many years' time by the techniques of the day,' he added.

As Dr Cary stood down, the trial judge Mr Justice Weatherup asked Mr Hedworth, QC for the Crown, if the bloodstain on Jennifer's underwear definitely belonged to her. Mr Hedworth replied that there was no evidence it came from anyone else.

★ ★ ★

Day twelve saw a familiar face return to face Robert Black once again. Retired Lothian and Borders Police Detective Chief Superintendent Roger Orr, one of the leading officers whose investigations in the early 1990s led to Black's first three murder convictions in 1994.

He took the witness stand to read out the statement of Laura Turner, the six-year-old girl whom Black abducted in July 1990. She afterwards told the police how, coming from a friend's house, she had had to walk right alongside Black's blue van that had been strategically parked to ensure that she would have to come close to it. Mr Orr read out her account of what happened next.

'He wasn't looking at me then but then he looked at me. I didn't know he was a bad man then. He said sorry but then he grabbed me round the waist and bent me over and pushed me under the chair of the van.'

Black, Mr Orr told the court, shouted at the little girl to be quiet, not once but twice, before slowly and calmly reversing the van down the road, making a three-point turn and going back the way he had come. He drove out of Stow and stopped at a lay-by near a disused quarry. He then pushed the little girl into the back of the van and molested her. Putting strips of tape over her mouth, he bound her hands and put a cushion cover over her head, tying it tightly around her neck. 'He then placed her inside a sleeping bag and zipped it up.'

Mr Orr went on to tell the court the dramatic story of how Black was spotted by a member of the public, his subsequent arrest and the rescue of the little girl – who was estimated to be twenty minutes away from suffocation. He told the court how Black claimed to the arresting officers that his action had been a 'sudden rush of blood to the head'.

The court heard about the array of items the police found in Black's van, which included pieces of girl's clothing, ties, tapes and similar material that could be used to bind and gag, plus a number of 'sex toys' and objects that could be used for sexual abuse. The jury learnt how a further search of Black's flat in Stamford Hill in North London uncovered two scrapbooks of child-pornography pictures and numerous black and white Polaroids of Black carrying out sexual acts on his person in front of a full-length mirror. None of this accorded with his claim of a rush of blood to the head.

Roger Orr then progressed to the cases of Susan Maxwell, Caroline Hogg and Sarah Harper and confirmed to the jury that Black's work records and petrol receipts placed him at both the scenes of the abductions and the locations where their bodies had been found. Mr Hedworth asked Mr Orr then to explain how records of Black's deliveries helped convict him.

When explaining details of the three cases Mr Orr particularly focused on how Sarah Harper's body was found floating in the River Trent near Nottingham a month after she disappeared. He then crucially provided a link with the Jennifer Cardy murder by stating that Sarah had drowned but may have been unconscious when put into the river. 'Put simply,' said Mr Orr, 'she was alive and capable of breathing when she was put in the water.'

★ ★ ★

The following day, Thursday, 13 October and day thirteen of the trial, began with all members of the jury, accompanied by the judge, and the prosecution and defence lawyers, visiting the two main locations relevant to the trial. (Black was not taken with them.) They first drove to Jennifer's home village of Ballinderry and went along the Crumlin Road, following the route that Jennifer had taken that day over thirty years before. The police then took them to the lay-by and they walked down to McKee's Dam, which had been cordoned off, and they stood at the water's edge while the judge, Mr Justice Weatherup, told the jury just where Jennifer's body was found.

As the fleet of people returned to court, the police took down the tape and left the scene; members of the general public had stopped their cars and stood by the dam, most undoubtedly aware of and remembering the horror that had once occurred in this tranquil setting. As they surveyed the pondweed-covered surface of the water, for many it was with deep sadness for the little girl who lost her life beneath it.

★ ★ ★

The group returned to Armagh Crown Court to see Roger Orr's second day on the witness stand. This time he read out to the court the details of the other known and confirmed young girl to have survived an attack by Black: in April 1988, fifteen-year-old Teresa Thornhill escaped from Black after a frantic struggle during which she fought and bit at him until a friend came to her rescue (*see* p. 106).

Teresa was walking home with a male friend when they both noticed a blue Transit van 'driving suspiciously', Mr Orr told the court, and after she and her friend Andrew Beeson had gone their separate ways, the blue van came back and parked in front of her. Teresa decided to cross the road and as she continued to walk, Black opened the van bonnet. 'He asked her if she could fix engines. At this time she was becoming quite concerned and quickened the pace. But she was immediately grabbed from behind, she didn't see it coming. It was a very strong bear hug, pinning her arms by her sides and lifting her off the street.'

As Teresa bit Black's hand and arm, she knocked his glasses off in the struggle. Mr Orr continued: 'She screamed continuously and struggled. In her own words she was fighting for her life.'

Mr Orr described how Black had then attempted to push Teresa into the van but she had blocked his efforts by putting her feet up against both sides of the door frame. Black became frustrated. 'He responded by saying "Get in, you bitch!".' Mr Orr finished with an account of how Teresa's friend heard her screams and came running, whereupon Black dropped her and sped off in his van, while they ran to Teresa's house.

★ ★ ★

On day fourteen, Monday, 17 October, the court heard tapes of interviews between Black and Northern Irish detectives in 1996 and 2005. As mentioned earlier, the 1996 conversations were with the then Royal Ulster Constabulary, who travelled to Wakefield in West Yorkshire to interview Black, whilst in 2005 the interviews were conducted in Antrim Police Station by the RUC's replacement, the PSNI (Police Service of Northern Ireland). Andrew and Patricia Cardy and Jennifer's older brother Philip sat in the public gallery and heard the recording of Black describing how he would stalk and watch children on the beach and then insinuate himself into their play.

'If they were burying each other in the sand I might join in, or something like that,' he said. He explained to the detectives how he would set up a scenario to gain the trust of a child's parents: 'I would ask them to watch my watch and glasses while I went for a swim.'

Whilst befriending the parents Black could obviously do no harm to the children, but he would watch them for a while before moving on to another potential victim. 'I would just observe them as long as I could and then carry on walking along the beach, keeping my eyes open for another opportunity.' When questioned about Jennifer, Black denied he had anything to do with her murder. However, he was willing to talk about stalking young girls when he was driving about for work.

'I would look at her and try to guess what age she was, maybe, I might park up for a couple of minutes and watch her. If she was walking a dog I would get out and stroke the dog or ask for directions.'

Black also freely admitted to a sexual interest in little girls and talked about his 'fantasies' involving the abduction of and sexual assaults on young girls. These he insisted were just fantasies and were never acted out in real life. But in reality these statements from Black were a type of coded confession, these were not mere stories, tales or fantasies. His claim that they were 'fantasies' was merely a tactic to talk about them without implicating himself. During the 1996 interviews Black refused to admit his guilt over the three 'Midlands Triangle' murders of which he had been convicted in 1994. The interviewing detective told Black that he had been found guilty of the three murders in what had been a fair trial, remarking, 'This isn't a conspiracy.'

'Feels like it.'

When asked by the detective what crime he had committed, Black replied, 'I've done things where I should have exerted a bit more self-control, that's all.'

When discussing the abduction of Laura Turner in Stow in 1990 he indicated this was one such example of him failing to exert self-control. 'I had no intention of keeping her tied up and gagged like that,' he maintained.

Quizzed on how he would have felt if the child had died, he answered, 'I think I would have been devastated, I think that would be the word.'

This was a devious effort to disassociate himself from the murder of a child in the minds of others. He claimed there were only three occasions when he lost self-control and he said these were:

1. When he was sixteen in Greenock in 1963 and he attacked the seven-year-old girl in the air raid shelter.
2. When he was nineteen and he molested a young girl whom he was babysitting.
3. The 1990 abduction of Laura Turner in Stow which led to his arrest and downfall.

Referring to the second of these, for which he was sent to borstal for a year, Black said something which could be analysed as having a double meaning:

'I did not like getting locked up and vowed I would never get locked up again.'

What did Black mean by this? He was of course trying to indicate that he never attacked another child until 1990 when he abducted Laura Turner. Or he could have been trying to back this up by pointing to the vast collection of child pornography he had built up in an effort to control his paedophiliac desires. On the other hand, his words could also have indicated his intention to ensure that no other child would tell of his attacks because they would not survive to tell the tale.

He followed his attempt to portray himself as an innocent man who had had three moments of weakness by talking of an incident when he had had the opportunity to abduct a little girl he found crying near his van. She had lost her mother.

'There was nobody in the car park,' he said, 'there was a hill behind the car park that hid the car park from the rest of view, it would have been quite easy to get her in my van. But I didn't. I took her by the hand and took her across the car park and she spotted her mother and ran to her.'

This incident may have happened, it may not have; however, it is irrelevant either way as it was a clear attempt by Black to distance himself from the labels of 'monster' and 'child killer', which he disliked – and he confirmed as much in telling the detective, 'I don't like the idea of people thinking of me as a killer.'

Trying a direct line of questioning, the detective put it to Black that he had murdered Jennifer Cardy and should just confess.

'Why don't you give your secrets up?' he asked.

'Cos I ain't got no secrets,' Black said flatly.

The detective then tried to get Black to empathise with the victims of such attacks in an effort to get him to talk.

'You too were a victim?' he prompted.

'Yeah.'

But Black would not budge at this point from the position of denial.

The detective returned to the subject of Jennifer Cardy. 'Who would have thought Robert Black, a delivery driver from PDS, would have done that?'

'I would like to help you but I can't.'

* * *

Before the recordings were played, a retired detective who had been part of the original investigative team was questioned by Black's defence counsel. David Spens, QC, asked retired RUC Detective Chief Inspector Stephen Clarke about a number of witness sightings of a blue van in and around the Ballinderry area at the time of Jennifer's abduction. The Crown were claiming that Black was driving the smaller, white Datsun van that was used primarily for the work runs like Northern Ireland – this line of questioning by the defence was an attempt to cast a shadow of doubt over that claim by implying it was the driver of a blue van that had been spotted in the area and not the driver of a white van who had abducted and killed Jennifer. However, Mr Clarke was able to state that all blue vans and other vehicles that were spotted in the Ballinderry area at the time were subsequently followed up, traced, accounted for and ultimately eliminated from the investigation.

The defence had another throw of the dice to play, however. Junior defence counsel Paddy Taggart then stood up and asked Mr Clarke if the police investigating Jennifer's murder had been able to identify a blue van reported to have been seen at the lay-by adjacent to McKee's Dam where Jennifer was later discovered. Mr Clarke said that police were not able to trace that particular blue van, but he remarked that many vehicles used the lay-by as it was very popular place to pull over for drivers, located as it was off the A1 motorway between Newry and Belfast. It was a good answer to a tough question. Many vehicles would have used the lay-by that day, the day of Jennifer's abduction; however, in the investigation that followed not all of them would have been reported to the authorities or even noticed.

When asked about the forensic value of re-examining the victim's clothing, Mr Clarke confirmed that any evidence from it was ultimately lost forever as the forensic laboratories where Jennifer's clothes were stored were destroyed in a Provisional IRA bomb in 1992. Mr Clarke then told the court that Jennifer's parents Andrew and Patricia (who were sitting in the public gallery) had donated Jennifer's red bicycle to a children's charity in Romania.

★ ★ ★

The fifteenth day of the trial, Tuesday, 18 October, heard from recordings of interviews between PSNI detectives and Robert Black made over three days in 2005. These dialogues took place at Antrim Police Station when Black had been taken in for questioning over Jennifer's murder while he was serving ten life sentences in Wakefield Prison.

The tapes revealed a strategy that Black seemed prepared to use during interviews. In an effort to talk about his feelings about child abduction and sexual activity with children without implicating himself, he talked about the two subjects as if they were a fantasy, a non-reality, a story that he would simply play over in his head like a dark movie of the mind where he was the director. The reality, however, was that the events he was describing were not fantasy but real-life events; events that he had taken part in. Before the tapes were played, Jennifer's parents Andy and Pat left the courtroom, to return after they had been played.

The exchange that took place as follows was between Robert Black and Detective Constable Pamela Simpson.

DC Simpson: 'You also mentioned that part of your fantasy, or in your imagination, included abducting a young girl.'

Black: 'I don't recall talking about that.'

DC Simpson: 'Well, if I could ask you, Robert, is that part of your fantasy?'

Black: 'It has been in the past, yeah.'

DC Simpson: 'Can you tell me about that?'

Black: 'I'd be driving along and see a young girl, I'd get out and talk to them, try to persuade her to get into the van and take her somewhere . . . quiet. I'd take her into the back of the van . . . and all that stuff.'

DC Simpson: 'What would happen then?'

Black: 'I'd drop her off somewhere, maybe take her back where I found her.'

DC Simpson: 'So, you're driving along in your van and you see a young girl that you're interested in. How would you then get to talk to her?'

Black: 'I might ask her directions, and then "Do you want to show me where it is?" That's the way it used to work in my mind. Cos in fantasies it always works.'

DC Simpson: 'And what type of area would you be in?'

Black: 'Either a quiet urban street or a rural surrounding.'

DC Simpson: 'So if she resisted and said, "No I'm not getting into your van", what would happen?'

Black: 'In your fantasies that doesn't happen. Things always work out the way you want them in fantasies. You know in your fantasies you never pick up an awkward customer. You're lucky that way.'

DC Simpson: 'What would be the ideal place, Robert, to go to?'

Black: 'Some place maybe like a picnic area, for instance. I might have a spot that I think would be an ideal spot that I've seen in the past and then I might be in that general area and I might see a girl that triggers off a fantasy, what it would be like to pick her up and take her there.'

DC Simpson: 'Would the lay-bys we talked about earlier play a part?'

Black: 'Some, but lay-bys are dodgy. You'd always have other people driving into lay-bys.'

DC Simpson: 'When you say they're dodgy, is it something you would consider?'

At this point Black went silent and did not answer the question. The exchange was undoubtedly a strong and

THE FACE OF EVIL

important one for the PSNI and prosecution to play before the jury. Black's description of this 'fantasy' could easily be made comparable with what he did to his three murder victims, but crucially could also be compared with what happened to Jennifer Cardy. Black's refusal to continue with that line of questioning was one of two moments during the 2005 PSNI interviews when he realised he had said too much.

This 'fantasy' could easily be viewed as a coded confession – something that the prosecution were eager to demonstrate to the jury. That those parts of the interview describing driving along and seeing a young girl, in an area of rural surroundings, persuading her to get into the van and the possibility of taking her to a picnic area or lay-by, could be compared with what was believed to have happened to Jennifer Cardy was not lost on the courtroom – in particular a statement from Black regarding the ideal spot that he might have seen 'in the past', about being in the general area and seeing a girl, which would trigger off a fantasy of taking a young girl to that ideal spot. It could easily be speculated that this ideal spot that Black had known of 'in the past' was McKee's Dam, the general area referred to being Ballinderry and its surrounding roads, only ten miles from McKee's Dam, and the girl he had seen who triggered off the fantasy was Jennifer Cardy. Ultimately, we know for a fact that Jennifer was taken from Ballinderry and then to McKee's Dam.

One of the few moments of the trial when Black showed any expression or body language – shifting uncomfortably where he was sitting in the dock, eventually looking down at the floor in, for him, a rare show of embarrassment – was when the items removed from his work van in Stow in 1990 were shown to the court: the sex toys and other 'aids' which were equipped for abuse. Black had been questioned during the interviews about the various items that had been found. Asked specifically in the 2005 interview about two child's dresses and a little girl's swimsuit, Black had described how he would wear these items when committing sexual acts on his own body.

> DC Simpson: 'The girl's one-piece swimsuit was size age eight to ten.'
> Black: 'I would have thought that was for a larger child than that. Cos I know I could get it on and I'm no nymph. When I was at home I sometimes put it on.'

When pressed about what he would do with a particular item specifically adapted for self-abuse, Black's calm demeanour gave way to an angry and more reluctant response: 'No, you obviously know what it was for. I'm finished talking about that. I've done. Done this before and I'm not doing it again.'

Despite this outburst Black also seemed, perversely, to enjoy aspects of the questioning, commenting to DC Simpson as she questioned him: 'I am quite enjoying watching you struggle.'

***

On day sixteen, the court heard more of the May 2005 interview recordings between Black and PSNI detectives. They started with Black describing how his fantasies, in his own words, nearly became reality only the once. The incident he was referring to was the 1985 incident with two young girls, two sisters whom he talked into getting in his van.

Black: 'Just the once. Can't remember when exactly. It was somewhere up around Carlisle way. I stopped and started chatting to these two sisters. I actually managed to persuade them to get into the van and I drove them round like towards where they lived and I actually went past and went round a big, like, another road that led into where the houses were and I turned round and parked up and let them out. I had to sort of talk myself into it then talk myself out of it. I would see a girl on the road and think, Could I, should I, will I? Usually it didn't go any further than that, no, too many people around, you know? Until 1990 and the roof fell in. If I'd known she was only six years old I wouldn't have done it.' Black laughed as he uttered this last sentence causing one of the jurors to jolt.

Before this exchange Black had told detectives that he had never explained his fantasies about young girls and abduction before. This was a blatant lie as Black had done just that during recorded interview sessions with the late sex crimes expert and therapist Ray Wyre in the early 1990s while awaiting trial over the Midlands Triangle murders and associated offences.

DC Simpson: 'And is there any particular reason why?'

Black: 'I don't know, maybe because I'm not exactly proud of the way I feel towards young girls. Like there's a part of me that knows I'm wrong, that knows that it's wrong, that I shouldn't be doing things like that, I shouldn't even be thinking things like that. But there's the other part that says, "You like it, go on." There's a side that says, "You're not hurting these children . . . they like it really."'

This account given by Black of his feelings about assaulting young girls certainly does not sound like the inner battle of a man dealing with a perverted fantasy; it reveals, rather, a man who knew that what he was doing was wrong but was determined to justify it.

Understandably, the interview recordings had by this stage become too much for Jennifer's mother; breaking down in tears, she left the courtroom weeping. Andy Cardy sat, head bowed down, before getting up to join his wife. After a short courtroom break the couple, with immense courage, returned to their seats in the public gallery to hear another recording. This time it was Detective Sergeant Pat McAnespie who put it to Black that he had abducted and murdered Jennifer Cardy.

DS McAnespie: 'There are twelve similarities between the Jennifer Cardy murder and that of the three child murders of which you have already been convicted.'
Black: 'That must be a coincidence because I didn't do any of them.'
DS McAnespie: 'We believe, having looked at the facts, that it proves you were involved in the abduction and murder of Jennifer Cardy.'
Black: 'No way.'

DS McAnespie: 'You're a man who accepts that he likes pre-pubescent girls, you're a man who accepts that he fantasises about abducting these girls, you're a man who accepts that he wants to carry out some form of sexual act on them, so you've got all the motive in the world. Isn't that right?'

Black denied he was involved and claimed young girls willingly got into his van in his fantasies.

DS McAnespie: 'Robert, let's face it now, there's not much chance of a child willingly getting into your van.'
[DS McAnespie had then produced a photograph taken of Jennifer on the day she was abducted. Jennifer is standing outside her home in the sunshine, smiling proudly at the camera beside her new red bicycle.]
DS McAnespie: 'You see Jennifer on her bike?'
Black: 'Was that taken close to the time she went missing?'
DS McAnespie: 'Shortly before it. That's the bike we are talking about. She got that bicycle for her birthday.'
Black: 'Looking at that, I would have thought she was younger than nine years old.'
DS McAnespie: 'Would you? Those are the same clothes, believe it or not, white socks, corduroy trousers, blouse. Did you ever see her, Robert?'

Black: 'No.'

DS McAnespie: 'Were you on the B12 and you saw that girl and you thought, Happy days, I'm in a van, open the door, throw her in, away we go?'

Black: 'No'.

DS McAnespie: 'No? Okay. That's what we say happened, Robert. We're saying that this is the perfect situation for you . . . You see her and you stop and you want to speak to her. What do you say? "Excuse me, wee girl, can you show me how to get somewhere?" And an obliging nine-year-old girl with nothing to fear says, "Yes, sir, I'll help you," and you talk to her, and your urge, your fantasy takes over.'

Black: 'No'.

DS McAnespie: 'She wasn't willing to go and you abducted her, you've crossed that line, fantasy one minute, then reality kicks in. You put her in the van and you have to restrain her. She doesn't want to go with you, she's not willing, why would she be? . . . Her bike was on the road and you think to yourself, If I leave that bike on the road someone's going to come along and see it, so you get out and throw it over the hedge.'

Black: 'No.'

DS McAnespie: 'And you think, Right, where do I go, and then you remember McKee's Dam.'

Black: 'No.'

DS McAnespie: 'You go to McKee's Dam, she's got a ligature round her neck, so possibly by that stage

she's possibly even unconscious . . . and she was
sexually assaulted.'

Black: 'No.'

DS McAnespie: 'Then you have the problem: What
am I going to do with the body? There's one thing
you could do, and you're at McKee's Dam and you
put her into the water . . . You couldn't have cared
less. Is that right?'

Black: 'No. I didn't even know of the existence of
McKee's Dam.'

The court then heard once again from retired Detective
Chief Inspector Stephen Clarke, the prosecution's last witness.

Mr Clarke informed the jury that he had reviewed all child
murders in Northern Ireland from over the last forty years
and, using four points of reference, compared them with the
crimes Robert Black had been convicted of committing. The
four points were as follows:

1. The victim was a pre-pubescent girl.
2. The victim was abducted from a public place.
3. The victim was murdered.
4. The victim was taken away in some form of transport.

'There was only one case that fitted the four criteria and
that was the case of the abduction and murder of Jennifer
Cardy,' he asserted.

Toby Hedworth, QC for the Crown, asked Mr Clarke if
he would confirm to the court that the Jennifer Cardy case
was the only such child murder in Northern Ireland in the

forty years since 1972 that matched the criteria linked with Robert Black's method of operation. Turning to address the judge, Mr Justice Ronald Weatherup, Mr Clarke confirmed: 'Yes, My Lord, the case is unique.'

Mr Clarke then added, 'The Jennifer Cardy case is also the only case that has never been detected.'

The defence opened their case with junior counsel Paddy Taggart informing the jury and court that Mr Black would not be taking the witness stand to defend himself. 'Mr Black will not be giving evidence,' he said.

Mr Justice Weatherup then asked the defence team if Mr Black was aware that the jury was entitled to draw an inference from the accused not taking the stand. Black's defence counsel David Spens, QC confirmed for the jury that Black was aware of it.

★ ★ ★

The defence team laid out their case on day seventeen of the trial, Thursday, 20 October. They called a lone witness and put their case to the jury. Dr Christopher Milroy, an expert forensic pathologist, gave evidence via video link from Malaysia, where he was on a lecture tour. In his evidence he said that the internal marks found on Jennifer's body were not necessarily proof that she was the victim of a sexual assault.

'It is significant there was no injury,' he said.

This attempt by the defence team to cast reasonable doubt on there having been a sexual motive for Jennifer's abduction and murder – and that it therefore could not be compared with the three murders for which Black was convicted in

1994 – was efficiently countered by the Crown during cross-examination, when Mr Hedworth, QC asked Dr Milroy if it was the case that sexual assault could be committed and not always leave marks or visible injuries. Dr Milroy agreed that it was, stating that it depended on the severity of the sexual assault. He also accepted that an injury could have been missed at the original post-mortem examination, techniques used at the time having been significantly different from modern ones.

'If you have the body of a young girl who is abducted in circumstances where there is no ransom note, one of the starting points surely would be, has this girl been sexually assaulted?' Mr Hedworth suggested.

The debate then focused on the stain found on Jennifer's underwear. The prosecution said that an experienced forensic pathologist had visually identified the stain as blood back in the 1981 autopsy. Dr Milroy stated, however, that it did not prove the stain was definitely blood, pointing out that a visual analysis was not as efficient as a scientific one; only a scientific test could have proved what the stain was. He added that decomposition fluids could have caused the staining.

When discussing Jennifer's cause of death, Dr Milroy said he believed that the state of Jennifer's lungs at the autopsy would support death by either drowning or asphyxiation. David Spens, for the defence, then asked Dr Milroy which of the two he believed was the more likely cause.

'Probably more likely than not it was drowning. I don't think you can express a strong preference for one or the other,' answered Dr Milroy, who also said that he believed that 'in all likelihood' Jennifer had had some sort of ligature wrapped around her neck.

With the conclusion of Dr Milroy's evidence the defence had completed their case – in just under two hours. The next stage of the trial was for both the prosecution and defence lawyers to begin their closing statements – summing up their case to the jury.

★ ★ ★

On day eighteen of the trial, Friday 21 October, Toby Hedworth, QC for the prosecution, was first to speak. He delivered a strong and confident closing statement, choosing Black's refusal to give evidence as his point of departure.

'There is one absolutely central and fundamental witness that I, on behalf of the prosecution, would have liked to have asked some questions. Questions to assist you in your careful and thorough and fair examination of this case,' he declared. 'But strangely, this witness is not dead. He is not infirm. He is not unable to come to court. He has in fact been here in the centre of this court for the duration of the trial. But he has quite deliberately chosen not to walk the few short paces from the dock to the witness box, take the oath, look you in the eye and answer these charges. You may ask yourselves why. Because, ladies and gentlemen, the prosecution would have some questions for Robert Black. Questions that, because he is guilty, he knows he cannot answer.'

During this verbal challenge Robert Black remained sitting in the dock with headphones on and wearing an expression that was the same as it had been for the majority of the trial – unruffled, impassive, indifferent, displaying no emotion. He would yawn occasionally, perhaps to show his lack of concern or interest in the events taking place in front of him.

Mr Hedworth then spoke of how Jennifer's murder whilst unique in Northern Ireland criminal terms, became part of a pattern when put into a wider British context alongside Robert Black's known crimes. Jennifer's killing displayed Black's hallmark and signature. 'In Northern Ireland Jennifer Cardy stands alone – she is unique. No one here does that sort of thing. But Robert Black does. And Robert Black was here on that day.'

A recap of the crimes for which Robert Black was convicted in 1994 followed: the murders of eleven-year-old Susan Maxwell from the Scottish borders in 1982, five-year-old Caroline Hogg from Edinburgh in 1983, ten-year-old Sarah Harper from Morley in Leeds; and the attempted abduction of fifteen-year-old Teresa Thornhill in Nottingham in 1988. The three murder victims were all found in areas adjoining lay-bys, like Jennifer Cardy. As Mr Hedworth outlined Black's crimes, including his arrest in 1990 for the Stow abduction, a juror broke down in tears at the harrowing details, prompting Mr Justice Weatherup to grant her wish for a break, and the court rose for a five-minute period.

When court resumed Mr Hedworth stated: 'That Robert Black was the abductor and murderer of Jennifer Cardy we submit you can and should have no doubt.'

He then went over the thirteen distinct similarities between Jennifer Cardy's murder and the six crimes of a similar nature that Black had committed whilst employed as a PDS van driver of which he had already been convicted:

1. Each victim was abducted at a time when Robert Black was in the area in connection with his employment driving his PDS van. This is really evidence of opportunity.
2. Each victim was pre-pubescent except fifteen-year-old Teresa Thornhill, who looked younger, as in eleven or twelve.
3. Each offence was committed during the school holidays.
4. Each victim was abducted from a public place.
5. Each victim was wearing white socks.
6. In each case, a vehicle was used to carry the victim away.
7. Each victim was carried in the direction of Robert Black's return to London.
8. Each victim was sexually assaulted or, we can infer, was to be sexually assaulted. In this case, this was disputed by the defence.
9. Each victim was killed except for the girls in Stow and Nottingham who were rescued.
10. None of the victims was grossly injured.
11. In all cases, except for Teresa Thornhill in Nottingham who escaped, there is evidence of disturbance of clothing. It was so in this case. As well as the possibilities of interference with the underwear there were some buttons missing from Jennifer's cardigan.
12. In all cases, except for the girl in Nottingham who

escaped, and Sarah Harper, who was disposed of not far from one, a lay-by was involved.

13. Sarah Harper like Jennifer Cardy had been placed in water.

Mr Hedworth continued: 'Jennifer Cardy's killing can be properly described as unique. And accordingly you may think a case set aside from all others in Northern Ireland. But it's not unique when added to what has happened in Great Britain where a tiny number of other offences are comparable. The abductions and murders of Susan Maxwell, Caroline Hogg and Sarah Jane Harper are comparable because they were all committed by the same man – this defendant Robert Black.

'Comparable because the stealing of young Jennifer from the roadside as she cycled to Aghalee, her murder and the dumping of her body in McKee's Dam had about it so many matching features to the other cases that . . . it bears Robert Black's signature and demonstrates that it was he who committed these offences. There is a strange paradox to Mr Black. He doesn't want to face the truth but equally he likes to talk, almost in a sense of boasting. He is arrogant. He enjoys control and talking about what he does as long as it doesn't lead to consequences.'

Mr Hedworth then reminded the jury of the 2005 interview between Black and Detective Constable Pamela Simpson, and how Black perversely told her that he was enjoying watching her struggle. Mr Hedworth then added:

'When he can wriggle he will. But ultimately he has to play

almost a game of cat and mouse with the officers and he talks in more and more detail of the so-called fantasy. We say this was no fantasy, this was a re-telling of what he had done.'

In concluding, the QC said the prosecution were certain that Black was in Northern Ireland on the day of the murder, and the evidence displayed during the trial proved it:

'Robert Black was available to and, we submit, did, abduct Jennifer Cardy and then did what he liked to do to little girls before discarding her, by now to him a useless body.'

As Toby Hedworth sat down on that Friday afternoon, his closing statement delivered and the case for the Crown summed up, the judge called an end to the day's proceedings, saying that the court would sit again on Monday when the defence team would deliver their closing statements to the jury.

★ ★ ★

Monday arrived, 24 October and day nineteen of the trial. Senior defence counsel David Spens, QC immediately went after the prosecution's claim that Robert Black was in Northern Ireland on the day of the murder, saying that they had failed to prove that was the case. As Andy and Pat Cardy and Jennifer's older brother Mark looked on from the public gallery, Mr Spens explained:

'The prosecution has simply failed to prove their case against Mr Black, they have failed to prove he was in Northern Ireland on August 12th, 1981, and in particular in Newry. Opportunity is the key in this case. On this the prosecution case is weak, flimsy and ultimately unsatisfactory. It has cracks that cannot be papered over.'

The defence counsel then called Black's so-called confession worthless, as he made it under a false impression of where one of the receipts was issued.

Mr Spens then laid out the differences as the defence saw it between Jennifer's murder and Black's other known past crimes, in an attempt to counter the Crown's list of similarities between the two.

He talked about how Jennifer had not been wearing a skirt or dress like all Black's other known victims and the fact that Jennifer was still wearing her shoes when discovered: 'Missing shoes were a tell-tale sign that he had been at the scene of a crime. The shoes were always removed.' He added that whereas Black's other known victims had been gagged, there was no sign that Jennifer had been.

Mr Spens then addressed the emotional nature of the trial. 'It must be very difficult for Jennifer Cardy's parents to relive all of this. You would have the utmost sympathy for her family and at the same time you would have absolutely no sympathy for Mr Black. Sympathy can play no part in your deliberations,' he said to the jury. 'You must assess the evidence coolly, calmly and dispassionately. Maybe some, or all, of you would like to convict him because of what you know about him. But,' he pressed his point, 'you don't decide verdicts on emotion; sympathy can play no part.'

He next reiterated the defence's position that there was no evidence that Jennifer had been the victim of sexual abuse whereas there was evidence of sexual interference in relation to Black's known victims. Mr Spens alluded to Professor Thomas Marshall's claim earlier in the trial of feeling under pressure to alter the analysis of his 1981 findings. 'Something about the prosecution case just does not feel right,' he said.

'What the prosecution are trying to do is fit a square peg – Mr Black – into a round hole – the circumstances of Jennifer Cardy's murder. It doesn't work.'

★ ★ ★

On day twenty of the trial, Tuesday, 25 October, the judge Mr Justice Ronald Weatherup addressed the jury. He reviewed all the evidence heard over the previous nineteen days, focusing on the evidence of Black being in Northern Ireland that day and having the opportunity to commit the crime; the witness testimony by the three expert forensic pathologists on the questions of Jennifer's cause of death and whether or not she was the victim of sexual assault, and the bad character/similar fact evidence based on Black's past convicted crimes and how they compared with the murder of Jennifer Cardy.

All the while, Jennifer's parents Andy and Pat, her brothers Mark and Philip, and her sister Victoria sat in the public gallery and listened.

Summing up his directions to the jury when considering their deliberations on reaching a verdict, the judge instructed them to decide the case on the basis of evidence rather than on an emotion reaction.

'All right-thinking people would be appalled at what they have heard,' he said. 'Those of you who have a daughter or a niece, or other young girl you know, would be appalled by what you have heard and would be concerned about what would happen – you of course would not want any children you know to be confronted by the defendant. You would have been totally outraged when told of his past convictions. You would of course want to throttle him or worse if he came anywhere near any member of your family. It's understandable given what you know about him, emotions can run high. But I want you to stop, step back and take care and I want you to be careful about what you do. I want you to remember you have to judge on the basis of evidence. I don't want you to consider the matter on the basis that he has been convicted of doing those things to young girls in England and Scotland, that means he's done it here. You have to be satisfied about his responsibility for this particular offence and not judge him on the basis of what you know about him.'

Concluding, Mr Weatherup said: 'You can't help but feel sympathy for the family and victim in this case. Nevertheless you must look at the matter objectively and consider the evidence.'

That afternoon the jury of nine women and three men left the court and returned to their base to deliberate. On Wednesday afternoon Mr Justice Weatherup was informed that they had failed to reach a verdict. He was sympathetic and informed the jury that they could continue their discussions and deliberations the following morning, a Thursday. He added that they were under no time pressure to reach a verdict. It was 3.30 p.m. The Cardy family made their way home that night still not knowing if Robert Black would be found guilty of killing their daughter. They undoubtedly hoped the next day would provide them finally with an affirmative answer and subsequent justice.

THE TRIAL CONTINUES

★ ★ ★

On the morning of Thursday, 27 October, their second day of deliberation, the jury met again. By midday they had reached an agreed verdict. They had deliberated for a period of four hours and fifteen minutes in total over two days. As the courtroom filled, Mr Justice Ronald Weatherup made it clear he did not want any outbursts when the verdict was delivered. The jury foreman stood up and announced the verdict: 'Guilty!'

A collective sigh of undeniable relief could be heard from the public gallery. Black simply sat there with not a flicker of emotion to indicate he cared about what was happening. Judge Weatherup then spoke to Black:

'You've been convicted by a jury of murder. There's only one sentence that will be imposed by law. That's the sentence of life imprisonment. Accordingly I sentence you to life imprisonment.'

Turning to the guards, Judge Weatherup ordered: 'Take him down please.'

At this point Pat Cardy broke down and wept as did a number of others present, an outpouring at the end of what had been perhaps the most emotional and distressing trial to have ever been heard in a Northern Ireland court.

The Cardy family then presented gifts to the prosecution team and in an extraordinary act of dignity and generosity of spirit embraced members of Black's defence team in an expression of respect, concluding what had been clearly, for all involved, a very difficult trial.

Outside the court a fleet of television and newspaper

journalists were waiting, hoping especially to hear what the Cardys had to say. In the midst of tape recorders and cameras, both filming and flashing, Jennifer's parents, surrounded by their children and other family members, spoke with amazing dignity and bravery words that will undoubtedly stayed with whoever heard or read them. Andy Cardy was the first to speak.

'When we lost Jennifer, it was awful but over the last six weeks, it was like losing Jennifer each and every day,' he said of the trial.

'For the last six weeks we've had to endure and listen to how Robert Black kidnapped, sexually abused and murdered our daughter,' he told the press. 'It has been absolutely horrendous. We heard things that, in all honesty, were not even in our imagination. We were confronted with the awfulness of her last few hours and what she had to suffer, it's been truly awful. We don't have any hate for Robert Black, I fear for him because Robert Black's end if he doesn't come to repentance will be an eternity with Satan in hell. That's just the most awful thing . . . to think that somebody has given their life over to sexual abuse and all he was up to. Jennifer was one of God's own, she was the apple of God's eye. Jennifer was a child of God and I wouldn't like to meet Jesus having harmed one of the apples of his eye.' Andy Cardy added that he believed Black should have faced the death penalty for the crimes he committed, but as a devout Christian he stressed that it was in a righteous way rather than a vengeful way. Listening to the man speak, nobody would have doubted his sincerity.

Jennifer's mother Pat then spoke to the press. 'Jennifer was the most happiest of little girls that I have ever known, she was so innocent, she was just so happy and she loved her family but Jennifer had a lovely thoughtfulness beyond her nine years and Andrew and I will not only never forget her but, yes, she is ever, ever remembered and always missed . . .' she said, later adding, 'And yes, Robert Black has done this awful deed but I join with my lovely husband and say that he will not destroy us. I will say this – that murder and death and trial and trauma are no match for the grace of God . . . I'll be really honest in I don't think we'll ever get closure because our daughter has gone but we have the relief of knowing the perpetrator of this gruesome, horrible crime has been brought to justice and that does give us a peace and relief.'

Andy Cardy then added: 'We would not have been happy if he had been convicted without a proper defence and we believe he had the best defence that could ever have been provided for a murderer . . . So we leave the court so happy that justice has been done and Robert Black will never again be able to harm another wee girl. He will be in jail until he dies.'

The man who had led the investigative team that had for the previous nine years laboured to build a case to convict Robert Black of Jennifer's murder, Detective Superintendent Raymond Murray of the PSNI said of the Cardys: 'None of us can imagine what they have suffered over the past thirty years or more recently during the past weeks of this trial when the horrific events of August 1981 were revisited.'

Talking about the length of time involved in building a case against Black including trawling through 560,000 petrol receipts to find the vital evidence, DS Murray explained: 'It has taken many twists and turns. At times we've been full of hope and on other occasions we've been frustrated by a lack of progress but we stuck to our principles and to our task and collected the evidence to convince a jury Robert Black is guilty. In the end it was good old-fashioned police work which brought this case to trial and secured a conviction. Today's conviction will ensure he remains behind bars for a long time to come.' Not for nothing was this investigation known as 'Operation Perseverance'.

DS Murray also said that it was not a case that had a silver bullet but was a case that was woven together with many strands of different forms of evidence; those strands ultimately built a strong and compelling case.

Robert Black returned to Maghaberry prison in County Antrim, only a few miles from the Cardy family home, found guilty in a court of law of another child murder, his fourth.

Two months later at the beginning of December, Black was in Belfast Crown court to be sentenced to a minimum 25-year jail term. Toby Hedworth, QC had called for him to be sentenced with a whole life term while defence QC David Spens told the judge Mr Justice Weatherup: 'This is one of those rare cases in which there is no mitigation and so I propose to say nothing in that regard.'

Mr Justice Weatherup addressed Black. 'On 12 August 1981 you abducted a nine-year old girl from near her home. This was an act of sexual predation. Whether you sexually assaulted Jennifer has been a matter of some debate but there can be no doubt that the abduction was intended to further a sexual purpose,' he said. 'Within hours of that abduction Jennifer had died by drowning as a result of your actions in placing her in water. You subjected a vulnerable child to unpardonable terror and took away her life. By the manner of that loss, you also wounded forever a family that treasured that child. It was a wicked deed . . .' Referring to the victim impact statements of Andrew Cardy and Jennifer's brother Philip, the judge continued, 'Her father speaks poignantly about Jennifer, of the family awareness of Jennifer's absence from all family occasions, and of the harrowing revelations in the course of the trial . . . a six-year-old who lost his sister [Philip] speaks of fear and dread, of a child's nightmare of the family being targeted again, of dreams of what Jennifer's last words were and how she would have struggled in her final hour alive. Taking a life of a family member takes away parts of the lives of many others.'

Black was then sentenced and led away back to Maghaberry to continue serving his life sentences. He would now be eighty-nine years old before he was considered for release.

The Cardy family spent some quiet time alone reflecting on Black's sentencing before departing the court once more to face the media amongst flailing umbrellas caught in the wintery weather of wind and rain, Pat Cardy, recently injured in a car accident, in a wheelchair pushed by her husband Andy.

AFTERMATH

Black appealed to overturn his conviction for the murder of Jennifer Cardy in January 2012, one month after his sentencing, with his lawyers arguing that Mr Justice Weatherup should not have allowed the bad character evidence of Black's previous convictions to be heard by the jury. But the court of appeal rejected his bid in June 2013, a relief for the Cardy family. The trial had cost over two million pounds but what aroused criticism from local politicians was the £5,500 spent on hiring a private plane, at taxpayers' expense, to fly Black from England to Northern Ireland for the trial.

Following Black's conviction in 2011 a number of things were discussed in public forums regarding the police in Northern Ireland's investigation into Black. The now late John Stainthorpe, the senior detective on the Sarah Harper murder investigation, voiced concern that it took so long for Black to be convicted of Jennifer's murder. He explained his views to the *Huddersfield Daily Examiner* on 28 October 2011: 'When we were hunting Black we did a search of his work records as a driver and were able to track him all over the country,' he said. 'We had ferry records and fuel receipts to show he was in Northern Ireland when this girl went missing. It put Black in the right place for the murders so I cannot understand why it has taken more than twenty years to bring him to court for this crime.'

This observation could perhaps be viewed as an unfair criticism particularly when considering the fantastic job the RUC and PSNI did in building a case against Black for trial. A former RUC detective Sergeant Abe Stockport, speaking to the *Scottish Herald* on 28 October 2011, gave some insight into why it had taken so long to convict Black of the Jennifer Cardy killing.

'There was no DNA or anything at the time but Black was a suspect because we were looking at long-distance lorry and van drivers. There was a lay-by along the Belfast–Newry road where lorry drivers would sleep for the night and he was seen there but there was just nothing we could do. We had nothing on him. At that stage the petrol receipts were not available and there were hundreds of other suspects. We looked at all those in the area with convictions for sexual offences. We worked on it for months and cleared up a lot of other, local, crimes as a result. It was a difficult time. Each officer might have been dealing with ten to fifteen murders at a time on their own. There was a team of twelve of us. I have dealt with throat-cutting cases, terrible violence, but this is the worst case. The memory of it has never left me.'

The day after these comments were published, DS Raymond Murray offered further explanation as to why the process of charging Black took longer than expected by some to complete, revealing that the May 2005 interviews with Black in Antrim PSNI station had taken a year to prepare. There is no doubt the evidence gained from that final interview was vital in gaining a conviction against Black. DS Murray explained: 'Black was the only prisoner. People were told if you have planned arrests please put them back slightly or bring them forward because these three days we are emptying the place, and we took over. We watched very, very carefully. We had a clinical psychologist watching too, we had Roger Orr watching as well because Roger at that stage probably knew him the best. He is a fascinating character, Mr Black, and we took their experience; redrafted our interview strategy and then we went.'

The PSNI, acting on advice from retired detective Roger Orr, avoided using terms like 'murder' and 'killer' as Black would clam up when such words were put to him. DS Murray explained, speaking to *The Express* on 29 October 2011: 'I don't know whether people noticed but whenever they said "murder" in court he took his earphones off. He can't cope with that word "murder" so the earphones came off and were set down. The irony was we never expected to get a confession. We did get a confession at the end of the day, it just took us a while to recognise it.'

Part of the thanks for getting that confession falls to the detective who interviewed Black in May 2005, Detective Constable Pamela Simpson, who managed to gain Black's confidence, as a result of which he responded better to her than he did to her colleague Detective Sergeant Pat McAnespie. This led to Black saying and revealing more than perhaps he intended. A further example of this was revealed in the BBC Northern Ireland *Spotlight* programme released after Black's death in 2016, when one particular tape-recorded interview between Black and Detective Constable Simpson revealed Black depicting a rural location in a fantasy that seemed identical in its detail to the exact location in Ballinderry where Jennifer Cardy was abducted. Once again Black was describing a real-life event but trying to protect himself by claiming it to be a fantasy':

DC Simpson: 'And, well, can you describe to me in your fantasy what the country situation would be like?'
Black: 'Well, it was just a narrow road, it was going downhill and way at the bottom of the hill where the road curved away. There was a house set back from the road a bit. And it was the only house in sight.'

Ultimately it would be used as evidence in his prosecution.

★ ★ ★

Following Black's conviction for killing little Jennifer came a renewal of those questions that followed his 1994 convictions: how many more victims had he claimed? How many more little girls had fallen victim to his predatory and murderous ways? Investigations into a number of cold cases concerning the disappearance and/or murder of young girls in the UK and in Europe were given fresh impetus. Following Black's conviction for the murder of Jennifer Cardy, Devon and Cornwall Police investigators renewed their efforts to solve the case of Genette Tate, who disappeared in 1978 in circumstances similar to Jennifer's abduction.

Roger Orr believed that Genette Tate's was the only realistic case left to pursue, whilst on the other hand DS Murray said that he believed the Robert Black story did not end with Jennifer Cardy and that there was probably more work to be done in relation to him and other unsolved crimes. In 2008, thirty years to the day after Genette's disappearance, the Crown Prosecution Service decided not to charge Black with her abduction and murder, as they felt a file submitted by Devon and Cornwall Police did not present a strong enough case to convict Black in a court of law. Many thought the Cardy conviction and the similar evidence between Jennifer's case and Genette's would bring renewed hope of a prosecution.

But how many more children did Robert Black kill? There is a long list of little girls who disappeared, most found murdered, others believed to have been murdered. Not all these cases could be laid at Black's door, although his name was mentioned from time to time, particularly in some press reports.

Between the two trials, in 1994 and 2011, two cases that were on the original list had been solved, and Black was eliminated from a third. These were:

1. Marion Crofts (fourteen) was cycling to music practice at school on 6 June 1981 when she was waylaid, raped and strangled. Every possible bit of evidence was kept by the police, and as forensic science advanced, much painstaking checking of DNA samples eventually led to a match being found: in 2002 Tony Jasinskyj was given a life sentence for her rape and murder.

2. Colette Aram (sixteen) was abducted, raped and strangled in Keyworth, Nottinghamshire, as she walked to a friend's house on 30 October 1983. Once again, it was thanks to advances in forensic technology that, years later, in April 2009, Paul Stewart Hutchinson was charged, and was sentenced to life imprisonment in January 2010 for her rape and murder.

3. Lisa Hession (fourteen) was attacked, sexually assaulted and strangled on 8 December 1984 as she walked home alone from a party. Nobody has been charged with her murder, but from 2011, with the advances made in forensic science, police have been able to eliminate a number of suspects whose DNA they've checked on the National DNA Database, including Black.

The other cases in question include the following, although my co-author and former Norfolk Constabulary Intelligence Officer Chris Clark and I dispute the likelihood of Black being the offender in some of them:

1. 8 April 1969, Norfolk, England: April Fabb (thirteen) disappeared when cycling towards her sister's home in the village of Roughton. Her bicycle was found in a field along the road she had taken but her body has never been found.

2. 21 May 1973, Lincolnshire, England: Christine Markham (nine) vanished while walking to school in Scunthorpe. Her body has never been found.

3. 18 March 1977, County Donegal, Ireland: Mary Boyle (six) disappeared while on a family visit to her grandparents' home in Ballyshannon. Black is known to have been just over the border in Northern Ireland at the time of her disappearance. Her body has never been found.

4. 19 August 1978, Devon, England: Genette Tate (thirteen) was abducted while she was on her bicycle delivering newspapers in the village of Aylesbeare. Her body has never been found. Black is known to have made numerous deliveries of posters to the south-west of England in 1978.

5. 22 July 1979, Essex, England: Suzanne Lawrence (fourteen) disappeared after leaving her home in Harold Hill. Her body has never been found.

6. 16 June 1980, Greater London, England: Patricia Morris

(fourteen) went missing from the grounds of the school she attended in Feltham, West London; her fully clothed body was found on Hounslow Heath two days after her disappearance. She had been strangled with a ligature but had not been sexually assaulted. The circumstances of Patsy's murder do not fit with Black's MO, and there is no evidence of him having been in the area.

7. 4 November 1981, Renfrewshire, Scotland: Pamela Hastie (sixteen) was raped and murdered. Her body was found in Rannoch Woods near her home in the Renfrewshire town of Johnstone; she had been strangled with a piece of string and had been attacked with a knife or similar weapon. A young man was charged with her murder and sentenced to life; this was ruled a miscarriage of justice and he was released in 2007. There was an eyewitness and he remains adamant that a man he saw running from the crime scene matched Black's description. However, the circumstances of this case – rape and the use of a knife – do not fit Robert Black's known modus operandi, and there is no evidence that Black was in the vicinity of at the relevant time, so the police have not taken him seriously as a possible culprit.

8. 20 June 1985, Germany: Silke Garben (ten) vanished on her way to a dental appointment in the town of Detmold in north-eastern Germany. Her body was found in a stream the following day; she had been sexually assaulted and strangled. Black is known to have made a delivery of posters to a British Army base located close to Garben's home on the date of her disappearance.

9. 5 August 1986, The Netherlands: Cheryl Morriën (seven) disappeared as she walked to her friend's home in the port city of IJmuiden. Her body has never been found. Black is known to have made regular trips to nearby Amsterdam to purchase child pornography – but these trips were during the early 1970s before he started to work for PDS, and there is no evidence to place him in the Netherlands in 1986, so he is not considered a likely culprit.

10. 5 May 1987, Île-de-France, France: Virginie Delmas (ten) was abducted from Neuilly-sur-Marne, in an eastern Paris suburb, on 5 May 1987. Her body was found on 9 October in an orchard in Mareuil-lès-Meaux about 22 miles away. She had been strangled, but owing to the extent of decomposition, it could not be determined whether or not she had been raped. Black is known to have made several deliveries in and around Paris on the date of the girl's disappearance.

11. 30 May 1987, Île-de-France, France: Hemma Davy-Greedharry (ten) disappeared when she went to buy a set square just down the street from where she lived in the Paris suburb of Malakoff. Less than two hours after she was last seen alive, her naked body was found not 900 yards away in Châtillon. She had been raped and strangled. Black is known to have regularly travelled upon the road where Hemma's body was found when making deliveries in northern France.

12. 3 June 1987, Île-de-France, France: Perrine Vigneron (seven) vanished on her way to her pottery class in the

village of Bouleurs; her strangled and decomposed body was discovered in a rapeseed field in the commune of Chelles, about 20 miles away, on 27 June. A white van had been seen in Bouleurs on the day of her disappearance.

13. 27 June 1987, Île-de-France, France: Sabine Dumont (nine) was last seen alive in Bièvres when she went to buy a tube of white paint from the bookshop down the road from her home; the following day her body was found in the commune of Vauhallan a few miles away. She had been sexually assaulted and strangled. Black was formally named in 2011by French police as a prime suspect in her murder.

14. 11 May 1989, North Rhine-Westphalia, Germany: Ramona Herling (eleven) was last seen walking from her home in the town of Bad Driburg to a nearby swimming pool. She never arrived at the pool and has not been seen since.

A number of these will be discussed in further detail in the pages that follow, in which Chris Clark discusses those we believe to have been victims of Black, and explains the reasoning behind our beliefs. His account includes a case that is very personal and close to home for him – the attempted abduction of his wife Jeanne when she was a teenager in the summer of 1971.

PART TWO

CYCLE OF OPPORTUNITY

(BY CHRIS CLARK)

11

COLD CASES

Following Black's 1994 conviction, a number of police forces, as mentioned earlier, came forward, all anxious to look into the possibility of Black being responsible for a number of other murders of young girls. Once the case of Jennifer Cardy could be taken off the list, with Black's conviction in 2011, police renewed their investigations into him.

* * *

I started to take a personal interest in Robert Black in 2010 when my wife Jeanne told me about an incident that had occurred to her nearly forty years before, when it became clear to me that she had nearly been seized and taken away.

Having always thought, since his arrest in 1990, that Robert Black was involved in the 1969 abduction and murder of April Fabb from my home county of Norfolk, I realised that the circumstances of the incident Jeanne recounted to me were identical to those of the abductions of April Fabb, Genette Tate and Jennifer Cardy – all girls out on cycles on a hot sunny day.

With this in mind I tried to piece together Black's life from 1968, when it is known that he moved from Scotland to London, to 1976 when he started driving for Poster Despatch and Storage (PDS),which is where subsequent police enquiries into his background started from.

On 22 March 1967, a month before his twentieth birthday, Robert Black was sent to borstal for one year at Polmont near Grangemouth. During his time in this establishment he formed a relationship with another young inmate who appears to have been a rapist or at least a potential rapist. Together they planned a series of sexual attacks on adult women. One shudders to think that his potential co-partner could have been someone of the ilk of Peter Tobin or Angus Sinclair, fellow Scots of a similar age to Black, each eventually convicted of a string of violent rapes and murders.

The Robert Black of the late 1960s was short at five-foot-seven, and athletic, with a wiry build; his straight, light brown hair was already thinning and rapidly receding, and he had a very strong body odour. He was an articulate, lonely, odd young man who spoke with a 'Sean Connery' Scottish accent. Upon his release some time around the end of March 1968, Black, now aged twenty-one, moved into a probation hostel in Glasgow; when he left there with two recorded convictions for offences against young girls there was no supervision and no follow-up: he simply disappeared under the radar, away from authorities' view.

After a brief period in a nearby bedsit and an arrest for loitering with intent to steal on 12 August 1968, which earned him an important 'mugshot' but no conviction, Black suddenly crossed the border into England and moved south to the anonymity of London. (My co-author Robert Giles has covered Black's days in London in more detail in an earlier chapter.)

There he first took a cheap bedsit at 24 Bergholt Crescent, Stamford Hill which he moved into before 10 October 1968. This is where he would have been residing when April Fabb went missing during the Easter holidays of 1969. This address is only two streets away from the East and West Reservoirs in Stoke Newington which serve North London: do those waters hold a grim secret? Two of his known victims, Jennifer Cardy (1981) and Sarah Harper (1986) were thrown into water – Jennifer into McKee's Dam and Sarah the River Trent.

Whether April Fabb was one of his earlier victims is not proven but her disappearance some nine years before that of Genette Tate and twelve years before the murder of Jennifer Cardy has glaring similarities to both. Black did not hold a full driving licence at this time but, importantly, he already had an extensive driving record from at least three firms in Scotland during the years 1964–1967, and, as will be seen later, had also incurred vehicle-crime-related convictions in 1972 prior to his acquisition of a full driving licence, which was obtained in 1976, and it is known that he had access to at least four vehicles at various times during that period: a white Hillman Imp, a blue Vauxhall Victor, a green Ford Zephyr, and a blue

Ford Anglia; there may have been many more, not necessarily legally acquired. By the time he was working for PDS, Black's knowledge of Britain's road networks was comprehensive.

12

THE APRIL
FABB CASE

On Tuesday, 8 April 1969, the day after Easter Monday, I was working a late-turn foot beat at King's Lynn when one of Norfolk's biggest mysteries occurred during that afternoon some 40 miles away in a quiet village in north Norfolk.

April Fabb, a shy thirteen-year-old a fortnight off her fourteenth birthday and on her Easter school holidays, set off from her home on that fateful afternoon in the quiet rural village of Metton to cycle the two miles to her eldest sister Pamela's home in Roughton, near Cromer, to give her brother-in-law Bernard a packet of cigarettes as a belated present for his birthday that had fallen on Easter Monday, but she never made it to the end of that quiet and little-used country lane.

Metton, close to Cromer, is situated in a triangle formed by the A148 to King's Lynn (leading to the A10 to London) and, nearer to Roughton, the A140 from Cromer to Norwich (leading to the A11 link road to London), while the third side of the triangle is the A47 between King's Lynn and Norwich.

April 1969 was a very sunny month, except in east Scotland and on the coasts of eastern England. Despite the sunshine, though, it was also a rather cold month and at times very windy, particularly on the south and east coasts on the 5 and 6 April, reaching gale force at times. Easter – 4 to 7 April – was very sunny and warm at times and the north Norfolk seaside resorts of Cromer and Sheringham were packed with holidaymakers; picnickers were abundant. On 8 April local temperatures reached 22 degrees Celsius, but the prevailing wind in exposed places made it feel colder and that is probably why April was dressed sensibly, wearing a green jumper, a wine-coloured woollen thigh-length skirt, long white socks and wooden-soled sandals. Her hair was brushed back into a bunch, tied with a brown crinkly ribbon.

April was seen at 2.06 p.m. next to a field where she had stopped with her bicycle to join two girls who were petting a donkey; she stayed there for a short while before continuing her journey, probably singing her favourite pop group Amen Corner's latest release 'If paradise is half as nice as heaven that you take me to, who needs paradise, I'd rather have you'. If so, it would have been prophetic as well as poignant, looking back.

She was last seen at 2.12 p.m. by a farmworker driving by in a Land-Rover, as she was about to turn right into Back Lane towards Roughton; just three minutes later her blue and white bicycle was found lying on its side where it had been thrown over a six-foot-high bank into a field in Back Lane. There was no sign of April – she had disappeared in the flicker of an eye, spirited away never to be found.

It was a world where a crime of this sort was a rarity and there being no record of other unsolved child abduction or murders committed from the time of Black's release 1968, this case strongly indicates to me that April was Black's first full abduction and murder, committed less than two weeks before his twenty-second birthday (which fell the day before April's birthday), utilising a motor vehicle of some description, and I am convinced that if we keep plugging away, eventually the missing pieces in April's jigsaw, which are likely to be found in London and not Norfolk, will provide sufficient evidence to point to Black's involvement. (Author update: Since June 2016, I have been working with a Norfolk-based medium who is trying to locate where April's remains are buried; this work is ongoing.)

Two vehicles were in the area during the material time that were never traced; they were a vaguely described grey car and a newish-looking red Mini with new-type reflective number plates; both have since been dismissed.

It later transpired that one of Black's favourite pastimes was to go to the seaside frequented by young children or to a playground and video or take snapshots of them playing – did he go to Cromer in Norfolk during 1969? It was reported in the press after his 1994 conviction that Black had visited Norfolk on a regular basis, but I can find no evidence of that, but it is my belief that Robert Black visited Cromer over that busy Easter weekend (there may be undiscovered photographic evidence amidst the collection seized after his 1990 arrest confirming this), and that on the Tuesday lunchtime rather than driving through Metton, he was sitting in his vehicle in the little-used Back Lane at a pull-in between two trees. He had probably just eaten or was consuming food when April rode into the lane behind him, and he saw his opportunity. He would probably have stopped her to ask directions, then perhaps quickly kicked her bicycle out of the way and, grabbing hold of her, he would have abducted her and driven off to an area where he could carry out what he has become infamous for. It now seems that he could virtually make children vanish into thin air.

That Black did not have a driving licence at the time did not, as we have seen, stop him from driving. He had been driving many years without a licence and generally seems to have managed to escape trouble; he was a competent, experienced driver and – as Ray Wyre learnt from him in interviews for *The Murder of Childhood*, 'His employment record has been substantially as a van driver, having had several jobs in the London area in this work.' He therefore frequently had the use of a vehicle.

Full details of April's story and the hunt for her are in a book written and dedicated to her memory, by one of my ex-bosses, retired Detective Chief Superintendent Maurice Morson, who inherited the outstanding enquiry from Detective Chief Superintendent Reg Lester in 1983 when Reg retired. Dedicated to April's memory, *The Lost Years* tests the original investigation.

Until April and later Steven Newing who both went missing

in 1969 with neither body being found locally, cases in the UK of abduction by a travelling paedophile were unknown, now there were two, one who targeted girls and the other boys. Prior to this, most cases of child murder that emerged from the 1960s were all committed in a radius around where the perpetrators resided – names that spring to mind are Ian Brady and Myra Hindley, Raymond Leslie Morris and Ronald Jebson

During 1968 many police forces had amalgamated, including the former Norfolk Constabulary, which fused with the former Norwich City and Great Yarmouth Borough forces to become Norfolk Joint Police. At the same time the Collator or Local Intelligence Office (LIO) came into being as part of Unit Beat Policing, which replaced the 'George Dixon' types, thus supplanting the local village bobby's knowledge of local people and criminals.

As the name local intelligence implies, it comprises intelligence about local criminals and local crime patterns, but includes little or no sharing of information outside that division or sub-division; indeed most of what I, as a serving officer in the force, knew then about April's disappearance came from the Norfolk newspaper, the *Eastern Daily Press*, popularly known as the *EDP*, and television.

It took another six years and the Baumber Report to look seriously at the sharing of intelligence at force and regional level, and nothing was geared up for the professional travelling criminal and the likes of Peter Sutcliffe or Robert Black who recognised no invisible policing boundaries.

April's criminal abduction and murder, although listed for

many years as a non-crime Missing Person enquiry without a crime file being raised, bears many resemblances to a number of other child-murders linked with Black that have been discussed in this book, in particular the 1971 attempted abduction of Jeanne Twigden, of which more below, the 1978 abduction of Genette Tate, and the 1981 abduction and murder of Jennifer Cardy. All four incidents involved young girls on bicycles in warm weather and rural settings. Following the disappearance of Genette Tate, Norfolk police were in contact with investigating officers in Devon, having noted the similarities between the two cases, but it took many more years before enough evidence could be collected in the case of Genette Tate, while April Fabb remains a cold case.

13

NEAR MISSES

AN ALARMING ENCOUNTER

In September 2014 a sixty-year-old woman I will refer to as J sent both Professor David Wilson and myself an e-mail stating that she had just seen a re-run of Professor Wilson's 2012 documentary *Killers Behind Bars*, featuring Robert Black, on the internet. She could not watch all of the programme as she believed that she recognised Black from one of the photographs of him that were shown as being the man who tried to abduct her in April 1968 (I believe April 1969) when she was fifteen years old, and when Professor Wilson said, 'There must have been others', she was inspired to get in touch.

J was cycling the two miles to her farmhouse home along very quiet lanes one evening from a riding school at St Lawrence near Bodmin in Cornwall on what was the A30/

A389 crossroads, where there was a garage and café, She became aware of a car that kept overtaking her and stopping ahead and overtaking her again as though the driver was looking for somewhere or was lost.

About halfway into her journey J noticed the same vehicle, now parked in a field gateway near a small bend in the lane, and as she neared it a man, the driver, appeared in the middle of the road and stopped her, saying he was looking for a particular farm. She told him that he had just passed it and tried to cycle on but was physically stopped by the man. She panicked and threw the bike down and ran but the man chased her and forced her back to his car. At that moment a car came onto the scene driven by a local farmer whom J knew and the man ran off. J was taken home by the farmer and the incident was reported to the local police. J later made a statement, but heard nothing more.

J said to Professor Wilson in her e-mail to him, 'Poor April Fabb and Genette Tate are often in my thoughts as they were on bikes . . . I never cycled the lanes again. If I could help in any way I would, I was stalked for several miles by a predator, it was not a chance meeting!'

I subsequently had a long telephone conversation with J and through me she contacted the Devon and Cornwall Genette Tate team.

THE JEANNE TWIGDEN CASE

Up until the time of April Fabb's disappearance and the next decade when Robert Black was on the prowl it was a rarity for children to be abducted and murdered. Any reports of children being enticed into vehicles after April's case were regarded by all East Anglian Police Forces as demanding 'high alert' action and subsequent transmissions of intelligence to their neighbouring forces.

Jeanne (who is now my wife) was nearly such a statistic and on this occasion certain members of Huntingdonshire Mid-Anglia Constabulary let her and the system down big-time. Her near-miss incident is what led to my personal journey in researching Robert Black and his early years from 1968 until 1976.

During the spring of 1971 Jeanne was a shy, just-turned-fifteen-year-old girl who could easily pass for a ten-year-old. On one hot Sunday early afternoon in May she cycled from her home in Offord D'Arcy, situated between Huntingdon and St Neots in Cambridgeshire, with her swimming bag some five miles to the open-air baths at St Neots via the quiet B1043 road, seldom used by strangers as it is by-passed by the A1 Great North Road. One village along the road is Great Paxton, situated just off the main A1 and some 50 miles from London.

After her swim and in the middle of the afternoon, Jeanne retraced her route back home for tea. When she was about a mile into her journey and close to the outskirts of Great Paxton she came across a dog lead lying in the carriageway and being an animal lover stopped to look at it. It is quite apparent to me, looking back, that the lead had been deliberately placed there in order to attract her attention and make her stop, and that Black, unknown to Jeanne had already targeted her when driving past; he had then planted the lead, before turning around and driving back. She soon became aware of a blue Mini or van travelling in the opposite direction, which slowed down and stopped opposite her, the driver of which was intently staring at her legs.

Jeanne started cycling fast towards Great Paxton, open fields on either side of her. The vehicle had turned and was now behind her, keeping pace before it came up beside her very slowly and then pulled in front still being driven slowly, forcing her to cycle at its pace – tactics very similar to those described by the woman I have called J.

After about a minute it drove off towards Great Paxton to an area sheltered by trees and undergrowth and when Jeanne next saw the vehicle it was pulled sharply at an angle into a gateway field entrance near a left-hand bend and the driver was out of the vehicle and standing by the rear offside of the vehicle. She describes him as a small, thin-faced man, clean-shaven and not wearing spectacles. The description fits the young man that Robert Black was then, just turned twenty-four.

She was by now panicking and instinctively cycled furiously past the parked vehicle on the off-side of the road. She then went into the driveway of the first house that she came to and there was no one in.

She got back on her bike and pedalled furiously into Great Paxton. Her would-be abductor had by now obviously been scared off, thinking that she lived in the house. Jeanne, still hysterical, knocked on a cottage door in Great Paxton and told the woman who opened the door what had happened. A bit later the woman's husband took Jeanne and her bike home to her parents. The local police were called and a male and female officer attended but basically said that there was nothing they could do as the man had not done anything! But for Jeanne it was a traumatic experience, which affects her to this day and with which she has never fully come to terms.

The modus operandi bears all of the hallmarks employed in the later abductions and/or murders committed by Robert Black, and was identical to that used with April just two years before and which would be used with Genette and Jennifer seven and nine years later. As far as Black goes, no photos have been released to the public as to how he looked then, so we are reliant on the 1968 image which bears a good likeness to the man Jeanne saw except that it shows him with his hair gelled. The 1968 photo bears no resemblance to how he looked a good decade later when Susan Maxwell was abducted and murdered, by which time he had put on weight and his hair had thinned further.

As far as the Mini was concerned it was dark blue in colour and either a saloon or, more probably, a minivan, which had rear doors for easy loading. An important fact that Jeanne remembered was that the index plate included the numbers 777. This could so easily have been narrowed down by permutation to identify the owner of this vehicle and there was a good chance that had the police taken the matter seriously and passed the details to all of their divisions and to surrounding forces via radio, telex and other means of communication used by the police, the offender would have been traced and the intelligence gained may well have solved other outstanding and future enquiries, even if the vehicle had been stolen.

Going from 1960 the registration number or index plate would have been made up of three letters signifying the local taxation office area, three numbers and no suffix. From 1963 it would have been made up with an A suffix and a yearly letter through to a 1971 model when it would have an H suffix. So the information Jeanne gave the police would have given them something to go on, at least if it was a company vehicle Black was using. By his own admission he frequently lost jobs through his poor time-keeping. But there were other ways of acquiring a vehicle: significantly, one of Black's convictions – on 22 September 1972 at North London Magistrates' Court – was for stealing cars and going equipped with a bunch of car keys. The circumstance leading to this conviction was Black's arrest on 26 August by PC 356 N Robertson as a passenger in a stolen Ford Zephyr car when he admitted another similar offence. Black had in his possession a bunch of car keys – but he was not driving the Zephyr, which raises the question, who was his co-accused? This criminal associate if traced could tell a lot about Black during this period including what they were stealing vehicles for and the areas they frequented.

14

A DISAPPEARANCE AND ANOTHER NEAR MISS

THE CHRISTINE MARKHAM CASE

On 21 May 1973, a cool Monday morning, nine-year-old Christine Markham vanished from a street in Scunthorpe after changing her mind about going to school that day. She had celebrated her ninth birthday the day before, and her father, Sidney Markham, said that she didn't want to go to school on the Monday morning. He added that she had played truant before.

Christine and two of her siblings, Susan aged thirteen, and Wayne aged ten, left their home in Robinson Close for school at about 8.45 a.m. Their mother Margery watched them set off for the bus stop. This was to be the last time that she saw Christine.

As they usually did, the three of them went to the bus stop in Avenue Vivian where the older two caught their bus to St Hugh's, leaving Christine to walk on her own the short distance to her school, Henderson Avenue Junior, five minutes away.

As Susan and Wayne left on their bus they saw Christine through the bus window turn around and walk back in the direction in which they had come. A number of sightings of Christine during that Monday morning were reported to the police, the last being from an aunt of hers who was on a bus going into town and saw her at around 10 a.m. on the A159 Ashby Road between the Brumby corner and the Priory pub, not far from the junction with Queensway, then part of the main A18 Doncaster Road, which linked the nearby Steel Works and five miles south-east with the A15, a direct route south via Peterborough and the A1 to Stamford Hill.

The aunt realised that Christine was making her way to Grange Lane South and hopped off at the next stop – however, Christine must have caught the bus going the opposite way and they missed each other.

A timeline of Christine's movements:

1. 8.45 a.m. left home in Robinson Road with siblings
2. Soon after, in Henderson Avenue Circle
3. 9.10 a.m. Near Scunthorpe United FC Old Showground
4. 9.30 a.m. Seen at junction Avenue Vivian/Long Road where a woman gave her 2p
5. 9.45 a.m. Seen junction Cliff Gardens/Oswald Road
6. 10 a.m. Seen by aunt who was on a bus into town, sitting on wall near St Hugh's Church in Ashby Road. The aunt

alighted at the next stop but Christine had gone by the time she reached St Hugh's. Someone had given Christine 5p for her fare to her aunt's address, Grange Lane South, where a neighbour fed her.

7. 1.00 p.m. The next sighting of Christine in Theodore Road is the last definite sighting and near to the house where the family lived prior to moving to Robinson Close, a two-minute walk away from her current home. Interestingly, the River Trent, now tidal-fed and much wider, flows not far away and feeds into the Humber Estuary and the North Sea – this is the same river that Sarah Harper finished up in at Wilford near Nottingham some thirteen years later in 1986.

8. There were numerous possible sightings of her in the course of that afternoon.

9. 7.30 p.m. possibly seen in Ferry Road near Sheffield Park, a five-minute walk from her home.

10. 11 p.m. possibly seen – which would make it the last ever sighting of Christine Markham – at the junction of Davy Avenue/Long Road/Robinson Road.

Of the last three sightings, the location of the 11 p.m. one was just a two-minute walk from her home.

My main reason for introducing Robert Black as a suspect in abducting and murdering Christine Markham is his 'guilty knowledge' of her case: in 1983 during a conversation (*see* p. 269) he included her name in a list of names of children that he was later convicted of, or is strongly suspected of, having abducted and murdered. The case of Christine's disappearance, although published in the local papers, never made the nationals.

ANOTHER NEAR MISS?

During January 2016 I received a message via my website contact page, from a woman whom I will refer to as M, who after reading recent newspaper reports about Robert Black and possible links to Norfolk and seeing my name quoted, wanted to tell me about an incident that occurred to her in Norfolk around 1976 or 1977 when she was a fourteen-year-old schoolgirl. Robert Black began driving for PDS (Poster Despatch and Storage) in 1976, and the East Anglian run was one of the routes out of London used by the company, encompassing the trunk roads including the A12 from London to Lowestoft, the A140 Cromer-to-Norwich, the A47 Great Yarmouth to Peterborough and the A11 back to London; Black himself also drove along the quieter routes interspersed between these roads.

M's family, consisting of her mother, father, elder sister and herself, one weekend stopped their car at a public house situated on a trunk road, possibly on the A47 on the Narborough-to-King's Lynn stretch and her parents and sister went inside, leaving M, who was underage, outside in the parking forecourt sitting on a bench alone with her dog.

She remembers very clearly that a van came past the pub and slowed down, while the male driver stared intently at her as he drove slowly by. He then came back in the opposite direction, again looking at her, and then turned round again and then drove into the car park. She remembers feeling very uncomfortable because he had driven past her more than once and doubled back. M lifted her dog up and put him next to her on the bench to act as a barrier as she was on her own outside the pub.

The man got out of the van but made no attempt to go into the pub, instead walking over to the bench. He then said, 'Do you mind if I sit down next to you?' M felt that she should get away from the man urgently and not speak to him, so at this point she leapt up and ran into the pub, crying, dragging her dog with her and frantically looking for her family. M's father was very embarrassed at the commotion and was more concerned about everyone looking at them than he was about his daughter's fright. So he did not go outside and investigate what he had been told, although her mother said several times following the event that she felt they should have reported it. Even though the incident was entirely downplayed at the time, it stayed with M for many years just as Jeanne's experience some five years previously never completely left her.

M said that the man was probably in his late twenties or early thirties (Robert Black was twenty-nine in 1976) and that the van was either white or dark blue, but time had taken the colour out of her memory.

She added that she had thought about reporting the incident to the police over the years but she felt that it would not provide anything significant and didn't want to waste police time, coupled with the embarrassment of reporting, in her words, a 'non-event'.

From what M has told me I am in no doubt that this was

Robert Black on an early 'scouting tour' whilst working for PDS, and it is my opinion that she had had a lucky escape. Due to the passage of time M could not be more specific about the exact date and location, but I advised her to report the incident to both Norfolk Police Cold Case Team for the April Fabb case and the Devon and Cornwall Police for the Genette Tate case.

15

THE DISAPPEARANCE
OF MARY BOYLE

'The Troubles', the conflict between Britain and Ireland lasted from the late 1960s until 1998, and during that time there was little or no cooperation between the Irish police, the Garda Siochana, and the Northern Ireland police, the Royal Ulster Constabulary (since renamed Police Service of Northern Ireland). The British border towns were fortified and there were police and army checks at most border-crossing roads including Belleek, part of which crosses the border south into County Donegal, but most of which is situated in Northern Ireland's County Fermanagh, and lies some 25 miles from Enniskillen, which housed a large British Army garrison and NAAFI shop.

As we know, Robert Black started working for Poster Despatch and Storage (PDS) during 1976, and that year visited the village of Annagry (in Irish, Anagaire), in the far west of County Donegal, before going into Northern Ireland to deliver his posters. While in Northern Ireland, he would often park his van overnight in one or another pub car park and drink at the bar, where he would befriend local teenagers. He carried on visiting the area annually until 1979, when he used the Belfast to Birkenhead (Liverpool) Ferry to return to England. During 1976–1979, to avoid the stringent road checks when entering County Donegal from the British side, it is more likely that he caught the Irish Ferry from Holyhead in North Wales to Dublin, where the Garda security was far more lax as the Irish Republic was not under siege and threat of terrorism. He would then use the Republic of Ireland roads to go across to the west and enter County Donegal via Sligo and the seaside resort of Bundoran.

Mary Boyle is one of Ireland's youngest missing persons at just six years old, and was once considered by both the Garda and UK police to have been abducted and murdered by Black whilst she was visiting her Gallagher grandparents in Cashelard near Ballyshannon on the southern tip of Donegal.

Thursday, 17 March 1977 was St Patrick's Day and Mary's family, including her twin sister, had travelled from Keadue, Burtonport in the north of County Donegal the forty or so miles to the quiet, isolated hamlet of Cashelard in south-east County Donegal, three miles north-east of Ballyshannon and four miles north of Belleek. It is also a 47-mile drive from Enniskillen in Northern Ireland.

The Gallagher farmhouse in Cashelard is on a hill with access along a narrow laneway and any view from the bottom road and Lough Columbkille is completely obscured by the terrain, trees and tall undergrowth. It is also hidden from view of the nearest neighbours, at the time the McCawley family.

On the following afternoon, Friday, 18 March, around 3.30 p.m. Mary Boyle's uncle and godfather Gerry Gallagher, after doing jobs at the front of the Gallagher house carried a heavy wooden ladder back to his neighbour Patrick McCawley some 450 yards away over marshy ground. His little niece Mary followed at a distance, her black wellington boots occasionally getting stuck in the mud, along the isolated bridleway shortcut between the Gallagher and McCawley houses.

About 70 yards from the end of this journey Gerry, with the ladder over his shoulder, was having to make his way through mud up to six inches deep; Mary, who was only four feet tall, hesitated. She then turned back in the direction of the Gallaghers' and Gerry continued his journey. Mary Boyle would not be seen again.

As the Gallagher house was out of sight of the McCawleys' and over 380 yards away over the rough terrain, it is reasonable to think that she could have found the nearer lane which connects the McCawleys' house to a quiet roadway to the right leading to Lough Columbkille and the A46 Belleek–Enniskillen road or to the left to another quiet country road which is a direct link to the N15 and Annagry 40 miles away – a good half-hour or more ahead of the her absence being noticed – and into the arms of her motorised abductor.

After about twenty minutes, around 4 p.m., Gerry Gallagher returned back home retracing his steps taken earlier and soon after he had got back he learnt that Mary had vanished. Both he and Mary's mother walked and drove around the country lanes, searching as many likely places as possible, while local people were summoned to assist.

At 6.30 p.m. the local Garda station in Ballyshannon was contacted and the Garda called in an army helicopter to conduct an aerial search whilst local people combed the countryside. As dusk turned to night the search was called off until morning.

Throughout the following day and during the following weeks, time and time again, all of the land, the waterholes, rivers and lakes were searched for miles around but to no avail; nothing, not even the Tayto Crisps bag Mary had been holding, was ever found.

Going back to the last sighting of Mary, this was in a quiet muddy lane about 70 yards from the McCawleys' and about 380 yards from her grandparents' home. These were the two houses in the immediate area and, to put it bluntly, either she was abducted and taken away in a motor vehicle or she wandered into a part of the countryside where she accidentally met her death. For me the former is the more definite taking that the whole area was searched early and searched again, and no trace of her has been found to this day.

This brings us to abduction, and the Garda first investigated the movements of local men who would have been known as potential suspects. All were ruled out – and that leaves a travelling abductor and Robert Black.

After an intensive investigation the Garda now believe that on the day Mary Boyle disappeared, Robert Black then aged thirty, may have been travelling in Northern Ireland.

An analysis of the employment records of PDS shows that he made deliveries in Northern Ireland at some time in the early part of 1977. It is my belief that on these early occasions, in 1976 to 1978, that Black used the safe-option voyage to Dublin and the Republic of Ireland roads to visit Donegal, before travelling east over the border and delivering in Northern Ireland.

There is evidence to show that Black was in Enniskillen, Co. Fermanagh, that Friday, 18 March 1977, helping to put up a poster billboard. Enniskillen is about 30 miles from Cashelard, a journey of less than one hour. A petrol receipt discovered by British police in 1994 shows that he bought petrol somewhere in Northern Ireland in March 1977, the exact date is not known, probably due to the receipt having faded with time.

Black was as will become clear a frequent visitor during the mid-1970s to Annagry and Dunglow in the north of County Donegal, visits which stopped after the IRA murdered Lord Mountbatten on 27 August 1979 by blowing up his boat in Mullaghmore Harbour, not far south of Donegal, as the British-registered vehicle Black was driving in the Republic of Ireland would now invite attention from the IRA. In the preceding years, however, Black is known to have frequented several pubs in the area, where he became drinking buddies with a group of young men and women. That there is documented evidence of Black having been there is possibly thanks solely to an unappreciated wisecrack. A normally tolerant garda was going through the routine of taking down the names of a group of drinkers left in an Annagry pub after closing hours, as reported in an article in the *Irish Independent* of 16 May 1999: '. . . The first name, Green, was a lady; the second name was White; the third name was Robert Black. The last man copped on to the irony of it and decided to throw in Johnny Blue. With a shadowy suspicion that he was being ridiculed, the garda charged them with after-hours drinking' – and Black's name was in the Garda records.

It has been revealed that during 1978 Robert Black had an overnight stay in Annagry with a family with children. The following morning he asked to borrow their car to buy a Sunday paper and drove along until he came up behind a young girl walking along. He stopped her to ask for directions to the paper shop, calling her to come closer to the car, then realised the child was a boy with long hair, asked for another shop and drove off towards Rannafast before circling back towards Annagry and attempting to stop a young local girl.

One of his regular parking spaces was the old Cope yard behind Big John's Bar (now called the Bridge Inn) in Dungloe. This yard is a regular truck stop, an open place guarded by the sea on one side and a warehouse on the other. Time and again Black and a regular group of innocent friends would go out together by car but however many of them there were he never offered anyone a lift or even took his van. On one occasion his van was already in the car park when they arrived and one of the girls approached the van and she thought she heard a crying sound coming from within; she assumed it might be a pet. Black wasn't in the van on this occasion, neither did he have a pet.

On another occasion, as they were leaving Big John's, one

of the girls headed towards the van and she was followed hurriedly by Black who became very aggressive and reprimanded her harshly for having gone anywhere near it. He seemed suddenly supercharged with hostility and she was frightened by his overwrought reaction.

The year after Mary Boyle disappeared, an exchange took place that is particularly sickening with hindsight, reported in the *Irish Independent* on 16 May 1999.

> [It was during] a conversation that occurred on one of his visits to a bar in Dungloe. One of the girls innocently referred to the Mary Boyle murder a year previously, and Black asked if some of the girls would show him where her house was. 'I want to see where her twin sister lives,' he said. When they declined, he became enraged and agitated. He was very insistent about them showing him the house. Thinking that he had a strange obsession with dead people, they refused to bring him.

On top of all of this information there is a conversation that Black himself had in a London pub in 1983, as reported to me by 'John' (*see* p. 269). In this conversation he spoke of girls murdered, and mentioned two Irish girls, one of them Jennifer Cardy, whom he was later convicted of murdering. The other one he referred to has to be Mary Boyle as there were no others.

On 27 July 2014 I appeared on a live linkup with Mary Boyle's mother Ann Boyle on Highland Radio, Donegal;

the full interview and Ann's views on the subject are within an article under 'Radio Interviews' on my website (www.armchairdetective.org.uk). Ann Boyle was pleased with my input but having heard a number of different theories on what may have happened to Mary has confused her over the years.

Since the broadcast, however, Mary's twin sister appears to be focusing on a more localised suspect and in 2016 she was engaging her energy in persuading the Garda to reinvestigate Mary's case as murder and hold an inquest with her suspect in mind. As much as I respect the family's views in this case, there appears to be quite strong evidence from various other sources freely available on the internet and elsewhere to lead me to the belief and conclusion that Black has to be the common denominator in what happened to Mary.

I mentioned above that it is known that Black was in Enniskillen on 18 March 1977, delivering and helping to put up posters. Cashelard is only about 30 miles west of there, a half-hour's drive along the Lough Shore Road. There is also the petrol receipt discovered by British police in 1994 that shows that he bought petrol somewhere in Northern Ireland in March 1977.

Other interesting testimonies that point to Black's involvement in the disappearance of little Mary Boyle include reports of a white van in the area. Indeed, Ann Boyle, Mary's mother, herself said that on the day Mary vanished, she saw a white van drive down the road away from the house.

In 2015, Tosh Lavery, a retired Garda diver, published a memoir, *Tosh: An Amazing True Story of Life, Death, Danger and Drama in the Garda Sub-Aqua Unit.* He writes about the Mary Boyle case:

> On the day of her disappearance, there were three brothers poaching from the lakeshore, the postman was doing his rounds in a white van, while another van was also seen in the area. A man cutting timber across the road [from the lake] said he saw a white van go past . . . A girl standing at Cashelard graveyard with her father and a local man saw a white van come flying round the corner and said that the man driving the van had a priest's collar on him, remarking that he looked like 'the kind of priest you wouldn't visit'. . .

So there is continuity of sightings of an unknown white van on the afternoon of 18 March 1977, travelling from the southern end of Cashelard from Belleek Road by Columbkille Lough past the Gallagher and McCauley homesteads to the northern end, travelling at speed past witnesses at St Mary's Church, Cashelard, heading towards the N15 and Donegal which route then continues along the N56 to Annagry.

When I spoke to Robert, my co-author, about this, he was quick to remind me of the 1980 photograph of Robert Black wearing a pullover with white piping around the neck, which at a quick glance would look like a priest's dog collar. Knowing Black's lifestyle and lack of care about his personal appearance and hygiene, it is quite likely that he already had this item of clothing some three years previously, in 1977.

16

TWO MORE DISAPPEARANCES

THE GENETTE TATE CASE

Thirteen-year-old Genette Tate vanished into thin air just after 3.45 on the afternoon of Saturday, 19 August 1978 whilst in the middle of holiday relief work delivering newspapers in Withen Lane in Aylesbeare, a quiet village situated in East Devon just off the main A30 Honiton-to-Exeter road some three miles south-east of Exeter Airport and less than five miles from the M5 motorway, which to the north links with the M4 that runs eastwards to London and westwards to Wales. Just five minutes previously Genette, or 'Ginny' as her friends called her, had been chatting happily a short distance away around a bend with two school friends just as April Fabb had stopped to talk with friends at the donkey field. One of the girls asked Genette for her mother's paper before she cycled off round the bend and out of sight. That was the last time anyone saw Genette, apart from her abductor. Five minutes later the girls came across Genette's cycle abandoned in the middle of Withen Lane and the contents of her bag, newspapers, lay scattered in the road; Genette had vanished off the face of the earth.

Launching what was to become the biggest operation ever mounted by the Devon and Cornwall Constabulary, all available resources were activated in the search for Genette Tate.

Immediately officers were rushed to Aylesbeare, an RAF helicopter was called in and the massive investigation to find out what happened to Genette was under way.

The village hall was taken over as an incident room and for the next six weeks more than eighty officers combed the fields and woodlands within a five-mile radius of the village. They were joined by Royal Marines and during one Saturday afternoon more than 7,000 members of the public responded to an appeal for help in searching nearby Woodbury Common.

Further helicopters, an RAF reconnaissance aircraft equipped with the latest photographic equipment, mounted officers from Avon and Somerset, and police dogs from West Mercia specially trained to sniff out human remains, all joined the search, covering hundreds of acres.

The Force Sub-Aqua Unit mounted an operation to explore 387 gravel pits, ponds, wells and streams in the area. Hundreds of barns, ricks and silage pits were thoroughly searched and acres of undergrowth cleared as the hunt widened.

A team of seventy divisional and regional Crime Squad

detectives mounted intensive enquiries in and around Aylesbeare, nationally and abroad.

Senior detectives from Norfolk and Devon and Cornwall forces conferred on the close similarities between Genette's disappearance and that of April Fabb some nine years before.

For many months Genette's disappearance attracted tremendous local and national publicity. Pictures of the missing girl and the story of her disappearance reached almost every town and village in Britain through newspapers, television, radio and (ironically, considering Black's employment) thousands of posters issued by the force.

One local television station set up a special telephone line inviting the public to call with information, but not a single clue as to Genette's whereabouts emerged.

The teams of searchers were eventually disbanded and the incident room switched from Aylesbeare to Heavitree Road Police Station in Exeter. Detectives continued the painstaking work of sifting through the masses of information that had accumulated, in the hope that somewhere they might find the key to the mystery. Eventually, the Missing Person enquiry ground to a halt and was wound down after amassing more than 20,000 nominal and motor vehicle cards in the indexed filing system.

In 2002 DNA belonging to Genette was found on a jumper kept by her mother, which would allow her body to be identified quickly if discovered. During 2005 some twenty-eight years after her disappearance, fifteen years after Black's arrest and imprisonment for abduction, and eleven years after his triple convictions for murder, Robert Black was finally investigated by Devon and Cornwall's newly set up Cold Case Team and interviewed in prison over Genette's kidnapping. He denied any involvement. In 2008 Devon and Cornwall announced that Black would not face charges in the case of Genette Tate.

During 2011, following Black's conviction for the thirty-year-old murder of Jennifer Cardy, Devon and Cornwall Police were given fresh hope and impetus in Genette's case.

Their Criminal Cases Review Unit have been slowly building a case against Black and he was again interviewed at the end of 2014 and once again during 2015. The matter was being decided by the CPS Complex Case Unit as to whether they had enough evidence to prosecute Black for Genette's abduction and murder when he died in prison.

On 25 October 2016 BBC News reported that Black was the 'only suspect' in the case, but died only days before he could be charged. Her parents have now been shown a 500-page dossier of evidence. Genette's father John Tate said the report contained information gathered by experienced former officers from Devon and Cornwall Police. Mr Tate who lived in the village of Aylesbeare when Genette disappeared, said: 'I am now convinced that Robert Black was the culprit.'. . . Black always denied any involvement in Genette's disappearance, but interestingly new information includes a 'jail confession' to a member of prison staff. In a conversation, Black mentioned to the staff member that he had visited Aylesbeare. The staff member replied that he had not heard of it and asked, 'Aylesbury?' But Black stressed it was 'Aylesbeare'.

TWO MORE DISAPPEARANCES

Black was particularly attracted to girls on bikes as they were vulnerable and made easy targets because they could roam away from village centres. It is highly improbable that Genette was his first murder victim when he was thirty-five years old considering the acts he committed when he was a sixteen years old.

There are some close similarities between the abduction and disappearance of April Fabb, the attempted abduction of Jeanne Twigden, the abduction and disappearance of Genette Tate and the abduction and murder of Jennifer Cardy. Of the classic trio that provide a basis for crime detection –Means (or Method), Motive and Opportunity – all that is missing is opportunity in two of these cases. These two cases (April Fabb and Jeanne Twigden) having been committed prior to Black's employment with PDS, there is no evidence of opportunity in that it is not known whether or not he was in the area. In Jennifer Cardy's 1981 case opportunity was established by Black's employment record and fuel receipts placing him in Northern Ireland at the time of her disappearance.

There is, however, strong circumstantial evidence in the shape of petrol receipts and witness statements to place Black in Exeter, less than 10 miles from Aylesbeare, on Saturday, 19 August 1978 and during the school summer holiday; additionally, in 1996 a woman came forward and told police that she recognised Black from newspaper photographs as being the man she had seen at Exeter Airport, only a few short miles from Aylesbeare, leaning against a red Transit-style van watching her children, on the day Genette vanished; he had then driven off towards Aylesbeare. The woman made up an e-fit and it bore a striking resemblance to how Black looked then. A red Transit van was one of the few vehicles to come into the Genette Tate enquiry and was seen leaving the village at speed around the time of Genette's abduction.

This, coupled with similar fact evidence, if put before a jury as a kidnapping, as in the Cardy, Maxwell, Hogg, Harper murders, should in my opinion have been sufficient to convict Black on a charge of kidnapping and then be assessed as to whether a conviction for the murder of Genette would be safe. But once again, he escaped justice, when in April 2016 the Crown Prosecution Service (CPS) said Black would not be charged as it does not charge dead suspects.

THE SUZANNE LAWRENCE CASE

During the summer holiday of 1979, on Saturday, 28 July, fourteen-year-old Suzanne Lawrence, a pupil at Neave Comprehensive School, left her home in Leamington Road, Harold Hill near Romford in Essex with her younger sister Michelle, aged thirteen, saying they were going to stay with a girlfriend in Dagenham, some seven miles away.

Michelle returned home on Tuesday 7 August without Suzanne and told her mother Pauline Lawrence that they had been staying at someone's home in Highbury, North London. Pauline told the *Romford Recorder*, published Friday, 10 August 1979: 'Michelle has been back with the police to Highbury but she cannot remember the house where they stayed or even the surname of the girl they were staying with. Suzanne has never done anything like this before, we have not had any arguments. She is only fourteen but likes wearing make-up and looks a lot older than she actually is. I will not be able to stop worrying until she is back safe and sound.'

That same article stated that police had stepped up their hunt for Suzanne who by then had been missing from home for three weeks, and were working on the theory that Suzanne could have joined up with a travelling fair after one of her brother's friends reported seeing her at a North London fair in Highbury Fields. The police stated: 'Suzanne has some connections with fairgrounds and we are making several enquiries along these lines.'

On Friday, 24 August 1979 the *Romford Recorder* printed an article under the banner 'Police Fear for Girl's Safety': 'Police say they are gravely concerned for the safety of a 14-year-old Harold Hill girl who has been missing for four weeks. A massive search for Suzanne Lawrence of Leamington Road has drawn a blank, and her natural father, who lives in Surrey, is appealing for her to contact him.'

Two thoughts on Suzanne being yet another victim of Robert Black are:

That she was last seen at Highbury Field Funfair only a mile and a half from Black's haunts and on the doorstep of the A1 and A12, both roads Black used for deliveries to the north and the east. Funfairs, like playgrounds and the seaside, were favoured by Black as places to observe children playing about. In all likelihood, Suzanne would have been hitchhiking back to Harold Hill and he could have offered to give her a lift.

And that the local newspaper, the *Romford Recorder* was the only newspaper that ran Suzanne's disappearance, yet some four years later during a conversation Black had in the Red

Lion pub, Stoke Newington, in 1983 he mentioned, in the course of talking about better-known cases of abducted and murdered girls, a girl from Essex who was murdered – this has to have been Suzanne, an obscure case going back some four years. Working on the premise that Suzanne would have been hitchhiking back to her home and Black gave her a lift, there would have been conversation prior to his finding a suitable isolated location in which to attack her, so he would have known at least her name.

During a senior police conference held in Newcastle in July 1994 to discuss other unsolved cases possibly victims of Black, the name of Suzanne Lawrence was added to the list.

17

ACROSS THE CHANNEL

THE SILKE GARBEN CASE

Silke Garben, aged ten years, was last seen on 20 June 1985 in the garrison town of Detmold in Germany on her way to a dentist's appointment. She was a very pretty child – similar in looks to Jennifer Cardy although with lighter-coloured hair. She failed to turn up for her appointment and it seems certain that she was snatched on her way there.

She was found the next day, face down, dumped in a stream near the army base and had been sexually assaulted and strangled, just like Jennifer Cardy and Sarah Harper, and, strikingly, she died of drowning but was most probably alive though unconscious when dumped in the water – like Jennifer and Sarah. Silke, like Sarah, had been subjected to a brutal sexual assault with horrific vaginal/anal injuries, the pathologist reporting a 6-centimetre tear in her vagina.

The details of the murder, injuries and disposal of her body are almost identical to the modus operandi used by Black, who made two trips to Germany that year, one of which coincided with Silke's abduction and murder. He was working in Essen, and Detmold is 105 miles towards Hanover. Black's main route whilst in Germany was from Hanover in the north-east to Essen in the south-west, using the German A2 motorway that links the two with another garrison along the way at Herford, which is only 18 miles from Detmold off the A2 at this point.

In 1985 British forces had large garrison towns at Herford, Paderborn and Gütersloh, all situated in a 20-mile radius of Detmold, so it is quite conceivable that Black would have been dropping off advertising posters for alcohol and cigarette at most if not all four towns, as well as the North Rhine-Westphalia base at Mönchengladbach near Essen and Osnabrück north-east of Detmold and Hohne near Hanover.

Edward and Kathy Rayson moved to the Dordogne in France during the mid-1980s and Robert Black was known to visit them; he also had access to a caravan in France.

In 1987 in the space of a few weeks four girls were abducted and murdered during May and June around the suburbs of Paris, which (with the help of a French translator), I detail below.

THE VIRGINIE DELMAS CASE

On Saturday, 9 May 1987, some time after 3 p.m., ten-year-old Virginie Delmas went down to play with friends in front of the block of flats where she lived in Neuilly-sur-Marne in the Seine-Saint-Denis suburb of Paris. It was the first time she'd been allowed out on her own by her protective mother but she would be nearby, just a few floors down, and it was a sunny afternoon with many people around. When Virginie did not show up later, her mother went down to look for her. There was no sign of the girl – her friends had not seen her – she had disappeared without anyone noticing. Her mother called the police. It was thought most likely that she had been abducted in a motor vehicle.

Five months later, on 9 October 1987, a couple picking apples found a body in an orchard in Mareuil-lès-Meaux in the Seine-et-Marne district east of Paris at a bend of the main A140 heading towards Meaux and the A1, which links to the Port of Calais. It was Virginie. Her body was naked and was too deeply decomposed for the post mortem to establish whether she had been sexually assaulted, but it found signs of strangulation and that she had been killed on the day of her abduction; her clothes were neatly folded next to her body and her shoes placed together.

The police checked the movements and alibis of several suspects on 5 May but found no connecting evidence. In 1997 investigations were dropped, but in 2005 a cold case investigation was reopened without success and no links were found by the French police between her murder and the three that follow.

THE HEMMA DAVY-GREEDHARRY CASE

On Saturday, 30 May 1987 Hemma Greedharry, aged ten, left her home on the Boulevard de Stalingrad in the Paris suburb of Malakoff around 3 p.m. with 10 francs in her pocket to buy a set square from a stationer's just at the end of her street. On her way home she vanished. There were eyewitnesses who saw her with a stocky man with wavy, blond hair. Less than two hours later, her naked body was found, on fire, in a bin liner behind a hedge, near a campervan in the car park of a council estate in Châtillon on the Rue Guynemer/ Rue Jean Mermoz intersection, only about 900 yards, or a one-minute drive, away from her home; strangely, her clothes were never located, which suggests to me that she was stripped, assaulted and killed by strangulation elsewhere before being put in a bin liner, dumped and set fire to using a combustible material composed largely of liquid styrene – a hydrocarbon found in the composition of many plastics and used in rubber, insulation, fibreglass, pipes, automobile and boat parts, food containers and carpet backing. There was no sign of its container.

Human blood group A+ was found under Hemma's fingernails – her own blood group – and semen inside her, but the DNA has not led to any advances in the investigation. On several occasions the investigators established suspects, a stonemason on whom styrene was found; a teacher already arrested for rape and indecent assault, but no charges have been brought against them.

THE PERRINE VIGNERON CASE

On the afternoon of Wednesday, 3 June 1987, seven-year-old Perrine Vigneron was abducted while heading to her pottery class nearby in the commune of Bouleurs to the east of Paris. When she had not returned home by six, her father went to fetch her – to be told that she had not shown up. Her naked body was found by a dog walker over three weeks later, on 27 June, in a rapeseed field near Chelles, only about 3 miles from the village of Neuilly-sur-Marne, from where Virginie Delmas was abducted just one month earlier; and near the dental surgery where Perrine's father practised. The farmer had sprayed the field on 6 June, so the body had to have been dumped after that date. The weeks of summer sunshine meant that the little body was too badly decomposed for pathologists to establish if she had been sexually assaulted, but it was clear that she had been strangled – there was still a ligature round her neck. Her clothes and shoes had been carefully placed next to the body just as Virginie's had been, but there was no sign of her glasses.

A white van had been seen in Bouleurs, and in the vicinity of the rapeseed field at the time of Perrine's dumping; Robert Black is known to have sometimes used a white van in his PDS work, as in the 1981 case of Jennifer Cardy. Eyewitnesses gave descriptions of the driver and the police issued a photo-fit in the hope that the man could be identified, but they drew a blank. In 2002 Perrine's body was exhumed and for DNA testing, but nothing came of it.

THE SABINE DUMONT CASE

On Saturday, 27 June – the day Perrine's body was found – Sabine Dumont, who was nine years old and the youngest of six children, left her family apartment in Bièvres in Essonne, south-west of Paris, to buy a tube of white paint for a picture she was painting for her new baby cousin. She was last seen, as rain began to fall, at around 5.30 p.m. by a friend. She was barely over a hundred yards from her home and then suddenly she disappeared without trace near the railway station, just a few minutes' walk from her home.

The next day, the 28th, after a night and morning of searching, police found Sabine's clothes, rolled into a ball, on the verge of the Route Nationale 118. It had rained that morning, yet the clothes were dry, suggesting that they had been flung there very shortly before. Her underpants and one of her trainers were missing. A couple of hours later, Sabine's naked body was found in a ditch at Vauhallan, also along the N118 but on the other side, near junction 7 along a stretch of road beside the railway, where there is a loop back towards Bièvres. That stretch of road had been inspected that morning, so she had clearly been left there only a few hours before the discovery. An empty white spirit bottle was found nearby, which was taken as evidence, as well as tyre marks, of which the police took imprints, and a number of cigarette ends.

The girl had died after being strangled and raped and her body had been set on fire with white spirit and was partially burned. Like Hemma, she had traces of blood group A+ under her nails – her blood group was O– – but A+ is common in France, and the discovery led nowhere. In 1999 French investigators at Nantes found a DNA semen trace on Sabine's T-shirt but to date it has not been identified from the FNAEG (the Fichier National Automatisé des Empreintes Génétiques – France's national genetic fingerprint database).

★ ★ ★

A judicial investigation was opened in February 2001 to verify the statements of a Dutch prisoner involving Michael Stocks, a Belgian lorry driver jailed in the Netherlands. Stocks died on 25 September 2001 after being burned in the workshop of the prison where he was serving a sentence of 20 years for the murder of three children. According to the information given to the French authorities by the Dutch police, Stocks admitted to a crime against a young girl in Mulhouse, a city in eastern France close to the Swiss and German border, but the French police were unable to find a connecting crime.

My thoughts are that the Hemma Greedharry and Sabine Dumont murders, both committed to the south of Paris, were by the same killer but that they were not Robert Black's work – unless it can be shown that he used styrene and white spirit for putting up billboard posters.

The Perrine Delmas and Virginie Vigneron murders were also committed by the same killer but are distinct from the other two, and these two I am linking with Robert Black: in both the MO is strikingly similar to that of the murders Black has been convicted of.

At the time the use of DNA in solving crime cases was in its infancy – since then, huge advances have been made in DNA profiling and there is still hope that these mysteries will be cleared up definitively.

THE RAMONA HERLING CASE

On Thursday, 11 May 1989 eleven-year-old Ramona Herling, wearing white trousers, a pink jumper and a denim jacket, left her home in order to walk the 500 yards to the open-air swimming complex situated at Brunnenstrasse 32 in the spa town of Bad Driburg set in the Höxter district of North Rhine-Westphalia in Germany, a 25-minute drive east along Highway 64 from Paderborn and a 35-minute drive south from Detmold, where Silke Garben was murdered in June 1985.She never arrived and has never been seen since.

Given that her sudden disappearance was in a triangular stretch of rural countryside and close to two British-Army-on-the-Rhine bases, coupled with the fact that an open-air swimming pool featured, there is every likelihood that this was yet another abduction and murder committed by Robert Black. It is also, interestingly, sandwiched between the 1988 failed abduction of Teresa Thornhill and the abduction of Laura Turner in 1990, which led to his downfall. Either way, if the German police authorities conferred with their British counterparts it should be easy to establish if Black was delivering posters in Germany during May 1989.

18

AN ENDLESS LUST
FOR KILLING

During 2012 I contacted the *Hackney Gazette*, the North London newspaper covering Stoke Newington, and on Friday, 17 August 2012 they published a full report about what nearly happened to Jeanne over forty years before. The article also asked any member of the public who might have any information about Black to e-mail me.

I only received one response – however, an important one as the following e-mail extracts show:

Date: Sunday, 2 September 2012, 12.08
Hello Chris,
As far as i can remember it was about 1983 when i saw Robert Black. My local pub was The Red Lion as it was named back then in Church St, Stokenewington n16 & i had seen Black in there a

few times, playing darts with the locals. One night i happened to be at the counter where he was sitting & i had a conversation with him. He told me a bit about himself, saying his name was Bob Black & how he was Scottish, i remember saying to him how his name was unusual as i had never known anyone to be named Black before. Talking about Scotland i mentioned about how terrible it was regarding the murder of Susan Maxwell, he agreed it was dreadful, & then went on to list a string of other murders & missing girls etc saying how they were equally as bad. Some of the names he mentioned i knew about from the newspapers but others i hadn't, & he said he was surprised that i didn't know about them, he seemed to be disappointed.

I would say he mentioned about 8 or 9 names one after the other & i was surprised that he had such a close knowledge of these crimes, but then i assumed he was one of those people who takes an interest & studies about murders & missing girls etc in the news & i thought no more of it. One of the names was Jenette Tate which he dwelt on saying she was abducted off her bicycle, also Jennifer Cardy in Ireland & he mentioned another girl also in Ireland. Then April Fabb & a string of others which i cannot remember, i did remember some but because time has elapsed i have forgotten them. That was the only time i had a proper conversation with him, other times i would see him there & i played darts with him once.

Date: Saturday, 29 September 2012, 17:47

Hello Chris, i didn't find out anything from the guys around Stamford Hill or Stokenewington, most of the people there now are of a different generation, those that would have met him are mostly gone to the happy hunting ground.

I used to live in Albion Rd when i was a teenager, lived at 207 for about 12 months in 1963/64 didn't see him then maybe he came later to Albion Rd.

The names that he mentioned to me in the Bar, in his low soft voice were April Fabb, Genette Tate, Jennifer Cardy, Susan Maxwell, I think he mentioned a young girl in Essex (cant think of her name) but i know she was murdered, & yes Christine Markham, i cant remember the names of the 2 girls in Ireland that he mentioned, & he also spoke of 3 or 4 more young girls just mentioning their names & saying how terrible it was that so many were murdered or missing.

It struck me straight away how it was very unusual for anyone to remember the names of these girls so well & the way in which he rattled them off, but again i would never have suspected him as he told me he lived in Stamford Hill & the girls were from areas mainly long distances away. He was a cool customer.

Regards John

With regard to the last e-mail it is quite significant that Black was talking during 1983 about the murder of fourteen-year-old Suzanne Lawrence from Essex who was reported as a missing person in July 1979 and was last seen at a funfair in Highbury, London and thought to have run away with it. Highbury is very close to Robert Black's then haunts.

Her disappearance only made the local Romford area papers and her name was unknown until after Black's arrest in 1990, certainly not a name made aware to Norfolk Constabulary Intelligence Departments. So there he is, talking about her murder some seven years before she became a known possible victim.

Again, Christine Markham who went missing in 1973 was not a household name during the 1980s outside of her native Scunthorpe.

The case of Jennifer Cardy made a small article on page 5 of the *Daily Express* on 15 August 1981 when she was still a missing person and there was no further British newspaper reference until 2002. She and Mary Boyle are the Irish girls referred to by Black.

In the course of 2012 through to 2014 I supplied Norfolk Constabulary and Devon and Cornwall Police with copies of my research material.

During June and July 2014 I had several newspaper articles published, which highlighted Jeanne's case and the other unsolved abductions that Black is suspected of.

In August 2014, to draw attention to the similar fact evidence of Jeanne's case in relation to others, I contacted Cambridgeshire Police and Jeanne was interviewed by a detective from their Major Crime Unit, but they didn't take the initiative and no liaison was made by them with either Norfolk or Cornwall and Devon.

During the autumn of 2014 I made e-mail contact with one of April's surviving family members, as a result of which officers of Norfolk Constabulary Cold Case Team arranged to meet me. I supplied them with the up-to-date research that I had collected and continue to do so.

In March 2015 I made contact with retired Lothian and Borders Detective Chief Superintendent Andrew Watt who was the senior officer involved with Robert Black's 1990 arrest for abduction and subsequent interviews for the Maxwell, Hogg and Harper triple murder investigation.

I outlined Jeanne's case by e-mail and Andrew replied stating, 'I am confident that the 1971 incident [Jeanne's] is Robert Black based on more than one point. He would be at the swimming pool [St Neots] looking for potential victims. This is part of his MO. He had a particular attraction to swimming pools.'

In a further communication he commented:

> I agree with you that Robert Black is a likely candidate for the 1971 attempted abduction. This has an uncanny similarity to the attempted abduction of Teresa Thornhill in Nottingham in 1988. This case was used at Black's trial at Newcastle in 1994 as I had asked that it be included in my remit to support the similar fact evidence in the murder cases and was an important piece of evidence. Teresa looked much younger than she actually was.
>
> As a result of conversations with myself and the late Ray Wyre Black it indicated that he stalked his

victims for lengthy periods of time before carrying out or attempting to carry out an abduction. According to Black he only moved when he felt it was safe. The first offence at Stow occurred after he had been following a child for some time. This was not the victim, however, but a girl called Mandy Wilson. For some unknown reason he moved his attention to the victim. On his own admission he had an unusual interest in pre-pubescent girls.

He also frequented swimming pools and indeed was employed at a swimming pool in London for some time . . .

Andrew went on in his communication to say that in his view Norfolk and Devon and Cornwall should connect the April Fabb and Genette Tate investigations with an overall SIO (Senior Investigating Officer) to examine evidence common to both cases.

In April 2015 I sent Norfolk, Cambridgeshire and Devon and Cornwall a copy of Andrew Watt's e-mails and I received a reply from Cambridgeshire stating that their Major Crime Unit had been in touch with Norfolk Cold Case and that they were now preparing a report in relation to the incident in St Neots involving Mrs Clark [Jeanne] and this information will be available for other forces who may be investigating Black.

During April 2015 I contacted Devon and Cornwall MIT (Major Incident Team) and outlined the Susan Maxwell case where Black's own photographs had helped to place him on that Scottish run at the material time, and suggested, if not already done, that they do the same with regard to any Devon photographs taken by Black in 1978.

I was in touch with the Garda Siochána in early 2017 about the sightings of a white van reported in the Cashelard area at the time of Mary Boyle's disappearance, and drew their attention to the high neck of Black's jersey from a distance resembling a priest's collar, as commented on by one of those who glimpsed the driver of a white van being driven at speed out of Cashelard.

On 13 January 2016 I was contacted by both the *Sun* and *Daily Mirror* newspapers and a double-page article appeared in both papers on Thursday, 14 January 2016. I reproduce the article (print version) by kind permission of the Mirror Group:

Evil Robert Black is feared to have murdered as many as 16 children in a monstrous 18-year spree – making him Britain's most prolific child killer.

Distressing new evidence links a dozen more child murders across the UK and Europe to the pervert, who died aged 68 this week serving 12 life terms for killing four schoolgirls.

He always refused to co-operate with police about other killings and took his sick secrets to the grave.

But a cold-case expert said yesterday that an individual who knew Black said he 'revealed information only a guilty man could have known' about a number of other child murders.

If Black's guilt is proven it would make him the most prolific serial child killer in modern British criminal history – slaughtering more than Moors murderers Ian Brady and Myra Hindley, who had five victims aged 10 to 17, as did Fred and Rose West.

Cold-case review expert Chris Clark, a former police Intelligence officer who worked on dozens of missing-child cases, said, 'In my opinion, Black was the only real suspect in these cases and more. His psychopathic tendencies were constant, his lust for killing was endless.

Yesterday *The Mirror* told how police were just weeks from charging him with the 1978 murder of Genette Tate, 13, of Aylesbeare, Devon, when he died on Tuesday of natural causes.

New evidence shows he was in the right place, at the right time, to have murdered 11 more from 1969 to 1987.

Driving a delivery van from 1972 to 1992, he had the opportunity to target kids, leaving little trace as he regularly crossed Britain and ventured into France, Germany and the Netherlands.

The informant, named John, used to drink with Black when he lived in Stoke Newington, north London.

He said the maniac reeled off 'eight or nine' names, including girls missing at the time.

They included April Fabb, 13, who vanished near her home in Melton, Norfolk, in1969. Black was quizzed several times about her but would not co-operate.

John said Black even told him about missing children who never made headlines, including Suzanne Lawrence, 14, of Harold Hill, Essex, missing since 1979.

Another was Christine Markham, nine, who disappeared in Scunthorpe in 1973.

Black was heavily linked to the disappearance of Mary Boyle, six, from her grandparents' farm in Ballyshannon, Donegal in 1977. Another was the murder of Pamela Hastie, whose mutilated body was found in Johnstone, Renfrewshire in 1981.

Mr Clark also unearthed evidence over more than five years of research linking Black to at least six murders in Germany, France and Holland.

The killing of 10-year-old Silke Garben in Detmond, Germany appears most strongly to bear his hallmarks .Silke vanished near her home in 1985 at a time Black was working nearby delivering posters for London firm Poster Despatch and Storage.

Her body was found days later. She had been sexually assaulted, strangled and left, by the side of a road [actually, face down, in a stream].

Detectives also believed Black was responsible for the abduction and murder of seven-year-old Cheryl Morriën in Amsterdam, Netherlands in 1986.

UK and French police also wanted to examine Black's involvement in the 1987 murders on the outskirts of

Paris of Virginie Delmas, 10, Hemma Greedharry, 11, Sabine Dumont, nine, and Perrine Vigneron, seven. Mr Clark said 'They bore the hallmarks . . . and he was in the country at the time.'

Black was jailed in 1994 for the murders of Susan Maxwell, 11, from Cornhill-on-Tweed, in July 1982, Caroline Hogg, five, of Edinburgh, in July 1983, and Sarah Harper, 10, from Morley, near Leeds, in March 1986.

In 2011, he was also convicted of the murder of Jennifer Cardy, nine, in Northern Ireland in August 1981. Det. Supt Paul Burgan, head of major crime in the Devon and Cornwall force, said a full file on the murder of Genette Tate was about to be submitted to the Crown Prosecution Service and Black would have been charged. Genette's father John, 73, said, 'I still hope and pray that we will get to the bottom of it.'

Black was finally caught bundling a six-year-old girl into his van. As many as 40 abductions, sex assaults and murders were examined as having possible connections to him.

Ray Wyre, who interviewed Black for his book, *Murder of Childhood*, said he had hinted about other victims. Wyre said, 'I have assessed many sex offenders and Robert Black is one of the worst that I have ever met.'

For further reading and ten associated articles on Robert Black, please visit my website: www.armchairdetective.org.uk.

PART THREE

THE STORY NEVER REALLY ENDS

19

SECRETS TO
THE GRAVE

It was the evening of Tuesday, 12 January 2016 when the news broke that Robert Black had died in Maghaberry Prison, situated outside Lisburn in County Antrim. I was sitting in my living room watching television when the news flashed up on the screen. The details would eventually come through that Black had suddenly collapsed after suffering a massive heart attack and subsequently died. He was sixty-eight years of age. I was in shock at the news and the suddenness of it. I immediately telephoned my co-author on this book Chris Clark to tell him the news in case he had not heard.

He wasn't home but his wife Jeanne was. Jeanne who, along with Chris, retired Superintendent Andrew Watt and myself, believes that she was almost abducted by Black in the summer of 1971 when she was a fifteen-year-old schoolgirl. I broke the news to her and she told me that if it was Black who stalked her and attempted to abduct her on that day forty-five years ago, she felt relief that he was gone. Chris phoned me back shortly after and we talked at length about Black's passing and how it meant that other families would never get to see him stand in the dock once again to be charged with other crimes.

The next morning I appeared on the Shaun Doherty show on Highland Radio alongside Andy Cardy, Jennifer Cardy's father. Later on that day I appeared on BBC Radio Foyle. Both programmes focused on Black and the crimes he committed and just like the aftermath in 2011, after Black's latest murder conviction, there were many unanswered questions surrounding Robert Black. Patricia Cardy, Jennifer's mother, reacting to his death told the *Daily Mirror* on 13 January 2016 how it was 'sad he's gone without so many other families getting a trial and a verdict like we did.' It was a sentiment shared by many, not least John Tate, the father of Genette Tate. Black had always been the prime suspect in her abduction and disappearance. 'I would have liked to have seen Robert Black go on trial charged with Genette's kidnap and murder but now that has been denied us,' John Tate said.

His words were even more heart-breaking when it was revealed that Devon and Cornwall Police were only a few weeks away from charging Black with Genette's murder: a fresh file had been sent to the CPS (Crown Prosecution Service) seeking permission to charge him; a decision was meant to be reached the autumn before but had been delayed and put back until the beginning of March. Police had traced two new witnesses one of whom made a statement regarding

Black's exhibiting strange behaviour back in August 1978 around the time Genette went missing. This, along with the added similar fact evidence stemming from the Jennifer Cardy conviction and the strong similarities between Jennifer's abduction and murder and Genette's disappearance, meant Devon and Cornwall police were increasingly confident Black would be convicted of Genette's killing. Sadly, and frustratingly, however, Black's death saw a long investigation fall at the last hurdle.

Devon and Cornwall Police had asked the Northern Ireland prison authorities to alert them if Black ever became seriously ill in the hope that a death-bed type confession to his other possible crimes might come from him, but his sudden collapse and quick death meant that did not happen. In all likelihood however, Black was never going to confess to anything even when faced with the prospect of imminent death – he would more than likely have kept his superior knowledge to himself in both a two-fingered salute to the authorities trying to charge him and in a perverse game of controlling the suffering of the families of all the suspected victims.

It was known within the prison service that his health was deteriorating; it was said that he had coughed up blood whilst playing a game of pool in prison but there was no indication that he was about to die or was even near to dying and he had been playing a game of cards with fellow prisoners shortly before he died. Black it seems had taken his secrets to the grave – even though it was not a grave he went into; instead he was cremated in a short ceremony which lasted just over five minutes in Belfast attended only by crematorium staff and a minister. His ashes it is believed were scattered at sea. The undertakers that handled the funeral arrangements had their premises vandalised shortly afterwards.

An interesting development arose after Black's death where a fellow prisoner in Maghaberry told authorities that Black had divulged information to him about other child murders. The fellow prisoner who himself is a convicted child killer became close to Black and was quizzed by police over what Black may have told him. There has been no further information released as of yet, however, to validate the prisoner's claims. So the same question continued to come up: how many more children did Robert Black kill?

In the early 1990s police looked at forty potential cases in which Robert Black could have been involved. That figure by 1994 had been brought down to under half that number with a possible list of seventeen deaths across the British Isles and European continent linked with him. Fast forward to 2011 following his conviction of killing Jennifer Cardy, the number was revisited and brought down again, this time to around eight other cases in which he remains a viable suspect. Somewhat irritatingly, certain sections of the media both in 2011 and after Black's death in 2016 continued to link his name with the murders of young girls in which Black had been ruled out as a suspect many years before.

After Black's conviction in 2011 retired Detective Chief Superintendent Roger Orr commented: 'He's not done them all, that's the thing. He's not a three-headed monster – he's a very dangerous guy – but he's not done them all. That's the reality because some of them that were originally referred are now solved, quite properly solved.' (*The Sun,* Friday, 28 October 2011.)

My co-author Chris Clark has – as seen in the last chapters – excellently covered the eight cases that he believes Robert Black was involved in over a twenty-year period from 1969 to 1989, and has detailed three attempted abductions where the victims were lucky to get away. In the next chapter, I am going to recap these cases as well as add some of my own observations – inevitably, this will mean some repetition of facts and circumstances, but covering the same ground over and over is part of the detective work necessary for piecing together what happened.

20

FILLING IN
THE GAPS

The first case discussed was the disappearance of thirteen-year-old April Fabb on Tuesday, 8 April 1969. As Chris says, Black could have been in Cromer over the preceding holiday weekend; perhaps he visited an Easter funfair (he abducted Caroline Hogg from a funfair in 1983), which would have attracted visitors from as far away as London, the capital city, where Black had been resident for over a year at this point.

Perhaps he was working cash in hand making deliveries or perhaps he was visiting beaches along the east coast of Norfolk. There would have been opportunities to photograph and stalk children and he would later, in interviews with the RUC officers investigating the murder of Jennifer Cardy, talk about the pleasure he took in looking at little girls as they changed their clothes on the beach, while he maybe pretended to be enjoying a walk or some fresh air.

As Chris remarks, there is evidence that he was driving and had access to vehicles prior to 1976; as said previously in this book he had his first delivery driving job aged seventeen in 1964, dropping off newspapers and magazines for the company John Menzies, amongst others. As Chris also mentions, Black was convicted of being involved in stealing cars and going equipped with a bunch of keys on 22 September 1972, three years after April's disappearance, and we also know he had access to a number of vehicles prior to passing his driving test in 1976.

So the lack of a driving licence in 1969 means practically nothing – Robert Black had the ability to drive and had access to vehicles in the course of a variety of odd and casual jobs, delivery work probably amongst them. Another clue to Black's involvement is the distance that April's bicycle was thrown into the field where it was found. Whoever abducted April would had to have had considerable upper body strength to have thrown the bicycle that far from the roadside edge. As a young man Black was a keen and active swimmer and footballer and also lifted weights in his room so it is highly likely that he had considerable strength.

The circumstances of the disappearance of April Fabb are almost identical to those of Jennifer Cardy over twelve years later. A young girl on a bicycle abducted while cycling to visit someone along a country road near her home. No witnesses, no screams heard and both bicycles thrown into the nearest field from the point of abduction. Both were taken away in a vehicle. Both were abducted on a sunny day during the school holidays, and on a weekday, April on a

FILLING IN THE GAPS

Tuesday, Jennifer on a Wednesday, at around the same time in the afternoon.

Metton and Ballinderry are two very similar villages in profile; they are, however, in separate countries that are considerably far apart – so if the same man was responsible for both crimes we have to be looking at an offender with geographical mobility and knowledge. and Robert Black certainly had both, even in 1969.

The reality is that girls being abducted from rural surroundings on bicycles was and remains a rare crime even today and Robert Black is one of the few individuals to have been convicted of such a crime. The problem is, though, that there is no actual evidence of Black being in Cromer or Metton or anywhere in Norfolk on that particular day – yet that does not mean that such evidence is not in existence. By the same token, there is no evidence that he was anywhere else on 8 April 1969, and until we know he was elsewhere, he cannot be ruled out either and for that reason he should remain a strong suspect for involvement in the disappearance of April Fabb.

* * *

The next case, that of the disappearance of Christine Markham on Monday, 21 May 1973, is the only case on our list that Chris and I disagree on. We talked about Christine's disappearance at length and in the end we mutually and respectfully agreed to disagree with each other. Whilst respecting and taking on board each other's viewpoints on the case we both ultimately had different theories and opinions on what happened to

Christine. Chris has outlined his reasons for thinking Christine was a potential victim of Robert Black such as:

1. Christine was a young pre-pubescent girl who went missing from a public place in an urban area not far from her home. In this regard her disappearance is similar in detail to the abduction and murder of Sarah Harper in 1986 and the attempted abduction of Teresa Thornhill in 1988 in Nottingham.

2. It is widely accepted that Christine was abducted. We can presume she was abducted for a sexual purpose. There is a possibility a vehicle was involved.

3. The geographical routes involved out of Scunthorpe as outlined by Chris and their links to London where Black resided at the time.

4. The conversation Black had with 'John' in the pub in 1983 – in which Christine Markham was one of the names that John, seven years before Black's capture, eventually remembered Black alluding to when talking about the unsolved murders of children. Christine Markham's disappearance did not make the national newspapers.

5. Was Black in the general Scunthorpe area doing a cash-in-hand delivery job?

My own view, however, is that Christine Markham was not a victim of Robert Black. There is no evidence at present to settle beyond doubt where he was on 21 May 1973; which means he could have been in Scunthorpe and then again he might not have been, we just don't know. It is widely accepted that Christine was more than likely a victim of abduction and whilst still classified as a missing person is sadly presumed to be dead.

The absence of a ransom note suggests a sexual motive, however, and whilst I accept Black could still be a possible suspect in her disappearance for the reasons put forth by Chris, and while I accept the possibility that she was the victim of a random and quick abduction by someone from outside the area and a stranger to the child (Robert Black would come into this category), I believe on the other hand the answer to her disappearance lies within the Scunthorpe area itself. Christine was described as a streetwise child who had played truant from school previously. Streetwise or not, the child was still vulnerable and I believe that someone that day took advantage of that vulnerability.

A vehicle may have been used at some point in her disappearance. It is impossible to know if she was taken away forcibly or if she was enticed away. Christine may have known her abductor and put her trust in them and that trust may have been betrayed. Then again, her abductor could have been a local but a stranger to Christine. The case is a frustrating mystery because although there were a number of sightings of Christine that day (as outlined by Chris in Chapter 14), there were no reported sightings of her in the company of a potential abductor or near any kind of vehicle. Despite 2,000 witness statements and 5,000 homes in Scunthorpe being thoroughly searched, Christine was never found and despite numerous arrests of an array of different suspects nobody has ever been charged in connection to her disappearance.

In 1983, on the tenth anniversary of Christine's disappearance her family switched off the light outside her home at night. It had been left on every night in case she came home. Robert Black was officially ruled out by Humberside police in 2004 and in May 2006 a cold-case review was launched.

After a renewed appeal for information, police received an anonymous letter which provided some new clues as to what perhaps happened to Christine and would point to a more local connection being behind her going missing. 'I would like to thank the person for the letter they have sent to me but it is really important that I speak to them personally,' Detective Sergeant Craig Scott from Humberside Police said on receiving the letter, quoted on the BBC News website in October 2006.

On the fortieth anniversary of Christine's disappearance – 21 May 2013 – it was revealed that the letter-writer claimed a relative had helped to dispose of evidence relating to Christine going missing but that anyone who could help confirm this was no longer alive. The letter specified that the evidence was buried at woodland near Metheringham, Lincolnshire.

Humberside Police at one point in 2012 considered digging up the area at that location but after a scoping exercise carried out by thirty police officers and teams of army staff, archaeologists and expert search investigators, the plan was abandoned for a number of reasons such as environmental factors and physical changes that would have taken place in the area over the forty years since Christine's disappearance meaning that it was unlikely anything would have been found.

'When people bury a body,' explained Detective Superintendent Christine Wilson in the *Scunthorpe Telegraph*, on 29 May 2013 'they generally dig where it is easy, but where it was easy thirty years ago it wouldn't be the same today. If Christine was buried in those woods, the area now has trees growing that were not there thirty years ago and ground levels will have changed. Given the time delay and the environmental factors, it would be highly unlikely to find any remains of Christine after all this time. However, that does not mean that we will give up. This file will continue to be reassessed and we would act immediately on any new information that came in as a result of this publicity.'

The disappearance of Christine Markham is a case that in comparison to cases of other missing children has received little publicity in the forty-plus years since she went missing and I sincerely hope this book can help generate new lines of investigation and lead to Christine's family and friends getting answers as to what happened to the little red-haired girl who played truant that day.

★ ★ ★

The next case on Chris's list is that of the disappearance of six-year-old Mary Boyle on 18 March 1977. The Garda (Republic of Ireland Police Force) along with the Royal Ulster Constabulary were both invited to bring their case files of any missing or murdered children to the July 1994 police conference held in Newcastle upon Tyne; the agenda of which was the exploration of the possibility that Robert Black could have committed other offences similar to the three child murders he had been convicted of two months earlier.

The RUC of course brought with them the Jennifer Cardy case, whilst the Garda brought Mary's case and that of ten-year-old Bernadette Connolly who was abducted whilst out running an errand on her bicycle near Collooney village in County Sligo on 17 April 1970 and her body found in a bog fifteen miles away from her home four months later in August. The Garda quickly ruled out Black as a suspect in the Connolly case but thought that further investigation in relation to Mary Boyle was certainly warranted.

Chris has outlined a number of reasons as to why Black could remain a possible suspect in the Mary Boyle case and certain sections of the media have continued to link him to Mary's disappearance after his conviction for the murder of Jennifer Cardy in 2011. A 2011 newspaper report claimed that in 2010 a witness had come forward, a woman claiming to have seen a man matching Black's description speeding out of Cashelard in a white van on the day of Mary's disappearance. This information was repeated in a further news report in January 2016 following his death.

In 2003 the Garda liaised with Devon and Cornwall Police and the PSNI in a meeting held in a hotel in Ballyshannon, County Donegal to discuss the similarities between the disappearance of Mary Boyle, the disappearance of Genette Tate and the murder of Jennifer Cardy, and the latest progress of each of their individual investigations into linking Robert

Black with those crimes. The Garda reviewed Mary's case in 2011 and the majority of parties involved in the Mary Boyle case agree sadly that little Mary was murdered and a number of different theories and scenarios have been discussed through the years.

The Garda after becoming aware of Black's movements around County Donegal in the mid and late 1970s (his name having appeared on a Garda charge sheet for after-hours drinking in a pub in Annagry, County Donegal) requested to question him after reports from people that claimed to have met and subsequently socialised with the smiling, scruffy Scotsman with the soft-toned voice.

In November 2014 gardaí arrested and questioned a former Irish soldier and convicted child molester about Mary's disappearance; however, the man denied any involvement and was subsequently released without charge. There remain two options as to what might have happened to Mary Boyle:

1. She was attacked and killed by someone from within the local area and near to where she was last seen alive on the hillside.
2. That on her return to the house she lost her sense of direction and made her way onto a local road where she was abducted by a travelling offender who came upon her by chance.

It is worth noting that in more recent developments Mary's sister Ann and Margo O'Donnell, the singer and a distant cousin, with the support and help of journalists, retired gardaí and others, have publicly stated that they believe they know who murdered her and that it was somebody Mary knew and that the answer to what happened to her lies locally rather than involving someone from outside the locality. In October 2015 Mary's sister Ann and Margo O'Donnell gave statements in a Garda station in Dublin relating to an individual whom they believe was responsible for killing Mary. Whatever ensues, we very much hope that the tragic mystery of Mary's disappearance can be resolved.

★ ★ ★

The next disappearance is one that has never been far away from the headlines. The abduction of thirteen-year-old Genette Tate on Saturday, 19 August 1978 has been linked with the name Robert Black ever since he was convicted of his first three child murders in 1994. Chris has laid out on Chapter 16 the details of Genette's disappearance, the investigative aftermath and the reasons why Black always was and remains the prime suspect.

There are other clues that point to his involvement. In 2012 John Tate, Genette's father, revealed in a television documentary that he was passed forward information that suggested Black bought bacon sandwiches from a roadside café near to Aylesbeare, which is would indicate some knowledge of the area. John said he had passed this information forward to Devon and Cornwall Police.

In 2001 it was revealed that Black had been talking to a fellow prisoner in Wakefield Prison in West Yorkshire and had implied that he knew what had happened to Genette. When the police were notified of this they arranged an interview with him but when it was put to him he clammed up once again and denied any knowledge of what happened to her. The officer, Retired Detective Chief Inspector of Cheshire Police Ken Lee who helped facilitate the interview explained in the *Mail on Sunday* in August 2001:

'Out of conversations Black was suggesting he was responsible for Genette Tate's murder. But as far as I can recall he did not make a direct admission. Once around the table Black was saying "I haven't done it. I don't know what you are talking about." . . .'

Another clue was the conversations Black had with criminal researcher and sex crimes expert Ray Wyre in the early 1990s while he was awaiting trial for the Midlands Triangle murders. One conversation saw Black bring up Genette while as the transcript that follows (from his book *The Murder of Childhood*) shows he was careful not to utter Genette's name and thereby incriminate himself.

Ray Wyre: 'What was going on?'
Black: 'I don't know. Maybe . . . there was that paper girl that went missing. I don't know where she was missing like, but it was all over the papers.'
Ray Wyre: 'Tate?'
Black: 'Yeah. That was her name, yeah. She disappeared. She never turned up.'
Ray Wyre: 'Yeah.'
Black: 'I suppose they've started thinking, How did he do it?'
Ray Wyre: 'And how do you think he did it?'

Black: 'Well, they found her bike, didn't they? He obviously persuaded her to get off her bike, or grabbed her off the bike, one of the two. Then got her into the vehicle and took her away.'

It is a fascinating yet frightening exchange. On the surface Black is talking about a nationally well-known case of a missing child yet he is careful to make it seem that he barely knows anything at all about the case: he refers to Genette as 'that paper girl', 'she' or 'her'. Black also never spoke the name of Jennifer Cardy during interviews with the RUC in 1996 or the PSNI in 2005. He could not say the names of these girls because to do so would, in his mind, be to incriminate himself. Black also alluded to the potential use of a 'vehicle' in Genette's abduction, careful not to mention the word 'van'. Listening to his words, there seems to be artificiality to them.

As Chris mentions in Chapter 16, a DNA profile of Genette was obtained in 2002 by forensic scientists from a jumper belonging to her that had been kept by her mother Sheila. This was compared with various items that had belonged to Robert Black to see if any trace of Genette's DNA could be found on them; unfortunately, too long a time had passed for any vestige of her DNA to be discovered.

Despite this setback, there remain the many similarities between the disappearance of Genette Tate in 1978 (making Black the prime suspect), the disappearance of April Fabb in 1969 (making him a good suspect) and the abduction and murder of Jennifer Cardy in August 1981 (a crime for which he was convicted in 2011). To remind the reader:

FILLING IN THE GAPS

1. All three victims had a similar profile: three pretty little girls all riding their bicycles when they were abducted and taken away, with a vehicle involved.

2. All three girls were abducted in the afternoon between the hours of 1.30 p.m. and 3.30 p.m.

3. All three girls were abducted along rural roads, only half a mile, or slightly more, away from their homes in or on the edge of the three country villages they lived in.

4. All three victims were abducted during spells of good weather, Genette and Jennifer in the summertime (August) and April in the spring (April).

5. All three disappeared during the school holidays: Genette and Jennifer were off school for the summer, whilst April was off for the Easter holidays.

6. April's and Jennifer's bicycles were thrown into fields from the point of their roadside abduction. Genette's bicycle was not thrown over the hedge but there are two logical explanations for this: a quick look of photographs taken back in August 1978 of Withen Lane from where Genette was snatched shows a very high hedge – the height of the hedge could have been at least part of the reason why Genette's abductor abandoned it along with the scattered newspapers on the tarmac. Another reason could be the layout of Withen Lane itself, the winding nature of the road meaning that somebody could have come round the corner at any time– so a quick getaway would have been essential.

7. As remarked by Chris in Chapter 16, the geography of the area and the road network links are significant,

especially when in relation to a travelling offender who liked to venture off motorways, like Black.

Aylesbeare, from where Genette was abducted, is near the M5 motorway, which is close to Exeter Airport; in 1996, as Chris mentions in Chapter 16, a woman came forward and claimed that on the day of Genette's disappearance a man at the airport, whom she recognised years later as Robert Black, was leaning against a red Transit-style van watching her two children, and when he became aware of her presence he drove away quickly in his van. If this man at Exeter Airport was indeed Robert Black then he was clearly in the vicinity of Aylesbeare, displaying predatory behaviour, that day.

Ballinderry, from where Jennifer Cardy was abducted is near Northern Ireland's M1, along which Black travelled towards Newry from Belfast once he was off the ferry, and then back again to the ferry, and the A26, which links to the A3 and A1, which was the road he followed when passing McKee's Dam where Jennifer's body was found.

Metton, the village from where April Fabb disappeared, was close to major routes such as the A148 road to King's Lynn and the A10 to London, and, nearer to Roughton, the A140 Cromer-to-Norwich and the link road A11 to London. London of course being where Black was resident at the time.

The bodies of Genette Tate and April Fabb were never

found. And while Jennifer Cardy's body was found there are two possible explanations as to why this should be. First of all, the bodies of Jennifer Cardy, Susan Maxwell, Caroline Hogg and Sarah Harper, Black's confirmed victims, were all found purely by chance by members of the public. There was an equal chance that their bodies would never have been found, especially in the case of the three 'Midlands Triangle' murders; it may just be by chance that the bodies of April Fabb and Genette Tate have not yet been discovered.

The second explanation could be that Black, for some reason, changed his MO in regard to the way he disposed of his victims. As is the case with April Fabb and Genette Tate, the bodies of the other earlier missing persons/abducted victims – for instance, Christine Markham or Suzanne Lawrence – have not been found. Assuming these are all the victims of an earlier series of crimes committed by Black, it might be that he was extra cautious in his earlier killing days to ensure the bodies would not be found – as they were in the post-1980 series of killings starting with the quick discovery of Jennifer Cardy's body – and traced back to him. Certainly, in the later murders, of which Black was convicted, the effort to conceal the victim's bodies wasn't great – they were dumped publicly with nothing covering them, discarded and cast aside in the most undignified and callous way, to be found – or not – by chance. Perhaps he started to leave his victims where they could easily be found as a way of mocking the police, to show he was invincible and could not be caught. If this was so, it was an over-confidence that would see him caught red-handed in 1990.

Genette's disappearance also bears similarities to the attempted abduction in 1971 of Jeanne Twigden, who, as we've seen, was stalked on a hot May Day afternoon after leaving an open-air swimming pool in St Neots, and nearly abducted as she rode home on her bicycle through the village of Great Paxton along the rural B104 road – which is adjacent to the A1 Great North Road that leads to London.

During 2003 PSNI and Devon and Cornwall detectives met in the West Country to discuss their joint investigations into Robert Black and the similarities between Genette Tate's case and that of Jennifer Cardy. Devon and Cornwall Police discovered a payment record or wage statement that suggested Black was working the South Coast delivery run that week in August 1978, a run that took in a series of towns and cities within which lies the village of Aylesbeare. Frustratingly, however, this wage statement was not sufficient evidence as it did not specify that the bonus was for the South Coast Run – it could also be interpreted as meaning Black did the Scotland work run that week as the two trips had a similar payment bonus structure. Even though it was believed he was working the South Coast run that week, it was not enough to stand up in court.

This evidence, whilst not conclusive, is interesting when considering witness statements – a report of a red or maroon car driving along that road, another witness's report of seeing a red Transit-style van speeding out of Aylesbeare village shortly after Genette went missing, the eyewitness's information in 1996 about the driver of a red van at Exeter Airport. Black was believed to have been driving a fire-engine-coloured

Transit van in August 1978. When these are grouped together, it definitely appears likely Black was in the South Coast/East Devon area at the time. Geographical profiling can also link him to the crime. Black had five main work runs with PDS as a van driver and committed the murders of Susan Maxwell, Caroline Hogg and Sarah Harper while on the Scottish/Northern run and the murder of Jennifer Cardy while on the Midlands/Northern Ireland run. Therefore it makes sense that he may have committed similar crimes on his other work runs, including the South Coast run, which took in the area from where Genette disappeared, and the East Coast run, which covered Norfolk and Suffolk in East Anglia: in Chapter 13, Chris tells of the attempted abduction a young girl, Jeanne Twigden, in Norfolk in the mid-1970s after Black had started working for PDS (the disappearance of April Fabb occurred before then).

Over the years, Genette's case file has grown so large that it has been kept in a twelve-foot-by-ten-foot document cage in the headquarters of Devon and Cornwall Police in Exeter. The paperwork involved includes 20,000 index cards in a filing system containing cross references and witness statements.

The initial 1978 search for Genette involved 7,000 volunteers from local holidaymakers to nuns to Royal Marines, who came to be known as 'Genette's army' as they searched the fields, moorlands, hedges and roads near her Aylesbeare home. Divers searched every dam, drain, pond, river and sewer for miles around and there was nothing left uncovered during a search around Aylesbeare which covered a four-mile radius.

A £23,000 reward was raised by the local villagers for information leading to Genette being found while a local vicar set up a phone-line for those who wished to come forward with any information. But it was all to no avail. In spite of her body not being found and her killer never convicted in a court of law, to many, for the reasons given by Chris and myself. Black is the man responsible for Genette's disappearance.

Even though Black died in January 2016, Devon and Cornwall Police still sent their case file to the Crown Prosecution Service, seeking permission to charge him with Genette's abduction and murder, in an effort to bring closure and some form of relief to Genette's family; however the CPS released a statement saying that they could not make a decision as they did not charge dead suspects

★ ★ ★

Another case covered by Chris in Chapter 16 is that of Suzanne Lawrence and this also has potential links to Robert Black. As Chris explained, she was last seen, on 28 July 1979, at a funfair in Highbury Field in North London, only a mile and a half from where Black lived. It is also worth noting that Black abducted five-year-old Caroline Hogg from a funfair in Portobello, Edinburgh just four years after Suzanne disappeared.

Chris also mentions how Black talked about 'a girl from Essex' during a pub conversation in 1983 and as Suzanne was from Harold Hill in Essex it does seem likely that it was her he was referring to.

★ ★ ★

FILLING IN THE GAPS

In Europe, there were several cases that displayed similarities to those of which Black was convicted. Chris has already outlined the details of the murder on 20 June 1985 of Silke Garben in Detmold, Germany and the links that make Black a considerably strong suspect, not least the horrific vaginal injuries suffered by the child, comparable to those inflicted upon Sarah Harper whom Black murdered just under a year later.

The murders of ten-year-old Virginie Delmas on 9 May 1987 and Perrine Vigneron on 7 June 1987 have also been looked at in connection with Black and for good reason as Chris points out in Chapter 17. Robert Black was working and holidaying in a white van in the northern region of France over six weeks in the May/June period of 1987 when these girls were abducted and murdered.

Witnesses reported seeing a white van cruising through the area at the time the victims disappeared. The appearance of the items of clothing and shoes beside the victims in these cases is particularly significant bearing in mind that the shoes and underwear of Susan Maxwell were also found neatly arranged next to her remains. Both girls, Virginie and Perrine, were found miles away from their point of abduction and clearly a vehicle was involved.

The murders of Silke Garben, Virginie Delmas and Perrine Vigneron all contain details that match Robert Black's MO as exhibited in the murders for which he was convicted. .

1. All victims were pre-pubescent, pretty, young girls and fitted Black's target victim group. The four ages of his

confirmed UK victims were, in chronological order of his attacks, nine, eleven, five, ten, fifteen and six; whilst the three little girls from Germany and France were aged, in chronological order of attacks, ten, ten and seven.

2. All three European victims were snatched near their homes in early/late afternoon time while going about normal daily activities – April Fabb, Genette Tate, Jennifer Cardy, Susan Maxwell, Teresa Thornhill and Laura Turner were all abducted or nearly abducted in early or late afternoon.

   Silke Garben was abducted whilst on her way to a dental appointment; Sarah Harper in Morley was heading home from the shop after buying some bread and milk when Black snatched her. Virginie Delmas was playing in front of her apartment building when she went missing, and Caroline Hogg was playing not far from her home in Portobello when approached and abducted by Black. Perrine Vigneron was heading to a pottery class when she was abducted, and Jennifer Cardy was heading for a friend's house, while Susan Maxwell was returning home from playing tennis with a friend.

3. The bodies of Silke, Virginie and Perrine were all found in public places with no real effort having been made to conceal them. Silke Garben was found in a stream off the River Rhine, face down and drowned; however, she was unconscious but alive when put in the water, just like Jennifer Cardy when she was put in McKee's Dam and Sarah Harper when she was put in the River Trent. Perrine Vigneron was disposed of in a field near a busy road, dumped in a manner similar to the disposal of Susan

Maxwell and Caroline Hogg, whose bodies were found in ground off lay-bys, whilst Virginie Delmas was found in an orchard, all of these places accessible to the public.

4. Silke, Virginie and Perrine were all sexually assaulted and strangled. Police believed Jennifer Cardy was strangled by her own cardigan to the point of unconsciousness before being put in water where she drowned. Like Jennifer Sarah Harper was alive but most likely unconscious when she was dropped in the river. The cause of death of Susan and Caroline was never known due to the state of the bodies when they were found, but considering Black in 1964 throttled a seven-year-old girl to the point of her passing out before proceeding to sexually assault her and then walk away, it is conceivable that Susan and Caroline died as a result of strangulation.

The brutal sexual assault on Silke resulted in her suffering a 6-centimetre tear in her vagina: Sarah Harper sustained similar appalling vaginal injuries. The motive in Virginie and Perrine's murders was clearly sexual as it was with Jennifer Cardy (bloodstain on her underpants, which were replaced on her inside out, and the zip of her trousers down), Susan Maxwell (underwear removed) and Caroline Hogg (found naked). It is hard not to conclude that these little girls were all murdered by the same individual – a sexually motivated serial killer of children, who seemed to prefer strangulation as a means of subjugating his victims.

5. Robert Black was found to have been in the abduction areas when all six of his confirmed UK-based victims

were snatched – proved through petrol receipts, delivery logs and wage statements. This played a crucial part in him being convicted as it displayed he had the time and opportunity to abduct his victims.

Black made two trips to Germany in 1985 and Silke Garben was abducted and murdered whilst he was on one of those trips. In an episode of the 2001 Channel 5 television series *Mapping Murder* that focuses on Black, Ray Wyre confirms that Black was in France when Virginie and Perrine were killed. He was working making deliveries in the northern half of France, which includes the two suburbs of Paris from where the two girls were abducted.

6. The presence of a van. Black was using a navy-blue van when he attempted to abduct Teresa Thornhill in 1988, and also used a blue van when he abducted Laura Turner in Stow in 1990. Black also was also using a van when he seized his four UK murder victims in the 1980s. A white van was seen parked in a field entrance at the spot towards which Susan Maxwell was walking when she was last seen before Black abducted her in 1982, Caroline Hogg was led out of the Fun City funfair by Black in 1983 towards a car park where a grey van was spotted. In 1986 a white van was seen driving around Morley the night Sarah Harper was snatched.

Black had access to several different-coloured vans while working as a driver for PDS. According to an article on him in *Real Life Crime* magazine Black was driving a white van when making deliveries in France in 1987 and witnesses reported seeing a white van near both abduction sites in connection with the two French cases. A vehicle of some sort was clearly used in the abduction and murder of Silke, Virginie and Perrine.

7. Silke, Virginie and Perrine were abducted and murdered in the late spring/early summer months of May and June. Three of Black's confirmed murder victims and one lucky survivor were abducted in the summer months of June, July and August (Jennifer Cardy, Susan Maxwell, Caroline Hogg and Laura Turner). Because of the good weather and the more active outdoor lives of children, and the school holidays, late spring and summer seems to have been a preferred hunting time for Black. All three victims on the Continent seem to have been abducted very swiftly and there were no witnesses to the abductions.

8. Black had already travelled to Northern Ireland on a number of occasions and in 1981 he snatched and murdered a child – Jennifer Cardy – and although Northern Ireland is part of the UK and they have the same culture, way of life and language, the journey there still involved travelling over the sea.. When in Northern Ireland Black was not just several hours down a motorway from his home in Stamford Hill, London. He was technically outside Great Britain, across water and in another country and had to get a car ferry back to England. If anything, this must have given him more confidence to abduct and murder a child. Unlike most of his colleagues, he was undeterred by the Troubles, which he probably realised were occupying

much police attention, and the deed committed, he was out of the country undetected and back home before his victim was discovered. It seems likely that he would have developed a similar confidence during his work trips to Germany and France during the 1980s, comfortable in the knowledge that he would be back in his home country before any suspicious glances could be thrown in his direction.

In interviews with Ray Wyre Black talked about how at the time of his 1990 arrest he had been planning a holiday to Bangkok in Thailand (where you had to assume he planned to abuse young children). After quoting this statement in the episode 'Crime and Motion' of *Mapping Murder* Ray Wyre explains in an exchange with the programme's presenter Professor David Canter how Black thought of his crimes not just nationally but internationally:

Ray Wyre: 'I think the country became his territory that he had control of.'

Professor David Canter: 'And he began to see that he could broaden beyond that, that he could go overseas.'

Ray Wyre: 'That he could go overseas, that's exactly what that statement is saying.'

As of summer 2017 nobody has been convicted of or charged with the murders of Silke Garben, Virginie Delmas or Perrine Vigneron.

The 11 May 1989 disappearance of eleven-year-old Ramona Herling in Germany, given the geographical location of her abduction and its circumstances, means that she too should be considered a possible victim of Black's, assuming that he was in Germany at the time. Devon and Cornwall Police are the current guardians of the file on Robert Black and might have documentation, such as petrol receipts and Black's work records, that would be helpful to the German authorities working on the case.

Another element that often crops up in discussions about the likelihood of Black being responsible for more unsolved murders and disappearances are the gaps in the timeline of his offending since he arrived in London in 1968. For example, if we create a timeline where we put in only the crimes Robert Black has been convicted of since his arrival in London in 1968, there are gaps between the crimes, which raises the question of whether or not he was killing undetected.

1968 – Arrives to live and work in London

1976 – Starts work as a van driver for PDS

1981 – Murders Jennifer Cardy in Northern Ireland

1982 – Murders Susan Maxwell in Cornhill-on-Tweed

1983 – Murders Caroline Hogg in Portobello, Scotland

1986 – Murders Sarah Harper in Morley, Leeds

1988 – The attempted abduction of Teresa Thornhill in Nottingham

1990 – The abduction of Laura Turner in Stow (victim is rescued and Black is finally captured)

Now if the other, currently unsolved, cases mentioned in this book are slotted in, the gaps are evened out or shortened.

I have put the unsolved offences in bold to differentiate between the two:

1968 – Arrives to live and work in London

1969 – Disappearance of April Fabb/Attempted abduction of girl in Cornwall

1971 – Attempted abduction of Jeanne Twigden in Cambridgeshire

1972 – Arrested in London in a stolen Ford Zephyr car with keys for going equipped

1973 – Disappearance of Christine Markham

1976 – Starts work as a van driver for PDS

1977 – Attempted abduction of a young girl in Norfolk – Disappearance of Mary Boyle

1978 – Disappearance of Genette Tate

1979 – Disappearance of Suzanne Lawrence

1981 – Murder of Jennifer Cardy in Northern Ireland

1982 – Murder of Susan Maxwell in Cornhill-on-Tweed

1983 – Murder of Caroline Hogg in Portobello, Scotland

1985 – Abduction and murder of Silke Garben in Germany

1986 – Murder of Sarah Harper in Morley, Leeds

1987 – Abduction and murder of Virginie Delmas (May) and Perrine Vigneron (June)

1988 – Attempted abduction of Teresa Thornhill in Nottingham

1989 – Disappearance of Ramona Herling in Germany

FILLING IN THE GAPS

1990 – Abduction of Laura Turner in Stow (victim is rescued and Black is finally captured)

What I have done here is not just attempt to fill in the gaps but present a type of profiling of the offender which I shall refer to as chronological profiling. This is where we think of an offender in terms of the number of times he kills or attacks and their frequency on a timeline, examining any potential gaps, and then see if there are linked cases that can fill in those gaps of offending. If there is a gap in the timeline of offending there may be a very good reason for it being there – apart from the obvious explanation like the offender being in prison – and we can rule that out in Black's case as following his year in borstal as a youngster he was not imprisoned again until 1990.

Another reason for the gap may be a change in the offender's personal or professional life that stops or hinders them from committing the crimes, at least for a period of time. Changes in the personal life of an offender very often involves a relationship with another person or other persons – this we can also rule out in Black's case, who had had no steady relationships of any kind past his one and only girlfriend as a teenager, and who had no family. As for Black's professional life, we know that he was continuously working (with the briefest of breaks in 1986) as a van driver for PDS from 1976 onwards, so his employment, during those fourteen years at least, was consistent. And from his point of view, there was certainly no reason to change his employment: as we have seen, it gave him the facility to work solo, to travel far and wide, and, as long as he made his deliveries correctly and on time, to go where and when he wanted.

There is no reason why all serial killers should want to kill all the time, or even on a yearly basis; even while they may always be on the lookout for potential victims. Some have cooling-off periods, and it is fairly clear that Black had these periods and we can explain the reasons why. These cooling-off periods differ in length depending on the offender and their circumstances. For example, there is nothing to indicate that in 1980 Black was involved in the murder of a child yet he is the prime suspect in the disappearances of two young girls in the two previous years (1978 and 1979) and we know he killed a child (Jennifer Cardy) the year after, in 1981.

The next year to show as a gap on the timeline where there are no known abductions or killings of children that can be linked to Black is 1984. It could have been a cooling-off year for him as six months earlier police were hunting the killer of Susan Maxwell (1982) and Caroline Hogg (1983) after connecting both cases publicly, so it would have made sense for him to lie low, especially since the police declared they believed the same man was responsible for both child murders. It in fact looks as though there is a three-year gap between the murder of Caroline Hogg in 1983 and the 1986 murder of Sarah Harper – but if we assume 1984 to be a cooling-off year and take into account the 1985 abduction and murder of Silke Garben in Germany the gap is shortened considerably.

Perhaps the huge publicity coverage and police work put into the Susan Maxwell and Caroline Hogg investigations from autumn 1983 and into 1984 is another reason to consider Black a suspect in Silke Garben's murder – did he seek his next victim overseas to steer clear of the investigative heat in the United Kingdom? We can apply the same logic in the second half of the 1980s: Sarah Harper's murder in 1986 once again saw nationwide publicity and a renewed and refreshed police focus, especially when it was eventually linked with the Maxwell and Hogg killings. So in the course of 1987 the investigation was ongoing, and with renewed vigour, when two little girls (Virginie Delmas and Perrine Vigneron) were abducted and murdered a month apart in France at a time when Black was working in the general area.

Did Black once again choose to offend abroad when the police investigation into his crimes was at its highest activity level at home? Putting these three continental killings into Black's timeline of offending reduces the gaps and makes them easier to understand. In 1988, two years after Sarah Harpers death he felt confident enough to attack again in Britain when he attempted to abduct Teresa Thornhill in Nottingham. However, the failure of that abduction and the amount of information thus given by his victim to the police would have meant once again a cooling-off period of two years until the summer of 1990 when he abducted Laura Turner in Stow. On the other hand, if we take into consideration the disappearance of Ramona Herling in 1989 in Germany – another possible return to the continent after a crime committed on home ground – it would close the gap between 1988 and 1990.

What we see when we look at the majority of these crimes,

solved and unsolved, is that Robert Black had the method, motive and opportunity to commit these crimes. Chris Clark and I are convinced that Robert Black was responsible for the deaths of more than four children. We believe that he was the most prolific and dangerous serial killer of children not only in the United Kingdom but Europe as well, not just in terms of the number of lives he claimed, but also taking into consideration the large geographical distances he covered and the number of years he was at large, undetected.

The Robert Black story never really ends – there are still so many unanswered questions over what other killings he might have committed and where some of his other victims may be. His death in January 2016, however, brought with it the end of any opportunity to charge him over more children's deaths, and leaves too many families still seeking to know what happened to their murdered or vanished child. Chris and I feel for all the children talked about in this book and their families. A big part of the reason why this book was started in the first place was to raise awareness, or keep this awareness alive, of what happened to these little girls in the hope that it will perhaps jog memories or prick someone's conscience into coming forward with information that may lead to these mysteries being solved.